ANNA UNCENSORED

ANNA UNCENSORED

A Story of Love, not War

Flashbacks from real life events

Roger Wilson

Lighthouse Publishing Limited,
Grieves Cottage, Drumelzier Haugh Farm
Broughton, Biggar
ML12 6JD,
United Kingdom
empower@lighthousepublishing.ltd

You can contact the author via email using:
roger.wilsonbook18@gmail.com

ISBN 978-1-910848-1-7-3

Cover Design by Cara Wilson
Typeset by Avocet Typeset, Somerton, Somerset
Printed in the United Kingdom

DEDICATION

For my talented wife Claire, who has been with me all the way on this journey.

To my daughters Natalie and Cara, and for Noah Annaheim Harbinson, who has just come into the family as a new great, great grandson of George and Dorice Annaheim.

To all the descendants of Grandmother Dorice.

Hoping that the remembrance of the sacrifices of those who served, and those who loved in The Great War will continue, through the generations to come.

Contents

Author's preface 9
Prologue 15
1 WAR, not LOVE 17
2 Egyptian Escapades 29
3 Those 'First' Meetings 47
4 That Ring 57
5 'S an Awful War 65
6 Marriage, Yeah or Nay? 75
7 More Than a Whiff! 93
8 Transport of Delight 101
9 Days of Leave and Love 113
10 To Fly 137
11 Pals, Prospects & Promotions 145
12 The Boys from Erin's Isle 159
13 Coloured Mist 177
14 About a Kiddums 189
15 Stunts 205
16 Matinees and Nights of Lov 221
17 4-Legged Friends 235

18 Some Bashes! 249
19 Adventures in Retreat 261
20 Sporting Days 279
21 Lines and Rhymes 291
22 Last Days 305
23 LOVE, not WAR 319
24 Afterwards 331
25 In Due Course 349
26 Epilogue 357
Author's notes and acknowledgements 364
About the author 366

AUTHOR'S PREFACE

Under the light from a single bulb, swinging from a twisted wire, the dank cellar of a Victorian villa, the walls green with algae, was a thrilling place for this eight-year-old to explore.

Among the rubbish scattered across the stone flags, I found a rusting metal box laying under a heavy blanket in the darkest corner, as if entombed in a graveyard of history. I opened the creaking lid covered in faded lettering

The smell hit my senses powerfully and lasts to this day; strong in my memory, and strong inside the ammo box itself.

A pair of well-worn, man-sized slippers, mildewed and rotting, lay on top. Underneath, old leather items smelling sweet and pungent like sweaty saddles including; reins, a map case and a holster. And then, deeper still, I found; stirrups, a broken pipe, a shaving brush and purple 'roneoed' documents caked in mud.

Then I saw old sepia photos cracked and with rusty pin-holes in the corners, showing a jolly fellow with his arm around a slim-waisted girl. And then, a photo of a large man in army uniform with a moustache, riding a horse. Many more fading photos, lay scattered and scarred. Pictures from another time, another place.

Deeper still; piles of letters all in envelopes with no stamps but addressed in a flowing hand to Miss Dorice Hookway, 1 South Parade, Bath.

Instinctively, I knew I had intruded on memories of both War and Love. Somehow tainted with death. With a shiver from the cold, and a spasm of guilt, I shut the lid and ran back up to my Grandmother Dorice's warm living room, to play again with her ancient gramophone. She was, as always, smoking 'Senior Service' cigarettes, and flicking the ash into an old brass shell-case by her fireside.

Our family never spoke about George Herbert ('Anna' or 'Bubbie') Annaheim, until the 1970's when we visited his grave in a peaceful WW1 cemetery near Cambrai in north France.

Among the rows of regimented gravestones, in Plot B1-6, we saw the evocative regimental crest of the Royal Munster Fusiliers, figuring a Bengal tiger on a bomb. Below is the name of my grandfather, Lt. G. H. Annaheim. 1st Royal Munster Fusiliers. Died 4th October 1918. Chiseled beneath; "In Loving Memory by Wife and baby Peggy at Bath England".

The latter was my own mother, who, like her father, was nicknamed 'Anna', starting from her service in a later world war, as a WREN. She took a cutting from the rose in front of the stone and kept it in her garden throughout her own long life. A memorial to a father never met, never known.

That ammo box and a battered valise found in that basement lay airtight and undisturbed (except by a boy of eight) for over eighty years, until it was ready to spur this story of Love and War. The numerous contents include trench maps, orders, aerial photos, journals and diaries, as well as more than seven hundred hand-written letters tied in packs with ribbons.

Anna wrote most of them to his true love, my grandmother Dorice, as well as to his brother, sister, parents and in-laws. The letters and diaries are truly 'self-talk', written with a freedom of expression that reflects his view of his life and loves. The letters were sent uncensored during WW1, and remain, to this day, as sweet kisses after death.

Half a million words of love and words of war have shaped this truly open and honest story of passion and adventure. Times appear so different, and yet also, so similar to our experiences and feelings today. Writing with Anna and Dorice's pictures in front of me show that the hundred years that have passed since the letters were written, demonstrate that war will always be trumped by love.

I do know him better than all those letters actually reveal. Better than, the diaries, school reports, memories recounted by family members, regimental histories and all the things that research on a life and a time, can disclose.

Reading those thousands of pages of handwritten letters and diaries, I realise that genes carry more than just chemical imprints of ones ancestors, but character traits one can recognize, and that surely have passed through the generations.

'Anna Uncensored' is more than a memoir or biography of an unnotable young Edwardian man. It is written as a 'ghost autobiography', revealing his thoughts, dreams and hopes just as he himself wrote his letters home. After these years of research, I know the man. I know him both on the outside and on the inside. I also happen to share some of his genes too. As an author, and grandson I feel that in this narrative, I am him.

Was the Great War a tragedy? It was nothing less. Yet it had its lighter sides, and even, a century later, the importance to families across the world has hardly diminished.

Knowing Anna from afar, I know how desperately he wanted to live and share a future with his wife and soon-to-be-born daughter. He lived a fully encompassing life, which, in that short span of war, brought him; friends, humour, jealousies, fantasies, scares and fears, but, most importantly; deep love. Like millions of others he joined up to do his duty, and like millions of others he just wanted to make it back to a peaceful life.

The alchemy of authorship leads to writing that will inevitably include truths, half truths, and exaggerations. Any human story, whether autobiography, memoir or novel, just like "Anna Uncensored", will forge these elements into a compounded whole.

I have based this story on the lives of the all the characters, using the letters as the key to the narrative. I have written it in his own words; not as a calendar of his life, but as a series of momentous flashbacks of his thoughts and happenings, as he himself would have seen and expressed them.

Mental flashbacks recently seem to have a valid scientific basis; with newly published research showing that a form of consciousness may still be present after the body has ceased showing signs of life. Brain neurons still function up to five full minutes after death. This electrical activity inside the brain could well replay lifetime recollections, while a process known as 'spreading depolarization' takes its course.

A few of the characters names have been altered so that living relatives would not feel compromised by this story. To these, and to the relatives of other families of those appearing, I can reassure them that the references have all come from the pen of the man himself, a mere hundred years ago.

Writing this manuscript has been an uplifting journey of discovery:

A journey of War and Love.
A journey of passion and delights.
A journey of sadness and joy, and then
a belief in Love not War.

This also is a journey that stays true to the man himself; George Herbert Annaheim ('Anna') 1892-1918

Roger Wilson, one of 'Anna's' two grandsons. 2018.

PROLOGUE

The date - October 4th 1918
The place - The old Cambrai Racecourse, Proville, Cambrai, France .
Falling beside his good pal the old Quartermaster, Captain Robert Baxter, and the 2nd in Command, Major Guy Nightingale; Lieutenant G.H. Annaheim is struck down in an 'untargetted' killing - if there is such a thing at a time of total war.

DYING?

As well as the 'ratatatat' of the machine guns of the 'planes zooming in the sky above, comes a new sound. Not a crump, whizz or a whoosh like that of the 'usual' shellfire landing nearby. Nor is it the pulsating drone of aeroplane engines themselves. Those are not new sounds. This is a sharp, brittle sound as this particular stray bullet lances downwards from the sky.

That bullet strikes his head, and 'Anna' curses his luck and the Bosche, in that order. Only inside his head. Not from his lips.

'The Hun in the sun' flying his multi-coloured Albatros 'biplane' only a few hundred feet above, is the cause.

And the Hun pilot never knew it.

Bad luck! After all the years of close shaves. And now standing right beside his pals astride the infamous Hindenburg Line, watching aerial skirmishes he is hit, and hit hard. With the war almost ended, this moment comes suddenly, and almost unannounced.

It takes just only several painful seconds, or at most a minute or two, for his senses to collapse completely. In that short time, flashbacks of his life occur. Not in any logic or timely order, but vividly, and with a speed and clarity that contrasts with the life-force, which is ebbing away so fast.

Flashbacks of a life well-lived, however short, and however many thousands of words he had spoken and written about his dreams and aspirations.

WASTED?

Just one of twenty million souls killed, wounded or missing from this Great War. A beloved hero only to his wife, his family, and his pals.

A man, who first lived for 'War, not Love' but later, came to love so passionately, that his priorities became 'Love not War'.

1

WAR, NOT LOVE

"... feel free to plan your life without care for this soldier-man"

We are off to Egypt! Penetrating smells swirl in my head as a vivid flashback hits me like a spark.

They are the pungent fumes of sulphurous smoke and black sooty steam from the ships and railway engines, filling the air, my nostrils and my mind. Trainloads of men, horses and stores are arriving on this dockside by the minute. It's all smells and noise and what seems to be organised chaos.

Most of the lads want France where the real action will be, and where the BEF will soon be going up against the Huns.

But for we volunteer troopers in 'A' Squadron Duke of Lancaster's Own Yeomanry (DLOY), it's Egypt to replace Regular Army Divisions. We are part of the East Lancs Division. Most of the men are from Manchester and are a mixed bunch from backgrounds so very different.

Me; I'm an outsider from Somerset – they call me "Anna" which is fine and occasionally "the Hun" which is not. So much for having a Swiss-German surname right now! I don't mind really – it is an adventure, and I am with my pals, and my beloved horse Jack.

It's already one month after war was declared. The whole squadron has signed for overseas duty, had medicals, and said farewell to jobs and families.

So now we are working hard at loading. Our ship is the Royal Mail Lines crack steamer Deseado. The only problem she is also carrying the Division and Battalion staff. They get the first class accommodation, and we troopers, get third class cabins. At least I get a bunk, sharing six to a tiny cabin on D deck.

My Jack is swung up in a cradle, and I manage to get him a sheltered line behind the bridge structure, with a canvas sheet either side. A kind of stall three foot wide and no room to lie down. But thank goodness he's facing on the port side; hopefully away from the west winds of the Atlantic and the sun of the Mediterranean. "Port out, Starboard home" they say, but there's not a lot that's 'posh' here.

Jack is quite restless, but I talk to him about the coming adventures. When I get a full sack of oats for his nosebag he is calmer. I must take great care of him because I know he will never let me down – whatever comes at us.

What a journey!

Sailing out into the Channel from Southampton at midnight is such a dramatic experience. No lights either in the channel or from the shore. Just a few stars stare through the dark clouds. It is morning and we link-up with a dozen transports, a couple of destroyers and, taking center stage, the powerful, black-hulled battleship HMS Ocean. It's a huge convoy. A great sight!

They say there are fifreen thousand troops on these ships, and I fully understand the pride in our Navy and, just for a moment, I feel envious of sailorman brother Eddy. I must remember to write to him as soon as we get near somewhere we can send post home.

I must also remember letters to Mother and Pa, to Dais and, of course, Katherine.

I need to think about her and 'us'. She is such a sport – we've been playing tennis at the Bath Tennis club, rowing on the Avon and riding together. But that's been when I've been back in Bath. Since, from 1909 – I was seventeem and just left school for the Bank – till 1912 when I was transferred to Manchester branch of the National & Provincial Bank.

We have had fun together, and she is my girl. She has my signet ring, so I suppose, it's a kind of promise or secret engagement. At least we do have an 'understanding'. But her parents, the Freemans, the chocolate barons, never liked me. No money, no prospects, and not a compatible religious upbringing. Her Pater said I have to earn five hundred pounds per annum to be in with a chance.

And I thought Quakers were meant to be a tolerant lot!

We do have fun. Kissing her and an occasional squeeze of her soft body. That's all though, as there's always a chaperone in sight. Dammit! The boys in the bank tease me; "Show me that picture of your girl Herbert", "When are you getting married Erb?" "What's it like Herbie, have you done it yet?"

All good fun, and I can take the joshing well. But it does make one think.

I stop worrying, as life is for the adventurous.

Goodness knows how long this war will last - months or years? Time is passing very quickly as we are busy aboard each day; reveille at 5am, then attend the animals - mucking out, feeding often by hand, vet inspections, trying to keep them cool with water, and be soothing so they are calm. For a trooper with his chosen horse this hard work is truly a labour-of-love. I don't mind this at all.

The Bay of Biscay, however is starting to live up to its reputation.

Brother Eddy once wrote to the parents describing a storm when on HMS Hindustan in the Channel fleet. He was sick for days and only helped by the sailors telling him to eat fried bacon and eggs to cure that deathly feeling. We are working like trojans as the storm hits hard. The convoy is lost in the sea and sky, which merge in the darkness and driving rain. The Deseado is being tossed about with a strange corkscrew motion. We poor Yeoman trooper fellows are working out on the decks to protect the horses, and getting soaked through.

No sleep for four days; just the salt spray lashing us for hours at a time. The noise is terrific from the wind and crashing waves that make the ship roll. Added to these near hellish sounds, is the mad honking from the seventy mules living in one of the holds below deck. That shrieking seems to often overpower the wild noise from the gale itself.

We set off with 142 animals, but this storm in the Bay of Biscay has done for twenty-six of the mounts. It is tragic to see a lovely creature going crazy, trying to stampede and tearing itself from its lines, snorting and pawing, before collapsing and having to be put down by a service revolver. Heaving a dead horse of fifteen hands over the ship's rail is an exhausting and sad business. But Jack has survived it all. I spend nights with him talking nonsense just to keep him calm.

I am no sailor, but I am proud of all my pals who are working like slaves during these nightmare hours of storm. Screaming horses, flapping canvases and loose lines. We lose many parts of our grooming kits like sponges and brushes, but we share what is left.

Entering the calm of the Mediterranean, I can now write letters home. From the first class salon we scrounge, I mean steal, some RML notepaper and a few postcards. The Squadron Major and Captain Bates are insisting on censoring the mail, so I am careful about places and names. Got them written to Katherine and my mother, and they are sent across in a huge sack to a destroyer that is leaving the convoy for Gibraltar. Let's hope they make it, especially the one to Katherine Freeman.

I hope I have said the right things, but we are at war. Who knows how long it will last?

At sea 16/9/14
My only dearest Kathy,
You know I am not a great letter writer, but I am writing to say how much I miss you, and how I spend lots of time remembering all the jolly fine times we have had together. Bow wow!

Hoping you are keeping chipper with all this war talk. We were all surprised when the call actually came. You will see the Royal Mail Lines letterhead here. This means I'm writing from a classy steamer – actually with my DLOY pals, about 150 of us. It's rather hot, often exhausting but quite an adventure and certainly different from working in the Bank.

We are part of the first Territorial Division to venture overseas; The East Lancashire Division, which is strange for a Somerset lad. All my pals come from Manchester or nearby. Our spirits are high now we are in calmer waters.

I cannot tell you much about this trip because of wartime orders and privacy, but just to say I am well and fit and Jack is in splendid shape after some turbulent times on this, his first sea voyage. I admit I have been a little seasick, but brother Eddy told me the cure years ago; to eat greasy food – no problems with that on this ship! Oooh oooh!

On the voyage I have been thinking a lot about our love and the difficulties that this longer parting will bring. In Manchester I felt able to visit you in Bath, and those weekends with you were truly topping. Woof woof!

You know you have been my only girl all these last years, and we sealed our special bond with my signet ring. You should know that I carry a picture of you close to my heart. I take quick looks at your pretty face whenever I can during the day, and take longer loving looks when in my cabin alone.

Now we are at war and I will be far away from you, so I feel I can't hold you to our understanding. It's not fair to either of us, even as hearts will be broken or at least very hurt. This war will last longer than Christmas, whatever the papers say. I have already seen military sights that are magnificent, and am in no doubt we shall beat the Bosche in the end. But when that is, and who will come home to dear old England is not to be revealed for sometime. Only God knows. And He's not telling.

I do believe we should halt our relationship and see what happens after the war. I know your family are Quakers and have a different, and respected, attitude to all this. Leaving my suitability aside. But your Pater did make it quite clear that I needed a salary of at least five hundred pounds per annum to secure your hand, and, his approval. While I would, in normal times, fight to win you and him over; as a bank clerk or even under-manager or as a Yeoman Trooper or with promotion if it comes, (as well as the Lord sparing me), it would take years to be accepted into the Freeman family.

As for you, dearest girl, I think you need to find your own destiny during these times and feel free to plan your life without care for this soldier man overseas.

May God keep You and Yours safe from this awful war situation.

Please write to me a line to let me know how things are with you, how you feel. I feel downhearted, but I do feel strongly right now that WAR COMES BEFORE LOVE. I wish you all the joy life can bring and hope we can remain pals into the future.

Sent with love and respect from your own
Bubbie xxxx

Mail to: Trooper G H Annaheim
Duke of Lancaster's Own Yeomanry
East Lancashire Division
M.E.F.
OHMS

p.s. Feel able to share this letter with your sisters and even your brother if you wish. It is not easy for me writing this after so many jolly times together – times that I will always remember most fondly.

Postcard to Mother and Father from RML Deseado
To: 8 Belgrave Place, Bath, Somerset.

Dearest Mother and Pa,
I'm writing this to you at sea on our way to somewhere hot. All well with my pals and the animals.
Will write when ashore.
Your loving son
Bubbie xxx

Thank heavens the mail got away. I'm still fretting about Katherine. Am I right to end things?

I chat to my best pal Marsden who joshes me "Women are all alike – so just love 'em and leave 'em – no worries"

I wish I had his attitude, but then he is a real 'swordsman' with lots of experience of these things. I am inexperienced in matters of the heart and find love a bit mystifying and often stressful. But that important letter has now been sent. I bet brother Eddy who is now twenty eight, and who left home for the navy when he was seventeen, knows a lot; a girl in every port for Naval Officers indeed. The Dirty Devil!

I love my family of course and my sister Dais especially. I must write to her about it all. Throughout all of my life my big sister has always been very close. I can talk to her about anything, while it's difficult, actually impossible, to talk to Mother and Pa about such tricky things. They still treat me as if I am a child. I am hoping that going off to war will change all that.

We are just passing Malta and another huge convoy heaves into sight. It's full of soldiers from the Indian Army, and, according to the rumours, they are en-route to France. Flags are waving, and bands playing. I swear I can see Sikhs or Gurkas with their colourful headdress. The lucky devils will get to cross swords with the Huns before we do.

The two weeks that have passed since we embarked in Southampton have gone so quickly. We've had drills with the SMLE rifle at some floating targets, and, more importantly, the Squadron has been issued with the 1908 pattern short sword. That shows we will be equipped for whatever comes at us, and, who ever we get to go at in war.

Rumours have started to spread, that since the German cruisers Breslau and Goeben got away scot-free to Constantinople in August, that the jolly Turk might need some sorting out.

All the kit will be ready in Egypt. Hopefully, tropical kit too, as the weather is scorching, and I am red faced and getting lots of ribbing about 'red Indians'.

Soon we arrive in Alex and our adventures are really beginning. The CO is keeping us busy, and our morale is high. We are a good bunch of pals, proud of the Squadron, plus we have our own mounts with us. Thank heavens for that. Jack is a true friend and is acclimatizing well. He keeps me company and helps me focus on this war.

LETTER WRITTEN AT SEA BUT POSTED IN EGYPT SEPTEMBER 30TH 1914 (Started 15th September)

Dearest Sister Dais,

You'll see that this comes on Royal Mail Line letterhead as I am still at sea – in the Med. You will have read by now, about the East Lancs Division of about 15000 men leaving, and that Egypt is our destination.

As well as rough seas, hard work to keep the animals fit, and military training, it has been an exciting time.

Tell the folks I am really fit and tanned – actually quite red faced for which I get ribbed terribly by my pals.

DLOY are the first territorial cavalry to pitch up overseas in this war, so we are very proud right now and longing for action of some kind.

I have to let you know I wrote to Katherine Freeman from the ship, suggesting we end our 'informal engagement'. I thought a lot about being away from her, and I decided it wasn't fair to either of us to stay together, when I might be overseas for years – who knows?

I know you didn't like her much, but also that Father didn't really approve (not sure if it wasn't a bit of religious bigotry from him). I thought I should tell you, as you are likely to meet her at the Club or somewhere in Milsom Street.

I should ask after you and the Carpenter and the boy. I do hope you are all fine and the War doesn't change things for you too much. I know we will give the Bosche a jolly good hiding. What, what! Must stop now as Bugles are sounding for boat drill…

September 30th
Dearest Sister

I'm getting back to this letter after we've arrived in Alexandria. What a welcome! An American battleship was alongside and they manned ship and their band played "God Save the King", then our band played Yankee Doodle music, and we all cheered while unloading. Jack has made it ok.

We are now in a clean barracks in Egypt (can't say where) with good stabling.

We've got issued with tropical kit so now feeling cooler,

but I wonder if I will ever get used to this intense heat. Will send a pic or two of me in the sun helmet! The pyramids look even bigger than the photos we saw at school and provide a wonderful backdrop to our training maneuvers.

Dear sister, I will finish this and try to get it posted – goodness knows how long it will take or even if it gets through to you. They say there are Bosche submarines in the Med already.

Please write as I feel such a long way from the family – (especially old Eddy who I haven't heard directly from, for over 4 years).

Love to you all in Bath and especially to you dear Dais and say all the right things to mother especially she's not to worry.

From your ever loving brother Bubbie xxxx

Send your letters to
Trooper G H Annaheim
DLOY
East Lancs Division
OHMS MEF Cairo, Egypt

I am wondering what will War duties here in the Middle East Force bring?

Apart from regular trooper duties, polo is making a big difference. I'm in the Squadron team with Marsden, Smalley and the Major himself. We are the team to beat – good sport too!

In Egypt, it's not just the heat of the city or out in the desert in the day; it's the smells that strike me so powerfully. Out here on the old racecourse at Heliopolis it really stinks! Horse smells are a joy, muck'n'all, with dubbin and polish on all the saddles and tackle, and, of course, man sweat from the pals! But this is different. It is an overpowering and constant stench of the native masses, camels and donkeys and that eternal smoke from the local charcoal bread ovens.

Marsden and I are ordered to GHQ to carry despatches to the Staff. We think we are chosen, as our mounts look smart and not suffering from sand colic. We ride through the streets of Cairo with pride; in full tropical uniform with rifles and swords sheathed and saddlebags packed with the papers. Invited to meet General Douglas and the other Staff 'red tabs', we are congratulated on our smart turnout. What a different life they have in the Shepeard Hotel – five stars all the way! We ride back to our tented camp!

Just ten days later, and we are both made up to Lance Corporal. Perhaps we really did impress the 'red tabs' – or was it that win against GHQ at polo?!

Today there are rumours of a sudden move to the Canal Zone, as not only have we declared war on the Turks, but they are said to be marching in their hoards towards the Canal itself.

War comes to us at last! What other pungent smells will it throw up?

I'm in the right outfit, and it's just as well I choose
WAR, NOT LOVE.

Exotic smells are disappearing from my senses.

What next?

2

EGYPTIAN ESCAPADES

"...it seems the friction of this event releases more of the perfumes from the bath oils"

I'm now blinded by a brilliant light, and feel an intense burning in my head. I am experiencing clear flashbacks in my mind of those baking days in Egypt. These 'escapades' light a fire and make a man of me.

The first weeks are all just Army routine; pure logistics:

Reveille 5.45am
Stables 6.30
Parade 9.30am

Then exercise horses, ablutions, rifle drill, semaphore training, then night or line guard. After my promotion to Lance Corporal, I am doing all of these regular duties plus; canteen corporal, saddlery corporal, and paymaster support.

The old bank clerk training is now coming into it's own. I'm good at lists and 'sums' – so I report; "All present and correct, sir"; whether it is kit; rifles, saddles, water bottles, or, whatever. The officers seem to appreciate simple accuracy, while the men are responding to my approach. This is firm, but human; and serious, but often with a lighter remark. I realise it's a kind of 'acting'; just like when old Williams let me manage the Branch, when he was off on his afternoon 'matinees'. I would 'play-act' being Branch manager and still get the pals to get the work done.

February 1916, and, action at last!! There's no time for play-acting now. This is what the months of training have been for. This is why we came to Egypt. They call it the 'Defence of the Suez Canal', but we in the Squad talk about beating the Turk back to Constantinople. For weeks we have heard of an Ottoman army approaching from their base in Beersheba, and crossing the desert to invade Egypt.

And now it begins.

1am reveille for the troop to be in full order for action. We move out to Guebba Station and entrain for Ismailia in open wagons, something for which we are well practiced. All is going well. Rifle holstered, sword sheathed and bandoliers, waist belt and pouches full of ammo. Dear Jack is ready to go; he's excited. He can feel the mood of the lads. And, I know He won't let me down.

Ismailia is a hive of activity. Indians, Gurkhas, Australians are all marching east up to the Canal. The Imperial Cavalry Brigade, with the 42nd Punjabis in their colourful uniforms are nearby.

We hear our own orders;
"Stand to your horses"
"Prepare to Mount"
"Mooooooouuuuuuunt"

And off we go. Not in drill formation, but in pairs. I am alongside Marsden, with Capper and Sullivan riding behind. A hundred troopers led by the Major Bibby, ride northwards about ten miles towards the crossing where there has been some action. We can hear the occasional artillery shell from the banks of the Canal.

It's 6pm on the 4th and we have just been told that the Turks have started to retreat. We are to bivouac at El Ferdan overnight. No rest as we set up horse-lines, grab some food and crawl under a blanket beside the horses. It's freezing and we aren't getting much sleep. The wind from the east is strong with sand swirling all around. Maybe this terrain is more suited to camels, but they are difficult creatures to ride and control, and are slower in the gallop. True cavalry are horse-mounted; fast in a galloping charge and more stable from which to fire.

Reveille 3am, and we move as a squadron to the El Ferdan Ferry. It's more of a floating barge that can take about twenty mounts and men at each crossing.

All across the Canal, and the Major leads us forward, and at last eastwards, into the desert. I've just spotted some dead Turks covered already in swarms of dreadful flies. No time for emotions as bullets and shells are flying around. There are abandoned rifles, packs and a couple of Turkish six pounder guns, as well as scores of starving, bedraggled mules looking lost.

Now; into line abreast and we could charge at any time, it's what I've practiced for four years, first in the Royal Gloucester Hussars and now with the Duke of Lancaster's Own Yeomanry.

This FEELS like war. It's hot; very hot, and the sky is murky with the stinging sand, but we start to see the enemy ahead. The odd bullet whizzes overhead, but there's nothing I can aim at. The Turks are running back eastwards into the desert. Pity really, as at the last summer camp in Greystoke in 1913, I was third in the shooting competition on combined sights at twelve hundred yards. Not bad!

Now, however, we have stragglers to be rounded up. They throw away their rifles and surrender straight away. The Squadron collects about forty Turkish soldiers and we start to escort them the three miles back to the Canal bank at a walk.

Pity we haven't caught a German officer. Pity we haven't crossed swords with a real fighting force. But going to war riding my Jack gives me confidence that this is just the start of a life of adventure. And now yet another freezing night under a blanket on the desert floor.

Back over the Canal, we hand over the prisoners to the Division and ride back to Ismailia before entraining for the Depot at Zagazig, after a refreshing swim for me and Jack in the Sweet Water Canal.

We have time now in the mess-tent here in Abbassia, to talk about how well we'd done in the 'Battle of the Canal', and how well we COULD have done if allowed to chase the retreating Turks across the desert. None of us were lost or wounded; so it was a success.

But no medals, no souvenirs and no shots fired at Johnny Turk. Just some nice words sent from the General about the 'men from Manchester'.

Finally, and after taking no less than four months, the post arrives from England including one letter I have been curious about:

Dearest Georgie,

I received your letter sent from the ship, and was of course really sad to read of your thoughts and your decisions.

I think fondly dear George of all our times together, and promise you I will never forget any of our 'special moments' at the tennis club and particularly those days when you rowed us 'sans chaperone' along the Avon to our secret place.

Dear Georgie, I know you are now somewhere hot and I do ask you to take care and come home one day safely. I do respect what you said about us, so I have sent your signet ring back to your Mater. You should know I wore it secretly round my neck when you were called away.

I think you are terribly brave to join this dreadful war, and I pray you are keeping safe. I will follow the fortunes of the Duke of Lancaster's Own Yeomanry, whenever they are reported, and I am sure you will do your duty with honour and bravery.

I shared the contents of your letter with my family, who were united in praise for your character, and manly spirit. They too share my prayers that God-willing there will be a swift end to this war.

I send you all the warmest wishes I can for your future and pray for your safety and happiness.

May God protect you.

Your dear friend

Katherine xxx

Well, that's that. She seems fine with the break. I think it is all for the best, but it seems we both have a place in each others' hearts. But it's time I focused on the present.

The CO, asks me about going for a commission. I tell him; "Yes please sir". That all gets delayed as I am falling ill.

Thank heavens for the Scarlet Fever. And such a lovely nursey – Judith Callow. How she helps me grow up. Night time moments of love, or is it just lust?

I have fallen in love with Judith here in Hospital 21 in Alexandria. Weak, red-faced, blotches all over – yes there as well!

She takes me under her wing. My temperature has gone down from 104 to about 100 in the first two weeks, and, we get to really know each other. She bathes me all over with cooled water – ALL OVER!

I tell her my life story (such as it is), including my break with KF. And she shared hers too. Coming from Shrewsbury, she has a slight Welsh lilt, is dark haired and has a shapely figure. Her smile is wicked, when the matron isn't around. It bucks me up no end. I know I am getting better already!

I was weak at first but somehow over these last weeks she has given me confidence and inner resolve. She says: "Go for the commission Georgie. It's a way for you to get back at KF and her family, who thought you not good enough". (And, of course, I can catch up with Eddy!).

Walking in the hospital grounds, I pretend to faint, and she lets me lean against her. She knows what I am really thinking and feeling. Then we start to laugh and we hold each other in a warm embrace. I squeeze her full figure and feel so much stronger. Perhaps I am getting better at acting!

After another three weeks in the hospital I invite her into town on her two-day leave pass. Alexandria has delights galore. Hotel El Agany is not far from the Hospital; with nice airy rooms overlooking the bay. She teaches me so much, gets me excited first, as she peels off her starched uniform, and then, starts on mine! We collapse onto the hard bed. And, I explore her body with relish. I am captivated by the mysteries she reveals in one long afternoon.

First time, I am not much good. I blame it on the Scarlet Fever. Being a nurse she understands these things. No acting here. It's the first time of real lovemaking; and so we try again, and again. Practice really does make perfect!

Afterwards, and pretty tired, we walk along the beach up towards the Port. A cacophony of noises, busy with animal-drawn traffic of all kinds, greets us up on the Corniche. Sailors envy the girl on my arm. That reminds me; I did write to Eddy about all this. Bet he's got a girl in every port, the dirty dog!

Dear Eddy Old Brother,

How are you old man? I read the Navy is doing sterling work across the world. And what a mad world it is right now. What! What!

You did China for a couple of years and now I'm told by Pa that you are on Home station. Did you learn the old Chinese lingo out there? I remember you were good at languages at old King Edwards – it must have been Pa's influence. Bow! Wow!

I haven't got my 'Gyptian' lingo sorted yet, and probably never will. Sport's the thing out here. I won the cup for jumping last Boxing Day and was cheered on by the Lancashire boys against the Aussies, New Zealanders and the occasional Punjabi or Gurkha.

There's no place for golf or rowing, but me and some pals have climbed the Great Pyramid. It was sort of mountain climbing. We found a radio mast attached to the top! I got selected for the Division polo team – the only Lance Corp amongst officers including a staff colonel! Should be good for promotion. What! What!

Actually, I've been listed for Officer Training here in Egypt so life should upgrade. Watch out old man, I might catch up with your illustrious career!!

How's the love life? I hear that sailor-men have a good time whenever in port. In Alex the jolly tars AND officers all seem to have a girl on their arm – or something!! Woof! Woof!

Did you read about the Suez stunt? Our Squadron got to cross the Canal and we picked up 40 or so Turk prisoners wandering in the desert. They didn't look so fit for war. My horse Jack behaved well and we came through it unharmed.

I'm writing this from a hospital in Alexandria where we are looked after by some lovely nurses. I caught scarlet fever but am now nearly recovered. Got my eye on a nice Nursey, now I've freed myself from Katherine Freeman. That was a bit painful but we mutually ended our 'pash' pretty much at the same time. Her people never liked me and there was always this Quaker business going on.

This thing with Nursey could be fun. Bow! Wow! I get bathed all over and lots of soothing attentions! They will soon let me out of here to explore Alex.

Well, old Man it's about time you wrote to me – Ma & Pa or Dais will give you the details. Dais is about to give birth to her second sprog. I wonder if it will be named George or Herbert or Edward or Charles – care to bet?? Stay well big brother

Sent with a hug from your wee bro'
Bubbie

Alexandria is so exotic. Walking out of uniform we pick-up thick loaf bread called 'kushan', lamb parts boiling in grease, and honey filled deserts. We are always being surrounded by noisy young urchins, offering us everything from their sisters, to exotic postcards!

This is all obliterated as I focus on Nursey and what will happen when I go back to the Division. There's probably no real future in it.

During these six weeks, visitors have come over from the Squadron – Bob a couple of times, and my old pal Marsden dropped in. He is up for Officer training too. He caught sight of Judith and gave me a wink – then one for her. The dog. I must update the parents on all this – well, some of it anyway!

Dearest Mother and Pa,

I hope all is well with you both and you get or got my occasional cards and the short letter after the 'Suez' stunt. I'm writing this from a military Hospital in Alexandria, Egypt. Don't worry – I'm not wounded or anything bad. I've got just a severe case of the SCARLET FEVER, which I am told will be fine after a few weeks rest.

My main news is that I have been recommended by the CO to go on an Officers Course at Zeitoun, here – so, before long, you will soon be proud of both your sons as officers and gentlemen. I wrote a letter to Eddie. Haven't heard from him for many moons. He must be still in Portsmouth the lucky dog. Still, the mail takes ages to get out here.

I think I should tell you both officially that Katherine and I broke things off – did you hear <u>that</u> on the jolly old grapevine? We wrote to each other at the same time and she will send my signet ring back to you at home. I don't know how I really feel, *but her folks never really wanted me in their family – not rich enough. She was a good sport putting up with me as long as she did while I was up in Manchester.*

She was jolly decent about it and couldn't see a way forward esp. with me over here for goodness knows how much longer. This war may last some time now the Ottomans are in.

By the way, the nurses are very kind and you should know my fever and swollen glands are almost gone now. I am allowed some light exercise to visit this really exotic city, Its different from Cairo – cooler and less hectic, so life's not so bad for a poor sick son!

My pals are all ok after the Suez stunt. Some up for promotions – I heard that Marsden is up for officer school as well – would be great to serve with him again somewhere – we met in the Yeomanry, years ago.

When you see Dais – tell her to write more often as letters are precious to me right now and say hello to the Carpenter.

As for you both, stay well. Don't worry, as Egypt is a safe billet. The pals (and the nurses) make it all OK, but I do miss my Jack – they tell me he is fine and getting good stabling and plenty of oats. Long term I hope to stay mounted as my animals are always there for me.

Dearest Mother and Father, I send all my love to you.

Your own son

Herbert xx

Officer School turns out to be a cinch. It isn't a long course, and there is a good crowd – mainly Aussies. Here at the Zeitoun School of Instruction we have lectures all day, and reading and study at night. Good food is served and there is time for sport too. I do well, as I have 'A' in marksmanship from the OTC at school as well as five years in the Yeomanry. Both count for a lot, and probably why I'm here.

We work together on tricky questions; 'how to discipline men in the field', 'how to march your men into action from trenches', and, 'how to retreat in orderly fashion'. Well, we shall see about that!

I mug up on hundreds of pages of 'Musketry Regs' and 'Infantry Training' but also am reading some 'lighter' material including some 'exotic postcards' bought in Alex and 'Spalding's Golf Guide'. I may get to play a round one-day with brother Eddy.

The Commandant, Lieutenant-Colonel Colston of the Grenadier Guards, interviews us all individually. He asks me about home, family and school. Then I jump in and say "I am very good with horses Sir, and have learned about the role of Transport Officer. That is, if I pass Sir, could I go to a Battalion that needs my skills from the Bank and the Yeomanry?"

He replies "Well, Annaheim, great care and judgment is used in the selection of a Transport Officer, as the duties are very difficult. They require energy, perseverance, good temper and ingenuity. Looking here at your record I see you are good at sports. Damned fine race you won last week, and, I see you played cricket and for your school."

No more was said.

Both Marsden and I have sailed through Officer School and I'm off to get a change of uniform. I'm soon to be commissioned in some regiment or other. Both brother Eddy, and myself are called Lieutenants now, but I should really thank 'Nursey' for her inspiration – in more ways than one.

I just await orders.

"From: HQ 29th Division 1-11-1915
To: 2nd Lt G H Annaheim
Please report forthwith to Division Base Depot
Mustapha, Alexandria. Railway warrant attached."

Marsden got one just like it. But for me, it's too late.

Again, I'm in Hospital. This time it's with the Mumps, and I've been sent to another hospital; Choubia, in Alexandria. The MO has informed the 29th Division that I will be 'hors de'.

The fight against the Turk is in full flow in The Dardenelles, but my old 'A' Squadron with pals Fox, Harris, Williams and the rest, are off westward into the desert to fight a new foe – the Senussi tribes of Tripoli. Lucky beggars.

It could be four or more weeks to get rid of this high temperature, massively swollen face and the aches all over. I'm so weak I can't even get interested in any of the nurses. I must be really sick!

Not a great hospital. Patients cry out in the night; some are badly wounded from Gallipoli, suffering malaria, enteric diseases, and worst of all, frostbite. The Aussie in the next bed dies in the night from his wounds, and some of the Irish fellows from the 'River Clyde' landings are in much pain as they are really smashed up. Poor blighters. Is this the face of war? I seem to have been lucky so far, but also feel guilt about not sharing it with my pals. I attend the Aussie's funeral.

The 42nd and 29th Divisions with many Lancashire lads and Irishmen have done glorious deeds out there on the peninsula. The papers say; "Lancs Fusiliers win six VC's before breakfast". And the Munsters got one as well.

Makes me realise this is serious business. I should be there. Marsden is out there now.

While I found adventure and joy last time I was sick in hospital, this time I am depressed and unhappy.

A letter has arrived for me at last from Marsden. It bucks me up no end. Apparently he is wounded lightly, has enteric fever as well as severe frostbite and got taken off the beach and shipped to a hospital in Malta:

Dear 'Anna' old man.

Well you may have heard that now it's my turn to get a 'cushy' and I'm writing from a hospital in Malta. The trenches in jolly old Suvla were flooded when I landed and then some amazing cold weather hit us all.

Well, to cut along story short I only lasted 10 days with the 1st Battalion Royal Munster Fusiliers, before me and no less than eleven officers and about eighty men were evacuated to the nearest hospital ship. This is a fine Regular Battalion, with a glorious history, but has suffered great losses and will need plenty of new men. When you are well, try and get posted to the Munsters. The Irish boys are fine fighters and the CO Geddes, a good sort.

How are you faring you devil? Are the nurses any good in that hospital of yours? I am expecting you to have stories 'a la nursey Judith' to share with me soon. Here, there's no luck on that front, because we are looked after by nuns, or 'sisters' as they are called. Yes they are nuns. No joy there at all!

Drop me a line asap. Good luck old boy

Your friend and partner in crime

Cecil M

Just remember the DLOY; "troop mooooouuunt!!"

I write to Mother and Pa, Dais, and again to Eddy, but I only tell him I've been reading up on Golf so we can have a game one day up at Lansdown or Bath GC. A letter arrives from Dais saying Eddy is off overseas (the Med?) in a destroyer so I won't hear from him for months I suppose. Just get a U-Boat or two while you're there!

Swellings gone, temperature down and the doc says I can move to a 'recuperation home', whatever that is. Turns out fine, and another Egyptian Escapade is unfolding:

A classy mansion on the El Gish Road, Alexandria has been converted into an officers 'rest house'. Single rooms, baths with nurses and servants to help, a library, and the company of lightly wounded and convalescing officers. Great food and drink too! There's a lovely view out to sea and these sunsets are wonderful.

She enters. It's the patron herself. She lives in the adjacent mansion and floats through the lounge chatting to some other officers. She has spotted me. And I her, of course.

Polite as 'a well brought-up Bath boy' should be, I rise and shake her hand and introduce myself. My hand is being held just a bit long. Hello, are we acting again? Later in the week, an Australian Captain called Reeves, a scarlet-faced Irish Major called Burke and I, have got invitations to go to her house for dinner. Seven pm; dress formal. This should be interesting.

Not much to record; all very elegant though.

Lady Dorothy de Worley is our hostess, and is surrounded by white clad servants all smelling sweetly of incense. The smell pervades the room. Sherry is served, but I make a gaff by asking for a whiskey. Too bad!

We sit for an elegant dinner served on silver plates by the attentive native servants. True British food, and I love every mouthful. The Aussie does all the talking, and, all the bragging. The Major drinks a couple of bottles of red wine, and his face goes even redder. I decide to keep quiet, polish off the food and just smile towards Lady D. She is wearing a kind of green silk kaftan you can almost see through. She smells divine, and is no more than say thirty. Oh oh!

She is a Lady of class, and they say married to a Guards officer in France – the Lord himself! She asks me politely about my war so far. I mumble about being in hospital twice already, how I rode against the Turks on the Suez Canal, and how I miss Jack.

"Ladies love a man who loves animals", I remember Marsden saying. She gives me a look, with the faintest of smiles playing across her exquisite face. This stirs something, and makes me think that this may be a more interesting rest-home than I at first thought!

As we politely leave to return to our billet next door, she holds my hand and whispers for me to come-by tomorrow afternoon at three. Old Marsden says; "Never refuse an invitation from a lady". Right.

Entering this exotic house I am announced by Kamal the butler, my heart beating so fast and so loudly I feel others can hear it. She walks across the room and kisses me full on the lips. Girls generally taste good to me, but this is sweetness of a whole new level. Forward perhaps, but graciousness personified. Wow! She orders "Kamal, show Lieutenant Annaheim to the blue bathroom". Bliss! A deep bath is already drawn. Cool and with some unguents and soaps seductively smelling of jasmine; over-ripe and rather physical. Kamal disappears and a few minutes later Lady D comes in.

I go red, not because I am in the bath naked, but because she is almost the same. There's a totally see-through white muslin robe hanging off her lithe body. I can see her full breasts and her wide dark nipples. Everything!

She sits on a stool beside the bath and says; "Let me scrub your back", and she takes a sponge and starts over. Just like dear old 'Nursey', but this time with even more urgency and intent.

"You are a cavalry man George, so tell me about your sword. Is it long?" I hesitate for a second before replying; "The Army call it the short sword but it's long enough. Why not feel!" She does and then; "Have you used it in anger yet?' I play dumb, but the blood is rising within.

Electricity is in the air, and my ears are aching, I am excited, and, as I stand up and she proffers a towel; "Come through when you are dry George", she says leaving the bathroom. I am standing in a soft white towel, covering a warmth that's burning from within and low down on the old torso.

As I follow her through to her bedroom, I am starting to tremble a little. She is standing naked in the half darkened room. She now comes over, pulls the towel away and grabs my buttocks. So I do the same to her, and we topple onto the bed. I cannot describe what is happening in detail, but some minutes later she murmurs "Do it from behind Lieutenant", and definitely moans a lot as I comply. It seems the friction of this event releases more of the perfumes from the bath oils. Glorious scent!

After that, she does most of it, sitting astride me holding my hands above my head. I lay back and just help while admiring the body of a really striking woman. She looks in tremendous form. And she is! It seems like she is like a moth to a flame!

Neither of us speaks for some time; we are smoking Turkish (enemy) cigarettes afterwards, not talking. I am thinking; I really hope I have given her the same pleasure she has given me.

The total experience has been like acting in some kind of play – a matinee performance indeed! Played in three – or was it four acts?

I feel I am 'a true swordsman' when she tells me just that. I won't fall for this beauty, just lay back and enjoy the experiences. She says; "George, your short sword really is powerful!"

This has to be the best convalescence ever!

My second Christmas 'Dejeuner' in Egypt, and my first in an Officers Mess. This time in Heliopolis as part of the Sixth Reserve Battalion of the 29th Division. What a riot! The mix of Australian, Irish and Lancashire Officers all ripping through the claret is a recipe for a wild time. The 'Abassia Blancmange' is already covering the walls before the coffee is served. A tremendous night – enough said!

A written order has just arrived;

To: 2nd Lt Annaheim G.H
Please report to Headquarters 29th Division Base Depot,
Mustapha, Alexandria. Forthwith.
Railway Warrant attached.
Captain Wickam for G.O.C Cairo District.
Abbasia 2/1/16

Training and 'resting' is over, and it seems like I'm off to war again; and it could be the Western Front at last. I am appointed Transport Officer to the 1st Battalion The Royal Munster Fusiliers, and we are sailing for France. How about some leave!?

These Egyptian escapades have ended after eighteen months. That's also the end of seeing the baking sun everyday.

That flash of brilliant light in my head has gone, as this flashback dies suddenly.

3

THOSE FIRST MEETINGS

"...when I met you in that 'first meeting',
I fell in love with you absolutely."

Oh Dorice! Such a pretty picture of you has just flashed through my mind! I always knew we were destined for each other, even from a very early age. The very first, 'first meeting' probably doesn't count.

Mother says we first met in Broad Street Bath when she and 'the little Mater' ran into each other pushing prams - about 1892ish. "You and Dorice shrieked at each other from pram to pram. Little did I realise you would grow up and get to know her so well!"

That's a bit rich, since she has been treating me as a kid for most, no, all of my life. She never really accepted my Darling Dorice as my only true love. That, is still making me cross.

Now on leave from France, Dais tells me all about Dorice Hookway; "Bubbie, she's a dear and pretty little kid and I will introduce you." I am not keen and said; "Leave it alone Dais, I'm not so keen, so please don't set me up - there's a war on. After all, that's why I said 'goodbye' to KF. And, after all, we're in a war."

Dais is her own person, and never takes no for an answer.

So, maybe, the real 'first meeting' is this arrangement by my dear sister, with an outing to Cheddar Gorge on a sunny day in June 1916 – twenty-two months since I left England for my Egyptian 'escapades'.

It is a nice ride in a couple of 'char-a-bancs', a walk up the gorge and a picnic on the grass. No alcohol provided, but I still play the fool as there are so many ladies there; Dorothy Adams, dear Dais and her old man Sid Carpenter, Mrs. Hookway, two maids and, the pretty little Dorice of course. All jolly fun, and I do try to steal a kiss in the back seat. Clumsy of me! Here is a girl with a beautiful face. She seems so fragile I just want to cup her head with my hands. A girl with a figure that is so stunning, I want to hug her and feel her curves up close. Am I a fool for being a bit too rough? But I must see her again.

I do, and it is one week later. We are off in Carpenter's automobile to Weston super Mare with Dais and Dorothy as joint chaperones for Dorice. The chaperones are good sports. They understand, and I am spending fifteen minutes alone with little Dorice in a shelter on the seafront.

What passes for conversation is me doing all the talking. Boasting actually; "I'm a cavalry man just back from 18 months fighting the Turks". "I love my sister Dais, we confide in each other, even though she is married to that dry old stick Sid Carpenter". "I won the challenge cup at the Avon rowing club. You must come out on the river with me."

Dorice is a little more open to my interest, which must be

obvious to her by now. Something sparks in me, and dear little Dorice lets me give her a hug. I try a tender kiss. She doesn't respond. I get a feeling that while she is not kissing me back, a spark crosses between us that says more than words, or kisses, can reveal.

So, from now on, my life takes a turn away from sport, horses, and the old Army. It turns wholeheartedly to this dear girl.

It is my last night of this first leave from France, and Dais and the Carpenter have organised a dinner soiree at 'The Towers', their impressive home up on Lansdown. The usual crowd are here, including my parents, colleagues of both Sid Carpenter and Mr. Hookway from the Bath Law Society, and Mrs. Hookway, and of course Dorice Hookway herself. The others, I don't notice, only this little Girlie herself.

And now she is singing. Beautifully, like a professional. I am quite choked and even tearful as this is the England I want to be part of, and she is the girl shining for me. I want her to become part of my life. I am frozen by obsession, fantasy, love. I must win her. What a voice! What a Darling Girl!

I leave for the smoking lounge with the rest of the men, but manage to slip away into Carpenter's study. Herc is a small card and an envelope. I write a secret note. How I will get this unnoticed to Dorice? I will find a way.

Late Wednesday night at the Towers

Darling dearest little Dorice
Its my only chance of writing to you and knowing you will get this scrawl without your pater or mater seeing it. Wasn't

it rotten having saying goodbye so soon, without being able to take you in my arms and hug you?

Dorice, you must know I love you. Do take care of yourself for me, and remember me when I'm gone.

You have just left my sister's house and I am terribly lonely. Goodnight.

Goodbye dearest little one
George H Annaheim
1st RMF
B.E.F, France

I take my parents home to Belgrave Place and return to Sid and Dais's house for the last few hours before I must leave early for the six am GWR train. And then back to the war.

It's two in the morning and Dais and I are sitting by the fire and it seems both of are agreeing Dorice is a sweet girl and a real 'catch'. I tell her that I have fallen in love with Dorice after these 'first meetings'. But does she love me? I trust Dais more than anyone in the world, and she promises to get the note to Dorice without Mr. or Mrs. Hookway seeing.

What will be the reaction? I can only hope for a reply when I'm back in France.

All these 'First meetings' have changed my outlook, and my life, forever. I write again:

Dear Dorice,

Just arrived at Boulogne and find there is no communication with the front today so I am staying here until tomorrow.

I am terribly homesick today and had an absolutely rotten journey. I was thinking about you all the way over.
Did you get the scrawl I sent you from Dais's place? I didn't

say half of what I wanted to.

Do write as I am dying to hear from you. The Carpenter remarked how well we got to know each other, and in such a short time!! Bow wow!

I don't know what it has to do with him though.

Cheerie Ho, Goodbye,

Ever Yours,

George 'Bubbie' Annaheim

I am writing again while at the Officers Rest House in Boulogne. I am keeping writing hoping a reply will arrive at the Battalion:

17th June 1916

My Dearest Dorice,

I cannot go to bed tonight without first starting a letter to you, but I am not going to post it until I hear from you as I have already written twice since I saw you!! My Journey so far has been absolutely rotten, simply and solely because I fell in love with you absolutely.

I passed your house at about 3.30am and looked up to see if there was a light on – no luck. Dorice, tell me you like me more than any other friends you have.

How I did enjoy the last few days of leave.

I wrote to your Pater as he told me to, but I also asked permission to write to you. Of course it doesn't make much difference if he tells me not to, but we shall have to think of some plan to outwit him.

I shall never forget our little trips to Cheddar, and, of course, to Weston s Mare! Mrs. Adams was a true sport!

I wonder how you will start a letter to me. Not "Mr Annaheim" for Heavens sake. While the pals call me 'Anna' or George, my family nickname is "Bubbie" from Herbert I suppose. I would rather like you to call me that.

Goodnight Girlie. I wish I could be in the old motor with you, even if your Mater and Pater were there!

The old Bosche are sending shells over my billet tonight. I'm off to the trenches at about 11.30 tonight.

Ever Yours,

Bubbie

The post corporal arrives with two letters from 1 South Parade, and one of which I shall keep safely as it is the first ever I receive from this darling girl;

Dear George, or may I call you Bubbie,

I received several lovely letters from you as you travelled back to France. Letters that touched my heart. I have asked Pater's permission to write to you, and he said it would be allowed.

Well 'Bubbie', I should tell you that our several meetings were important to me, as they seem to be to you. I had heard of you from your sister Dais Carpenter, who I have known as a friend for several years. Also my Pater and Mr. Carpenter are both solicitors in Bath and frequently see each other at their work.

Well, when we went to Cheddar, I saw this tall man in uniform, with a loud laugh and smiling eyes, who clearly was close to Dais. Then you looked at me with your watery blue eyes and my heart skipped a beat.

You certainly had some tales to tell about Egypt, but I was rather shy and just listened.

Then there was the trip to Weston. In that seafront shelter, I admit I melted when you held me captive by your stare. As your face came close to mine, my heart raced, my cheeks must have been rose-red, and I felt rather faint. When you kissed me, I just couldn't move, or think, or speak.

And then, at the party up at the Carpenters home, I could

feel the warmth and affection in your eyes as you listened to my singing.

But couldn't help remembering our time in the shelter, while I was singing 'Because'. You were a naughty boy in Weston, but I forgive you!

I am enclosing two little photographs of me that you may wish to keep.

I look forward to your next letter soldier-man.

Ever your

Dorice Hookway

I reply immediately:

My dearest little Girlie

At last I have received two letters from you. Thank you sweet Girlie. Cheerio Ho!

I am in love with you so much I can't wait for my next leave. What what!

Yesterday my Transport was inspected by the General, and of course he strafed me as these people are prone to do. I was feeling particularly glum and then your letters arrived. I thought you had forgotten all about me. And I was thrilled to hear from your dear self that you DO care for me! The pictures you sent of your dear self are absolutely topping and I am writing to Dais to give you one of me – maybe from Egypt.

I have sent you some buttons and badges on a shamrock from the Munster's, which we would wear in peacetime on our mess tunics. I wonder if you would wear them somewhere for me. I would like you to be a proud 'Munster's girl'.

Ever yours,

Bubbie Annaheim.

That first meeting, when the thunderbolt struck, I recall once again, one evening during the Loos 'stunts', when writing in my tent.

My own darling Dorice

I am just a wee bit unhappy tonight as there's been no mail today. Perhaps there will be two tomorrow morn! I shall never forget writing my first letter to you darling Dorice, four months ago.

It was very late and I was sitting by the fire talking to Dais after that special evening was over. I had taken Mother and Father home and Sid had gone to bed. We were waiting for an hour or so before I had to go down to the station and back to this old war. Dais said she had lots of things to talk about, but I only wanted to talk about 'you, you and you'. So I gave her that first scribbled note and asked her to get it to you in secret.

I do wish we could have been alone more than just those few moments.

Leave seems to be halted as we are in the Line; in and out, every few days, and it's getting quite 'busy' out here as the Huns are sending over tons of shrapnel shells. I have lost a few pals already, but we are doing daring things to keep the Boscheman guessing.

When I do come marching home it will be wonderful if you can meet me. You will meet me won't you?

I simply love the little snaps of you taken at Cheddar. You are evidently chewing cake and Sid Carpenter is handing something to Mrs. Adams, but you look simply a darling, as you really are.

I am going to sleep now with sweet dreams of your darling self.

Millions of hugs and kisses
Your own
Bubbie A.

A momentous and joyful time in my life as letters arrive that confirm that darling Dorice is truly mine:

Dorice my own Baby Girlie

When I met you in that 'first meeting' I fell in love with you absolutely. There's no turning back for me. I want you as mine. I can't really believe that it is YOU who is writing so sweetly to me.

Look here Girlie I will be straight with you. I was unofficially engaged before. But her parents objected to me so I did not see much of her and she didn't love me, and me not her.

I loved your last letter when you told me over and over again you loved me. By the way, when we met outside the ticket office in Bond Street, you looked absolutely "it". I could have hugged you there and then although my old headmaster was just across the road!!

I want you always to love me if you can and I think it will be like Heaven when I have you in my arms and actually hear you say 'I Love You Bubbie'.

All my love and kisses and hugs Dorice mine
Ever your own devoted
Bubbie xxxxxx

Those 'first meetings' changed my short life forever.

They were fateful, joyful and, I believe, ordained by God.

The picture in my head is fading, but will never disappear.

Oh, Dorice, where are you now?!

4

THAT RING

"Will you wear the ring on your dear little engagement finger?"

Anxiety is striking me hard. Like a bullet from above. It's about all the 'to-ing' and 'fro-ing' over THAT ring. For, one of the most anxious times of my life is wondering if she will wear it.

I have been such a fool at times, but I want her to love and treasure me, as long as I am fated to live. Life doesn't look too long now though, as this flashback recalls such worrying times.

I send the ring to her only a week after that 'first meeting'. I suppose I am impetuous, but maybe it is a way of erasing the past mistakes I made with my love life – such as it was. Besides, stories are legion of dead and wounded being stripped of signet and wedding rings AND NOT just by the Boscheman – our chaps too. Poor show indeed!

My darling Dorice,

You were a dear child to send me those two photos of you. I have been peeking at them all day. Do send me some more.

I have got a ring with my initials, but I don't wear it as I think if I was laying wounded somewhere some wretched

Bosche might cut my finger off for my ring, which would not be very pleasant.

Now may I send this ring to you to look after it for me? Perhaps if you looked at it you might remember poor old me. I cannot ask you to wear it as your Pater-well, may object.

Goodbye, my Darling little Girlie
With heaps of hugs and kisses
Ever Yours Bubbie

The signet ring is given to me on my 16th birthday when I leave King Edward's School, and start with the Bank. Apparently, it comes from some distant uncle on the Swiss side. I wear it till I am twenty. Now I've moved to the Manchester Branch, I have given it to Katherine. Her folks never liked me so I think it's a way of holding on to her. She told me that she wears it round her neck. It's an unofficial engagement.

Kathy sends it back in December 1914 to the Annaheim home in Belgrave Place, after my letter ending it all. Just as well.

It takes me a month, and about ten letters to ask dearest Dorice to WEAR that ring.

My Darling Dorice,

It's perfectly topping getting a letter every morning, you are a dear! So you thought perhaps I was only "flirting". No, I was – and am – truly in love with you.

I sent a couple of shamrocks for you and your mater to wear. WE are the only Regiment in the British Army to wear the shamrock on our hat – so it's something to be proud of I think! Please wear it on your bonnet.
Dorice Darling, I am going to whisper this;

"Will you wear my ring on your dear little engagement finger? I wish I could put it on myself and seal it with a kiss".

If I am spared to see you again, and you still love me then you are properly engaged to me. I must write to your Pater to let me have you absolutely for my own. He and your dear Mater might object, but if we love each other – well – perhaps they might acquiesce?!

Do you know what Dais says but you must not tell her I told you;"I hope we shall all live to see you two married". Wouldn't it be some honeymoon! I think if you were mine Darling all our life would be one long honeymoon don't you?

Tonight some of the fellows came out of the trenches and said "how's the girl Anna?" I wasn't kidding when I said; "Mine". They then polished off those wonderful chocs you sent! Marvellous pals the Battalion Officers!

I must now "allez aux trenches".

I love you with all my heart and have only you to live for.

Ever your own Bubbie

Please tell me about the Ring.

A short while later I write:

Dearest,

I am writing again, as, after I sealed a last envelope to you, I have more love and thoughts to send to you, the prettiest Girlie in the world.

The old Quartermaster is going up to the trenches tonight, so I can write to you again. I am not going to take unnecessary risks, 'cos I want to see you and hug you again; this time I will not be doing it against your wishes.

It was perfectly topping of you to send me a letter today, and containing ripping little snap of your dear self.

Now, I am still worrying about if you will wear the ring. Will you really wear it? I wish I could put it on your dear sweet finger, but I hope to see it there when I come home again. If anyone wants to know whose it is. Say it's mine, and so are you!!

Will you really wear it? You can get it altered if doesn't fit you. It actually belonged to some great, great, great grand uncle or other; some Swiss gentleman, probably called 'Gay-org' Annaheim.

Now I will send you a very small portion of Dais' last letter to me; "I think she is a dear little kid and you would be a lucky chap if you could get her. She was looking sweetly pretty on Friday......she was wearing your badge round her neck".

Dais and I were always great pals, I am so glad you are both pals too.

The Bosche are shelling this little village I'm in, but so far they haven't hit anything at all. It is great to sleep through it all. Goodnight my own darling little Girlie

Ever your own

Bubbie

Now I get a missive from my dear 'sis' Dais, telling-me-off; "it's unlucky":

Dear Bubbie,

It was wonderful hearing in your last letter that you are safe, and proud of your work in the Regiment.

Mother, Father and Sidney send you their warmest greetings and we all are following the brave exploits of the 16th Irish Division in the papers.

I can tell you that I met Dorice in Milsom Street, and we went for some tea together. She is a sweet charming girl and I know she is perfect for you. I have thought that for years, which is why we introduced you to each other.

But, dear Bubbie, sending her a Ring you already gave to Katherine Freeman before, is not a good idea. It is an <u>unlucky omen</u> for the future, and you must quickly write to Dorice and send a 'proper' engagement ring. I am so happy for you *that you have found in Dorice a lovely girl for keeps. Don't spoil it by giving her second-hand ring.*

If you send me some money I can go and choose a nice new one. Like you asked, I am sending Dorice some more photos of you – the ones from Egypt and some of your rowing exploits.

We have just heard from Eddy. He is paymaster officer now serving on a torpedo boat destroyer based in Salonika and seems happy with his life out there. Do write to him c/o HMS Adamant.

All our love to you, dearest little Brother, from the Annaheim and Carpenter families, and especially from me, your ever loving sister Dais. I pray for you every night.

Ps write soon

Dais gets a 'fiver' to buy a proper engagement ring – but the engagement is still secret:

My very own darling little Dorice

I don't know how to thank you sufficiently for your ripping letter and the topping parcel which turned up ok. I am quite cheery umps! I quite understand that the ring I gave you isn't good enough but it will do Dorice until I find a substitute won't it? I knew you wouldn't mind, even if it was made of iron.

However, Dais did write and strafe me for giving it to you, it's so rotten, but it's the only ring I ever possessed in my life. You know Dorice, I was never actually engaged to anyone, but we will both forget what happened before we met each other. Bow wow!

Let us both pray that the day I will be allowed to look after you and you will be my loving little wifie, may not be very far away.

From you own old B

I've now got the courage and write to Dorice's parents. Luckily I really think they like me. The "old man" himself is just a topping fellow – quite different from my own father. Mr. Hookway likes his whiskey and is a real man whom I respect and whose company I enjoy. I would happily serve with him in the Army. Mrs. Hookway – "the dear little Mater", is a sweet lady, and anyone would enjoy her attentions as his mother in law. She is a dear.

That feeling of guilt regarding the ring however, is still haunting me, so I am writing a 'confessional':

My very own darling little Girl,

Something is worrying me very much indeed today. It may make a huge difference to the amount you love me!! Sounds dreadful! but still it's on my conscience. I hope it won't make any difference though and you my darling will love me just as much as you did before. Now you must write immediately and tell me so that I may be happy once more. Now for it!!!

The ring you are wearing my darling little child was kept for sometime by the other Girl whom I liked before I met you. To the best of my knowledge she never wore it cos her people objected to me very strongly!!

A few years ago, before I went to Egypt, when I was in the Bank in Manchester, I simply gave it to her as a keepsake. I always wore it before she had it, and I wore it when she sent it back. Somehow I didn't think it mattered much but I certainly think I ought to have told you when I sent it to you. I only meant you to keep the ring until I was able to get another for you.

Dais knows the other girl had it and told me it was bad luck to give it to someone else, namely "You" my sweet-heart.

I shall be jolly anxious to have a reply to this. Still I cannot imagine you strafing me, my darling. Perhaps I deserve it though.

Now I am going to cheer up and hope for the best.

Ever Your own loving Bubbie.

Of course, darling Dorice replies with reassurance about 'that Ring':

My Very Own Darlingest Bubbikins,

I had a ripping letter from you this morning sweetheart mine, for which I send you a big kiss!

How are you soldier boy? I hope you are taking care of yourself for me. Bubbie, do take more care Darling, don't be too reckless, but I musn't strafe you.

I want to tell you once and for all that I love the 'old ring', because it is part of you. And it is only you I want to be with and care for you the rest of my life.

Let's not go over the past friends that we had, but think to the future, our future together. Rings are just for show, but a wedding ring will be MOST welcome Darling Bubbikins!

Oh for 'apres la guerre'. I just want to kiss you and hug you and tell you how tremendously I love you.

May God bless you Sweetheart Mine, and keep you safe and sound and may he bring you home to me again very very soon.

With all my love and all my kisses and millions of hugs.

Ever your very own loving and true lickle "Baby Wifie" xxxxxxxxxxxxxx

Oh how I wish we were really married. Soon my Darling!!

The flashback of these anxieties of years gone by, even now, doesn't resolve that mistake of that Ring. Still, Dorice has it safe, and like she said all those months ago that it's part of me, that she can keep.

That ring, is only one thing to worry about.

Oh, God, how I wish I had longer....

5

'S AN AWFUL WAR

"...although I have come through as one of only five officers left in the Battalion, my chances of surviving are rather limited"

The sounds of the bands of the Lancashire regiments at Southampton docks as we board 'Deseado', jump into my aching head again.

Going off to war is an adventure I have my pals, my horse, and a chance to see the world. And, to experience war at first hand. Proudly.

The Duke of Lancaster's Own Yeomanry has a long, but 'checkered' history; (starting back in 1700 and something), as a civil militia for home duties, including the infamous charge against the crowd of people in the "Peterloo Massacre" of 1819. After that, it becomes quite famous for positive support for King and Country. Assigned to the Imperial Yeomanry force it sees action in the 2nd Boer War up to 1902.

In Egypt, war is not all noise, bullets and excitement. It is spent mostly on drills, exercises, mucking out, and boredom. At first, it's all the sports suiting me best. But then there have come 'Escapades' during my sickness and hospital stays. They definitely suit me alright!

Here in France in 1916, I am seeing a different face to war; experiencing all that the latest advances in industrialised warfare, which is hurled across the Line by each side. And, from the air as well!

I am seeing desperate French and Belgian peasants looking lost, disheveled and starving. I am seeing beautiful countryside ravaged by all the mechanisms of hate, and, I feel, I am personally being singled out by a series of Boschemen with their shells, bullets and bombs at all times of the day and night!

As I write daily to Dorice, I share as much as I can with her, minus the real horrors that are extant out here:

My darling,

I have just come back from the Line. I was wishing that could find you here. That would be nice wouldn't it? I wonder Dorice, my sweetest wife-to-be whether there are any other folk who love each other as you and I?

It is a strange world out here. I can hear the old Bosche machine gun going quite plainly;"poofp, poofp, poofp", and now the "crack, crack, crack" of rifle fire and then the "crump crump" of high explosive shells, and then the "whiz whizz" of shrapnel. Earlier on this evening there was the very uncomfy sound of; "phizz, phizz" from bullets. It means they are coming a few inches or just yards from you.

It may sound quite weird to you that I write this, but it is rather weird that we stay alive out here by listening to all these sounds, near and far; and, we can work out our chances just by sounds alone.

I should rather talk about Love, but this is an awful war darling. But we are winning and then you and I will be together for the rest of our days.

Goodnight sweetheart, I send you millions of hugs and kisses.

Ever your devoted

Bubbie

Pals and men are falling around me, as well as horses and mules killed and injured beyond saving. And then there is the stench. It's indescribable, pungent and putrid – horrible.

Yet the job itself is one I love. The duties of Transport Officer give me freedom like no other role. I don't have a Company Commander to report to, just the Colonel. I am working well with Baxter the old QM, and I still have my horses, thank goodness. The men are proving a tough bunch; hard working when sober, but difficult when drunk. Yet we do have a good understanding and mutual respect; so discipline is rather good. I am also on very good terms with the CO, who is now putting me in for a permanent Commission.

After our first efforts up at Loos and Hulloch, we are attacking the front at Ginchy, and I now am seeing a brutal face to this awful war. In just two days we are down to five officers and three hundred men after our successful, but bloody attack. After merging with the 8th Battalion we are again up to strength with forty officers and almost a thousand men. I write to Dorice to share these thoughts from right up in the trenches at Ginchy:

My Own Darling,

Don't have a shock when you see this paper; I am writing to you with all I've got here as I sit with some Pals in a very 'hot' spot in the front line, in a spot that is being shelled and bombed at present!

I cannot imagine a more uncomfortable position to be in.

The noise is absolutely terrible, but the only thing on my mind is your dear self. The Battalion are in-the-Line and really in the thick of it, and I have just brought up the rations to find many less men here than started out.

I will write more when I get out of this Hellium, but the good news is that today I saw hundreds and hundreds of German prisoners; very big fellows but absolutely broken after having had a terrible time of it.

Some of the sights I have seen here show this is turning into an even more awful war. Oh for the day when I can kiss you and kiss you and you will be all mine.

'S an awful war, but I am quite safe.

Goodbye my Darling

Always your devoted Bubbie

Months are going by, and as we move around this country, I reflect on another year of war. It gets even more stressful, as new and fiercer implements are used to grind-out more territory, and to do more harm each other.

We are winning in this sector, which they call 'Passchendaele'. The mud and slime are as never before; making this job physically harder each day and night. We take Wytschaete, (for which all the men have a favourite nick-name!), but the losses are high again, including many of my pals.

Can this war get any more gruesome I wonder? I must try and stay cheerful in my letters for those at home, whatever I feel inside:

Dear darling little darling Girl,

I received your wee letter yesterday that cheered me, as I am so happy that you still love your old 'Hubbie-to-Be'.

It's a perfectly rotten old war and Heaven knows how

long it will last now the Russians are retreating. Suppose the Bosche will now send all their guns to this side and it will be "take me back to dear old Blighty", and the sooner the better. The Bosche are using lot of gas shells now – a new sort which burns your eyes out!! S'an awful war Dearie!!

Well, let's talk about love. There are only two things to talk about – Love and War, and seeing I am banned from talking about the latter, well, here's to Love!

Leave WILL come round soon and we will be happy and alone, caring for nobody else at all. Our little world away from this awful war will be just you and I.

This war will last all winter I think but what does it matter as long as I am alive and get leave occasionally – should come soon unless there is a push and then might get delayed. Bow wow! Cheer up Girl, you must always be thankful that I am alive and kicking!

I am writing in a tent painted so the whiteness won't be seen by Bosche aeroplanes – oooer! It smells rather badly but I am near my men and horses and everything in the garden is lovely.

Oh oh, the post corporal has come so I must say goodbye Darling Girl – in haste.

All love and kisses from you adoring

Bubbie xxx

Days of action pass by in a kind of nightmarish dream. No rest, no sleep; just work, work, work. All done under the most intensive shellfire I can ever remember:

My darling little Girlie,

I dunno,'s rotten! You say you don't get my letters, while I am getting yours quite well now. Nothing has happened to me, darling one, I cannot even get a 'cooshy one'. I am a little tired; as I am not getting much rest and the work right now is particularly difficult up near the front. If I was wounded and unable to write, I would get the 'Padre' to write a line for me; that's what he's for. Or my pal the Doc-man.

If I told you of all my adventures you would call me, well, some names. But I am lucky.

The other day I went to a neighbouring town and left at 11.45am. On the way back I thought the old Bosche was dropping a few more than usual in these parts. Well, the bombardment started at midday, and altogether two hundred people were blesse etc. It may be in the paper, it may not. I cannot tell you the name of the town, but it starts with an A. Anyway sweetheart, it was lucky we left it when we did. My horse and groom were standing in the town square most of the morning, and soon after we left, the square was 'finished'. Bow wow!!

It's a real shame about the post not getting to you, as I am writing as never before; literally every day. They will turn up I am sure – it's this awful war!!

Goodbye darling I am off to the trenches, don't worry, in a day or so it will be much safer as we will be out of the line.

With one big hug and a one long kiss on your dear sweet little lips

Ever your own devoted
Bubbie xxxxx

The war goes-on into a third year, and we still seem to be stuck around the same old parts of France:

Darling little one,

Lots has happened since I last wrote a line. We have been in a Push – a real 'stunt'.

I suppose you know where, and I'm alive – not even a scratch. It was terrible, absolutely terrible, and far worse than all the other stunts like the Somme, Loos, Hulloch, etc.

We must have had 90 casualties in one day!! So you can guess the size of the Battalion now. I have only been able to send some field pc's to let you know I was alive. I walked through a Bosche barrage the night before last and never thought I'd see dear old England again. Still, they can't hit me (touch wood) and, I am here, after a bath, clean, and in my right mind (more or less), and loving you Girl such a tremendous lot. I am still both QM and TO so my work is 'cut out' for me, but I will do my best to write whenever I can grab a moment.

Leave will surely come soon, as will the second pip!! Your old 'Hubbie' seems to have forgotten how to write so we'll just have to win the war and learn to write 'apres'. Bow Wow!!

The dear old Docman is still alive although he too has had a terrible time lately. I have been soaked through in these clothes for a whole week, but they have dried as it has stopped raining.

Goodbye darling Dearest Wifie. Your photo has been with me each step and each ride all the time. It and your letters are keeping me merry and bright though; 'S an awful war, Dearie!!

I love you and love you and love you.

All the kisses in the world and thousands of hugs and cuddles.

Ever your own loving Hubbie
Bubbie
xxxxxxxxx

Into the fourth year of this awful war, and things are getting more dangerous than ever. The Bosche 'Spring Offensive', which becomes our 'Great Retreat', brings me even closer to death than at any time in my short life. Dense clouds of gas, huge shells, flamethrowers and machine guns fired by

Bosche 'Storm Troopers' are just part of my horrendous experiences during these 'Adventures in Retreat'.

Losses are enormous on our side, but it is the intensity of this, more 'open' warfare, that shocks us all.

Between March 21st 1918, and early April, the 16th Irish Division, including the 47th and 48th Brigades are decimated, and we are standing before Amiens with so very few men. Brave deeds have been done, but they will probably never be recorded, such is the confusion and losses we have suffered.

There is talk of amalgamating the 1st and 2nd Battalions. Actually, it does occur, but has lasted merely a week before we start moving north and west as separate Battalions.

Resting and refitting is slowly taking place, and as I recover my strength and health, I realise this is a brutal total war. Although I have come through as one of only five officers in the Battalion, my chances of surviving intact are rather limited.

It is thus time to not only muse on these bad prospects, but to make some preparations. I am deeply depressed and particularly melancholy, so I prepare a letter to Mother and Dad and ask Baxter to send it in the future – if I don't make it through this awful war.

10/4/1918
Handed to Baxter for sending should I not come through.

My Dearest Mother and Father,
I hope you never get to read or even see this letter – because if you don't then I would have survived this awful war.

I decided to write this one to you, and ask my good pal Baxter, the QM, with whom I have experienced many months of total war, to get this to you as quickly as possible.

The last few weeks have been especially difficult and tremendously horrific. The Battalion is now down to 5 officers and just over 200 men, while the 2nd Battalion is reduced to just three officers and have lost nearly all their men in the fighting retreat. I have used every ounce of stamina and tenacity to get through with my men and animals, only to find out that so many of my pals have fallen. I cannot begin to count them, as it would hurt so much.

Maybe the Good Lord, who has just looked after me for so long, has decided my turn has finally come.

But if you read this, dear parents, then you will know I did my duty to the end. I want to tell you that I am sorry for all the problems I gave you as a boy, and more recently, as a man.

I know I wasn't so good academically and I reflect that this must have been especially painful to you, Father, as a professor and teacher of such a slack boy at old King Edward's.

You have been good, kind parents to Eddy, Dais and I, and I could not have wished for a better upbringing. Thank you. All the 'issues' between us were my fault and I regret all the 'anxiete' I must have given you.

So if you are reading this I would like you to be content parents of a 'soldier-boy' who fought for the King, and dear old England.

I have been a proud cavalryman and an even prouder officer in this, one of the finest Regiments in the Army. The bravest men I ever met have been Munsters; fighting behind a shamrock and a Bengal tiger – tigers indeed! The Bosche really do fear us in Battle.

I want you to promise me that through your sadness at me falling, that you will always take care of my Darling wife Dorice. I realise you were shocked by our swift courtship and marriage, but this is a great war after all, and grabbing happiness seemed to be the thing to do before it was too late. I have had the happiest year of my short life with Dorice, having fallen in love with her so deeply and completely. It is my thoughts of her that have kept me alive for so long, 'til now. Now it is over she will be distraught and she may be with child-who will be a true Annaheim, and, your grandchild.

I beg of you to take care of those I love so much; yourselves, Dais, Eddy and of course, especially, my darling wife and any 'wee A'.

These thoughts make me cry because Dorice and I had such plans for the future; plans that would have made you happy too.

Dorice's Mater and Pater are fine people and always treated me like a son, so I implore you to be friends and true pals with the Hookways. I loved them as 'family' too

Dearest Mother and Father, I realise this is inadequate by way of expressing my deepest thoughts and feelings. If you are reading this I have prayed that you both have long healthy lives and now, not be too sad. We will meet in another place; as is God's design.

My sincerest Love to you
From your son
Herbert (Bubbie) xxx

I write a similar 'what if' letter to Dorice together with a loving poem, which I wrote at this same time; which I also give to Baxter. He will only post these in case I don't come through.

Well, he will have to do that now, and it seems there will be no band music for my exit.

'S BEEN AN AWFUL WAR!

6

MARRIAGE, 'YEAH or NAY'?

"Do tell anyone who wants to know...
I am your future husband!"

"Da Dum Dee Dum – Da Dum Dee Dum".

Is that the noise of my officer pals bawling-out Mendelssohn's Wedding March at an impromptu and rowdy "bash"? The CO is on leave, and I have just returned to the Battalion after my wedding in April 1917.

The pals are marching into the mess are led, of course, by Marsden – the cad! "Here Comes The Bride" indeed! So they all know about Dorice and me 'tying the knot'. What they don't know is all the anguish of the decision to get married in the first place. Marriage, yeah or nay? A journey of it's own.

By July 1916 I am already 'fishing':

My very own darling sweetheart Dorice,

I am looking forward to tomorrow when I hope to get a line from you, as there was 'nixo' today.

I've just come back from the Line a little earlier than usual, and there were only a few bullets knocking about. I was riding my dear velvet-nosed DoriceII, and tonight she was scared of the hundreds of rats which in these parts are as large as kittens.

Dais wrote and said how she will look after you for me. Did she give you that little miniature of me yet? I won't want you to always wear it. But I like to think of it next to your heart. I am sure it will be comfy there! You can kiss me then occasionally. And I can kiss you there; when you take it off! Bow wow!!

We had a top hole time on the last days of my leave, and until you wrote, I didn't realise how much you loved me. You DO know how much I love you?

Do tell anyone who wants to know (esp. your kissin' cousins!) that I am your future Husband who loves you vey much indeed. I want to be your best pal, and, your Hubbie.

In your last dear letter, you said; "we might elope". Well, we'll see Dearest. There is this war that has to be won, but at least we are winning, in this sector anyway. I must also win over your Pater and dear little Mater to the idea.

One thing for sure is that, you are Mine, and that we will be happy together.

As I fall asleep in my little cot I send you a Teddy Bear Hug.
With all my hugs and kisses, dearest little
Girlie Mine. I adore you.
Bubbie xxxxx

Dennis Symons 'stirs the pot' from Salonika where he has been with the 6th Battalion He wants to know when he's to be the 'best man'! I reply that he should remember that I'm to be his 'best man' too, as we agreed years ago when we last met in the Royal Gloucestershire Hussars. A good school-chum too. He is on his way back to re-enter Bristol Medical School, after losing a hand to the enemy out there – Bulgars I suppose. Perhaps we will have a "Double Wedding Event"!

Thinking all this through, I am beginning to secretly have doubts as to the timing:

My own darling little Lady,

Some mail today! One from 'my Girlie', one from 'big Sis' Dais, and one from my future father-in-law; although, he may be unaware of it at present.

There is no question about it; I am merry and bright today.

My dear big sister Dais suggests; "that you and Dorice should get married when you come home!!! On five pence??!! (Even though I have been saving quite a bit).

Seriously dearest, I have been thinking that it would not be quite playing-the-game to get married while this wretched war is still on.

You see, (much as I should long to have you all to myself and you become 'Mrs.A'), well, I should have to come back here, and anything might happen. Then you would be a pretty little widow, and perhaps widders don't get married again as often as girls – so you see your life would be spoilt.

Now, if we get married when the war is over and I am alive, (cos we can't get married if I am under the ground) then we shall always be together. Don't you think it's by far the best idea?? I am getting quite serious right now.

Darling, leave has started so coming home is getting nearer and nearer. I have promised myself it isn't fair to go away and probably get pipped. So I mustn't think any more about it. Dais just sparked something in my brain. She is a bad girl – she puts all the naughty ideas in my head!

Meanwhile Dearest, all is quite quiet apart from when I take up the rations each night. Shelling, mortar bombing and sniping are just 'part of the job' 'S an awful war, dearie! But I will be home soon.

Goodnight my sweetheart.

All my love and kisses and cuddles too
Ever your devoted
Bubbie xxx

Times change, and the war is getting ever more dangerous for me, and my men. But as our loving letters continue, it is clear that Dorice and I should risk all. For love and marriage, and, for however short or long that may be. So, now, after the Ginchy 'stunt' on the Somme, I write to Mr. Hookway with a straightforward request to marry Dorice:

Dear Mr Hookway,

I expect Dorice gave you a bit of a shock when she mentioned "marriage with me"!! Well, I want to act straightforwardly with you, and if you think it best to wait until the war is over, well, that's enough.

I haven't ever asked you if I may have her! You know I will do all in my power to make her life a happy and contented one. Will you send me a letter expressing your views!!! I don't mind how much you 'strafe' me!!

Your letter will make a difference to my next leave. Will you tell me this, on my next leave may Dorice become officially engaged to me so that we may see, at any rate, a good deal of each other? If not, I don't care much about coming home.

Well, I can only apologise for not writing to you before, but I just found time to occasionally drink "your jolly good health".

Very best wishes
Yours Sincerely
George Herbert Annaheim

My proposal goes off the same day!

Darling Wifie-to-be

I kiss your photo every day even though I am in a tent and can't pin it up. I want to take you into my arms and kiss and hug you, as Dorice, I do love you. Darling will you marry me during my next leave? That's that!! If you agree!

I promise to be a good and dutiful husband forever and ever more and more every day. I propose we "allons" for about three to five days and then spend the rest of the leave in Bath. We must talk about these things now Sweetheart Mine, 'cos there won't be much time to discuss it when I come home.

Will you answer my question re allowing me to look after you for life in your next letter. I shall love to hear what your Pater says about it to me!!! 'Cos as you probably know, I wrote (or rather scribbled) and asked for his candid opinion. My Mother wants me to wait until "après la Guerre" mais, ce n'est pas possible, n'est-ce pas? Bow wow!

Now Girlie, for this effort you must write me a long, long letter 'cos – well I loves ye see!

All my love and kisses
Ever your devoted and loving
Bubbie xxxxxxx
Ps please tell Dais I will write to her tomorrow.

Her 'auld man' <u>is</u> allowing us to get 'officially engaged' as a start, thanks to the positive intervention of 'the little Mater'. Meanwhile my own parents are divided. Mother, with her negative and 'pious' views about "the consequences and risks of the war", and saying, "what if you got wounded for life?"

Father, at least says he thinks; "Dorice is better for you than Katherine Freeman, as she was really rather dull, while Dorice is really a lively girl". Good for him at least, and, at last. I get a sermon from them nevertheless!

Another hiccup on the way; as during a 'stunt', when it impossible to write; Dorice 'strafes' me about spending my time; "dining with the Colonel, rather than writing to your dearest love". Is it possibly that her cold is upsetting her, or is it that silly mistake I made in sending a picture of me in Egypt with my arm around 'Nursey'? Or, just a bad time-of-the-month?

Well, I write to placate her, and keep up my desires for us to be married:

My own dearest little Darling,

I am sitting on the ground writing on a little box and, 's not very comfy. Now it is resolved, thank goodness. After all the worries out here about 'who gets the Transport job'. There were three of us up for it including a Captain from the War Office and I was a lowly 2nd Lieut. At least that is now settled. I've, got the job. Bonski!

Darling I'm sorry you were a bit cross with me! I've never been cross with you. Did you think I didn't love you anymore? That's not so darling. I can't help loving you and loving you, so there!!

I write whenever I can, and even when I'm a little worried (like about my job, or when we're in the middle of a 'stunt'), and, I wasn't, or haven't, been dining with the Colonel.

Baby Mine, I love you and adore you, and crave your letters. I know my own are so patchy, usually so, after 'a whiff of gas'.

Darling, from the moment we met, and also when we are together forever, I promise to be a good little boy! And, I will never give up on wanting you for my own wee Wife.

There is that photo of the "Egyptian Affair", but you must realise that in that campaign, I hadn't met you yet Dorice Darling. Well, I have been an angel, since then, and I promise to love you and adore you more and more every day, and, forever, and ever.

Girlie Mine, forgive me for all I have said and done that has hurt you. All my kisses and hugs

Ever your own devoted

Bubbie xxxxx

Leave is stopped for months this winter 1916, with a constant in-and-out of the Line up here in the Spanbroek sector. Rather tiring, and we are deep in mud and filth. I get a short leave at the New Year, and we have cemented our engagement with a ring bought in the Corridor in Bath. We are talking marriage again, but there are lots of family issues that I now have to sort out on my return to France:

My dearest Darlingest Dorice,

I am very happy now that we have talked 'shop' together. I was sorry we had to put up with all that family nonsense on my short leave. It did make me anxious and unhappy, but now things look much cheerier. It was rather extraordinary that you and your Mater imagined you were not welcome at my home. I will tell you honestly, Dorice mine. They did not want me to get married on that leave and even borrowed thirty pounds from me to stop us in our tracks!

They both love you Sweetheart, but I have absolutely finished talking to them. Dais loves you, I know Father loves you, and, as for Mother, – she doesn't count – although she likes you. She apologized for all the things she said which were foolish. What's more she didn't like Carpenter at all and said Dais wouldn't be happy, but, as always, she's wrong!!! How very cutting of her to say she liked Katherine Freeman!! She knows that I never loved KF as I do you. Just ignore her foolishness!

I am free of all that 'anxiete' Darling, and am going to

make 'it' happen on my next leave. By the way, one thing I am NOT going to do is the thing you said in your last letter; "Get another Girl"!!

I am very satisfied and I know THIS ONE is with me and will be with me – throughout our lives together. I am yours; body and soul, as you are mine.

All my hugs and kisses I send to you.

Ever your own true Hubbie-to-Be

Bubbie xxx

I am having a bit of a change of mind as we are preparing for another big 'show', working day and night, and practicing for attacking the Bosche again. Somewhere, sometime, soon.

Should I go through with this marriage idea when the chances of getting more than just a 'Blighty' seem ever present? Dorice is a brick, and writes daily as if we are already "Homme et Femme":

My own dearest darling soldier-boy!

Thank you so much for another dear love letter. I was so glad to receive it, though I would prefer it if you yourself would come marching home again!

Bubby mine, I love you so, and am so sorry about all the 'family troubles' you had on that last leave.

Listen, soldier-man, nothing has changed between US, see? We love each other, and our lives our entwined forever, so all will work out well, I am sure. We will get married on your next leave, or jolly well elope! My Mater and Pater are now all for it – so what's to stop us Darling?

I don't need riches and fancy rings and things-although the story of 'THAT ring' still makes me smile! We can live here at 1 South Parade, in the room upstairs until this war is over, and then you will have a job again with a salary, and we will live together as cozy as cozy can be. I just love you and want you so. So there!

Don't get down or lonesome darling, or I will just have to come over and slip into your tent one night.

May God take care of you my Darling Man, and keep you safe and sound for me.

Sent with all my love, kisses and hugs .

Your ever loving and true Wifie-to-be.

D xxxxxxx

This reinforces my determination; and with Dais back in Bath to work out how to arrange things for us, my spirits are high.

Once again, it's illness that sets the pace of love and destiny in my life. Writing to the 'little Mater' from the Boulogne Hospital No 14, and recovering well from Measles:

My Dear little future Ma,

I am coming home again!! And I KNOW that this time it will put you out somewhat!! You see, now, and with your 'auld man's' permission, I am coming back to marry your precious (to you AND me!!) daughter! My darling Dorice!

It will be a rush I know, but I am so very excited that things are in place thanks to your dearselves, and my sister Dais, and everyone.

The doc has cleared me from infecting anyone with the "measles" so I am free to travel home and will get 10 days – Bliss!

You won't be frightened this time if I send a telegram to Dorice with the time of my arrival, but she need not come to GWR Bath to meet me, as she may catch cold.

Dais seems to have arranged so much of the 'doings', while

Dorice has invited Kiki up from Torquay to be a maid or something. My pal from school, Dennis Symons, will come over from Bristol medical school to be 'best man'.

I am very excited, and want you to know that if it were not for all yours and Mr. H's kindness to me, this wedding could never happen.

When I arrive, I will look terrible as all my kit is still with the Battalion, but dear Dorice has ordered me a new uniform so any photos might well be alright on the day.

Having spent nearly a year thinking and dreaming of 'our best day' I just want to thank you for everything, send you a dear little kiss, and am looking forward to seeing you on Wednesday.

Goodbye little Ma
Your future Son
Herbert xx

The wedding just seems to be going off in a whirl. The bride looks BEAUTIFUL, so sweet and so very young, while I look a bit grey and haggard. Frankly I am feeling like a 'string of cheese', after that time in Hospital, but I am doing my best to be merry and bright. My tears well-up as the speeches are made as the wedding breakfast flashes by. I am at breaking point, but will just hold out for our honeymoon by the sea.

It is a glorious honeymoon, but all too short. Meeting too many relatives including Dais and her brood, Dorothy and hers, and the famous Aunt Roy who runs a Naval officers' rest home in Portsmouth. It all seems to eat up the time. Always there are relatives around – if it's not cousins, it's aunts! We write to my parents, of course;

Royal Beach Hotel Southsea 5/4/1917
My dearest Mother and Dad,

We were both delighted to hear from you, and you, in turn will be glad to hear we are having a great time and quite topping weather. We were unable to have a compartment to ourselves all the way!! Never mind, the train was full, but still it was an enjoyable journey. I heard from my pal, the best man, that he is still infatuated with Kiki, the 'best girl'!

We thought the announcement in the paper was quite good and we are almost looking forward to coming back to Bath to be stared at by everyone!

Dorice and I thank you, dear parents, for all your help in getting us through. We are deeply in love and share our dream of a peaceful and loving family life after this old war is over.

Dorice says she is writing tomorrow, we are just off to see some Aunt of hers in Portsmouth; Roy by name. We will return to Bath in two or three days.

Goodbye, and Best Love from Dorice and Your own loving Son,

Herbert

Well, it's done. I am a married man! I am pleased that all the angst is over – (apart from this awful war!). And, I do feel dear Dorice fully understands the risks that come with it. The first one being that on our honeymoon she catches the measles! Not the best of starts to be sure, but ours will be a long and fulfilled life together, whether Army, or Bank.

That, is yet another conundrum to be solved! Another time, and another place, to workout that one.

Back with the Battalion, I get a lot of misplaced and 'naughty' humour from the fellow officers – especially at mess gatherings! My men are respectful, and obviously have learned about my wedding from the post-corporal, who must have noticed by now that my outgoing letters are addressed to 'Mrs. G H Annaheim', and no longer to 'Miss D Hookway'! All my Irish fellows are mostly married themselves, and probably therefore think I will be 'softer' with them from now on! We'll see!

Dorice, my own darling little baby Wife,

I'm so sorry my letters aren't turning up for some days. I just cannot understand it. Meanwhile, my little Girlie, I am alive and kicking.

I am dog-tired after a long night up to the trenches under some Hun strafing. But all is well, just a lack of sleep. The strafe is still going on – 'dash the war'. I am just looking forward to our next honeymoon, and we will be selfish with no relatives around this time. I bought you something, which I will put in a parcel – a nice pair of silk stockings. Marsden advised me to get black ones, so I hope you like them. Bow wow!

The Brigadier Major (Red Tabs an' all) came riding along just now and yelled out in front of everybody; "How's the your little Misses getting on?"

I couldn't think whom he meant at first, and then it dawned on me that he meant 'Mrs.GHA'!! So I said; "Very well thanks!!"

He told me his missus was just recovering from measles too. I was horribly proud, you know, for a 'gentleman with red tabs' to go out of his way and ask me how my darling little wife – YOU – were.

The Docman always used to say ;"Well Anna, how's Dorice?", but now it's; "how's Mrs. George?". I won't repeat what dear Marsden says!

Since I left after our blissful honeymoon, I have read your letters over and over again, and I am so glad that Kiki and your dear parents haven't caught the old measles as well, since you last went to press.

The war will soon be over and then darling Babs we can start housekeeping. Oooer! Get another husband!!

Goodbye dearest darling and bestest Wife in all the world.

May God Bless you and protect you as he is protecting me. All my love and kisses and hugs and TUDDLES!!!

Ever your own Husband

Bubbie xxxx

The Colonel is back from leave and I will have to tell him about my marriage. We are walking together and talk a lot about Bath; so I tell him. This is a relief, as he is decent about it, although usually not keen on young officers getting married. However he seems desperately keen that I should obtain a Permanent Commission, so I will just let things slide. He is keen for Dorice and I to meet him and his wife sometime in Bath. Let's just see. But I write to let Dorice know all is well on that front at least:

Dorice, My darling Wife,

I have just returned to my abode and found a nice long loving letter from you. You said; "thank you for the "a la" postcards of girls in undress uniform out here". All the ones I sent back are OK and I don't think your strict Pater will object to them.

There's a devil of a row going on at present. Someone must have annoyed the Boscheman, and he's sending over a few "crumps", but we are sending back an almighty hail of fire by the sound of things. The sound is really loud, but I am concentrating on writing this to my darling wife!

I must away for a short time and run up to see the Colonel. Bye Bye for the present.

Later I write:

Well Darling, here we are again, and I also have good news that the CO now knows I am married and he says he would like to meet "My little lady in Bath when we are on leave together". Bow wow!!

Relief all-round Darling Mine. Monck-Mason is a dear old thing, and, I think actually quite fond of me, which is rather strange in this here old Army! Rumour says he was a young Lt. in the Army in India and was divorced out there due to some scandal.

We have been married exactly 24 days – whoops dearie!! And I feel they are the happiest days of my life. Babs, I do love you so very dearly and I still pray that you may always love me as you do now.

God Bless you 'cos yer Mine. All my love Babs I adore and worship you. Getting married to you sweetheart is the best thing I ever did!

Ever your Loving Husband (!)
Bubbie xxxxxx

With marriage has come all the 'baggage' of family relationships – good and bad. Dorice is spending at least a day a week with my parents; which is especially sweet of her, since all their objections to our marriage so recently expressed hurt her terribly – me as well.

The best man Dennis, and bridesmaid, cousin Kiki, seem to be close to 'an affair'. I must write and put in my 'halfpenny-worth' on all this:

My darling little Wife,

How I love writing that!

I got two topping letters from you this morning Sweetheart, and one from your (and now my!) esteemed cousin Kiki. Do you mind if I answer her last effort darling? It struck me she doesn't treat her new cousin with sufficient respect!! I will enclose one for her in your letter if I get time.

I like the description of the "something" you are making; sounds jolly nice and, may I see it, when I get home please?

Kiki is of course the limit and I can only say it was a good job the best man went back to Bristol, or I know what would have happened! Bow wow!! I'm sure Kiki wouldn't have minded him putting her to bed!!! If only he had realised! By the way, I like her just as a cousin, no more than that, but then you have several more for me to meet! Get another cousin!

I often tell my friends out here; "I've been married one month", and they say; "Yes you old 'so-an-so' Anna, and you go and give your wife measles on your honeymoon!" Well, I couldn't help it, could I sweetheart!?

Dad sent me the local rag and sent a letter saying he and Mother say now, that I married with their consent. I didn't really. Father said: "well you can get married but you have not my consent and I cannot help you!" Ooooer!! Now, they seem to have changed and everyone is merry and bright. What what!! ?

My second pip came through just before we were married, so darling, you were married to a Full Lieutenant on your wedding Day!

I am longing for our second honeymoon, darling. That's the one that will last all our lives together as a long and happy time. It is rather cruel that you and I, Sweetheart who love each other so much, are not able to be together. 'S an awful War, Dearie! But I must thank Providence that I am alive. Everybody seems to be going under.

Well, Babs, I am turning in now as it's lights-out as there is a Bosche raid overhead. I wish I could see you lying in bed waiting for me. Gosh, I do love and adore you my

dearest and bestest wife in the whole world .
Ever your loving and devoted Hubbie
Bubbie xxxxxx

So there it is; everything with the relations, with the marriage and with the wedding, means 'everything in the garden is fine'.

Actually, after a nasty gassing during the Bosche counter attack following the Tunnel trench success, I do go a bit 'wobbly' about marriage; this time, well after the wedding. A kind of war-induced depression I suppose:

Darling dearest Wifie

I've written one letter, but it doesn't seem half lovable enough. I can never write my thoughts. I lie in bed (wood and rubber netting!) in the early morning and long for you. Thinking if I turn round I shall see your pretty little face and long to take it in my hands and place a long kiss on your dear lips.

I trudge along a road and try to imagine you are with me when I come back from the 'run' to the trenches wet through, I try and imagine that you will be there waiting for me in my hut with your arms outstretched. But there's no YOU when I arrive. Your little photos are all around the hut with the one I love standing on the table for everyone to admire as they enter my abode!

The guns are roaring tonight. It's pitch dark and I am alone; always alone when I write to you my wife. You are part of my life now. There would be no happiness, nothing to live for without YOU. I have seen other young husbands out here and wonder if they love as much as you and I. Some of the older fellows don't worry about their wives and seldom write, and I wonder if I will always love and worship you as I do now. I think perhaps I am in a strange mood tonight after a 'little gassing' from the Boscheman.

A little homesick, of course, but whenever I am alone my thoughts are of YOU, wondering if I will make a really good husband as I want to do, and if you will love me all of our lives as you do now.

I am so grateful that there is little differences in our ages, so we will grow up together with the same ideas. I feel an awful kid right now, with responsibilities both out here to my men and at home with you as my darling wife. Seems a lot.

This is a terrible life out here for a young fellow. Little or no exercise, or else inhaling gas, and living more or less underground, with poor food. Too much drink, and voila, yet we live and look pretty fit on it all!!

I should have done something mad ages ago if there was no YOU. Many a time I have been tempted to ask the CO to allow me to go on a raid, and then I have thought of YOU and what might happen, so I carried on with my job and dodged the shells.

Was the Hubbie you pictured in your mind before we met nicer than I?? Girls do always picture their 'Hero' but I wonder how often he turns up. I don't profess to be a hero, but I would like to know if you are disappointed in this way. Shall I ever attain the perfection of the husband you had on your mind before we were even engaged?

Gosh! What an extraordinary mood I'm in tonight. Don't bother to answer these mad questions Sweetheart!!!

I'm coughing a lot, and so very tired, I must off to bed

Always your own adoring

Bubby xxxx

I have no doubts really. Only those about 'the legacy of this war', and how it has affected our lives up till now and, as well as, into the future. Despite my absolute tiredness, I should only think about all the love we share.

The "Yeah" decision for this predicament was absolutely right. We have had about five hundred days married to each other, and so far, less than forty days being physically together as man and wife. What wonderful days.

Hence, I have few regrets, and certainly none about this "Yeah". Dorice has been a brick all along this journey, but now I can't wait for this damned war to finish. It will finish for me soon.

There it is again; Da Dum Dee Dum… Da Dum Dee Dum… 'cept it's not the Wedding March.

Is it the Funeral March? No, it's machine gun bullets from that Hun in the Sun.

7

MORE THAN A WHIFF!

"... one of the funniest things I've seen – these fellows trying to put on their gas helmets after a serious rum ration!"

I seem to have a vivid greenish/yellow fog in my head. Horrific.

It's damnable stuff – this Hun gas!

I suppose I'm lucky that I'm not dying by drowning slowly in my own bodily liquids, caused by such chemical perversions. Yet another flashback;

Starting at a walk, a 'whizz' goes by close. Jeepers it's a sniper – from across the lines – they are sneaky and always around. Up to a trot then another 'whizz' – closer this time and from the same source – the bastard. And then a different shot – from a different direction – this sniper must be one of ours – the bastard. Surely he can recognise a British officer riding by?!

Up at HQ, it appears my ride is wasted – apart from the excitement of being sniped at. "Would I now go across to visit the Leinsters on our left and sort out some remount issues – apparently; "There is a belief that they are getting the best". Dear old QM Baxter. Thanks for that comment! I will have a devil of a row about this later, as I know our mounts are the best in the Division.

As I ride another few miles across the barren countryside, we come across ground that upsets DoriceII – she gets quite agitated – yet this is the quietest ride of the day. I find out later, as tears stream down her and my face (and I got an itch), that this area had been shelled by Bosche lacrymatory shells, earlier in the month.

I write about this to dearest Dorice, because even from our early 'courting days' in 1916, I promised to tell her everything that is on my mind:

My Dearest Darling Little Girlie,

Thank you for your sweet letters, Dorice darling which I read over and over again whenever I get a spare moment.

I had the most exciting times last night. I was told to recce a track to see if we could get the limbers across. I was there alright but was being sniped at by our own as well as the Germans (cheerio dearie!!)

I rode through an area that had been shelled by 'lacrimator' shells. The fumes are still in the ground after their 'tear-making stunts'. Your eyes smart and tears flowed down my face. My little pony that I now call DoriceII, didn't like it at all, and we had a nice little gallop out of that district up to HQ.

I now have nine photos of you hanging on the wall of my little hut, as the roar of the guns gets ever louder. I am going to sleep now to dream of you.

Ever your own
Bubbie

The gas alarm gong, which is just a shell hanging on a chain, is always a nuisance especially right now, as I have just climbed into my cot at three am and am trying to fall asleep. I turn the men out with gas helmets on and then we stand-to all night. At least they say the gas doesn't affect animals if they stay still, and, it is good that gas masks are now being issued for the horses and mules which are a better solution than just blocking their noses with plugs.

Darling Dorice Mine.

I had to finish last nights' letter to you in a hurry because there was a Gas alarm and I had to rush off and wake up all of my men and turn them out with their gas helmets on. We 'stood-to' the best part of the night. It is quite possible for the gas to come over any time now because the wind is favourable to the Bosche and he doesn't hesitate to use it directly he gets the chance. The animals are ok if you don't move them about, and there are masks for them too.

They use this gas before they raid our trenches, as it causes difficulties for our men to be able to fight back. It seems to disable rather than 'pip' those who breathe it, but nevertheless it certainly is not used for a picnic!

Thank you for your 'everyday letters', I can tell you it makes everyone else so jealous when my letter arrives every day. My servant will chase all over looking for me with it in his hand.

I must away now darling Dorice
All my love hugs and kisses are all yours
Ever your devoted
Bubbie xx

Out here on the Somme front, the gas attacks are intense, and, just about all of us have 'more than a whiff' of the stuff. It seems to make your mind a bit 'fuzzy' and your attitude a bit 'down';

My Dearest Wife to be,

All the gongs in the district sounded again yesterday and we all rushed about trying to find our gas helmets. The majority of the men were sozzled when the fall-in sounded. One of the funniest things I've seen – these Irish fellows trying to put on their gas helmets after a serious 'rum issue'. Mad as hatters, but fierce fellows my Irish Lads!!

As it happens no shells landed nearby. But *at the same time a gas shell hit the Battalion HQ and no less than 7 officers and 4 messmen, as well as my friend the dear old Docman, were gassed and evacuated to the casualty station.*

Luckily, I have heard that they will recover quite quickly.

Sweetheart mine, I love your letters and many thanks for the parcel too, which turned up in good condition. As for the story on leave; I can only tell you that it is all cancelled right now, as the 'stunt" is on. It will open again soon dearest.

Some fellows did get leave, but then got killed or wounded even before they left here. No wounds – no funerals What what!!

Darling as I fall asleep, I dream of better times and just want to hug and hold you close to me

Goodnight Darling Girlie

Ever your own

Bubbie xxx

It seems that we all have a gas-head today The old CO, Lt-Colonel Monck-Mason is gassed but is not evacuated. He is a true legend in the Division, with a history of action in the Indian Army, and Africa as well.

Really nasty stuff is this new devilish Bosche mixture of chemistry. They say its something like chlorine and phosgene together in one shell. They call it 'white star'. I can't help remembering the old chemistry lessons at school; when the decrepit Science prof at King Eddie's, made Chlorine gas, by pouring acid over some purple crystals inside a kind of double bubble glass apparatus. It stank then, and stinks now.

Darling Little wifie,

In the same old blooomin' place! I am taking the evening 'off' tonight because last night I had a pretty rotten, or shall we say trying experience.

Just as I was unloading the rations at a sort of broken down farmhouse, a nice big fat gas shell landed on top!! The lads donned their gas helmets and we and the animals stood as still as possible. I started to put mine on and found nobody could hear me when I shouted so I had to take it off again.

It was terrible and I immediately thought of a 'blighty stunt avec gas'.

Well, a rush of air from an ordinary common or garden shell seemed to clear the air somewhat and we pushed off. Then another shell landed in a ditch alongside as we pushed off. It was a dud as luck would have it, and instead of being in Heaven, I am writing to you my dearest darling Baby wifie. By heaven I mean of course I mean at home with you of course!

Tonight the QM Baxter is going up. I was a little gassed and fortunately the dear old Bosche allowed me to sleep until midday! I am taking the animals a few miles back tonight as it looks like a 'dirty' night.

Sorry this is so short Girlie mine, but I will write again tomorrow something more loving.

Ever your own and true

Bubbie

The Bosche are using a frightful lot of gas shells now. It's much worse stuff than it used to be. Stuff which seems to burn your eyes out!! We call it Mustard Gas. Somehow we live with this dreadful nuisance, and casualties seem to be less, until the big pushes.

Here they come streaming back from the Line in their hundreds, with eyes bandaged and holding on to the man in front. It's a sight of war, which will haunt me forever. Some of our finest fighters go back in this way and few of them ever return to the Battalion. I lost two men Sullivan and Mahoney, but no horses. This evil chemistry seems to attack and burn into exposed skin. Thank heavens I'm not in a kilted Scottish regiment!

My Darling Little Wife

Last night I had to bring the rations up through a gas barrage. (whoops dearie!!). I thought it might bring a 'blighty' but up to going to press – no luck!! I lost two men with banged up eyes- they have been evacuated to the special gas station near Calais.

The remainder of us who went up have all got bloodshot eyes! It looks as if we've been having a night out!! This mustard gas doesn't take effect for twenty four hours or so. When I wake tomorrow I may not feel very well. I'll let you know tomorrow. I do have a 'gas head' but it might be 'the auld stuff'!

This morning; 'Spect you will wonder how 'my gassiest man' is getting on. Well, I'm still carrying on but don't feel very well. I don't want to go sick if I can help it. My eyes are better and don't burn so much, but I have a queer little pain in my chest. Not bad enough for a 'blighty'. The Doc-man told me it has some kind of arsenic in it, but the old science teacher at school would know, I'm sure.

I have just come back from the line again – it isn't 'too bon' up there. There's still plenty of gas about.

I am jolly fed up at present. I just want to fall asleep on your dear wee breast. Oh for leave!

The gas is quite OK and I don't think my eyes look very 'groggy' (not like last year eh?) I can't tell you the exact number of men from the Division who were gassed, but it was really hundreds! And I got great praise from the 'old Man' because I only lost two men and no horses. I'll tell you about it when I get home.

Things are much cheerier with the men; as together we have come through, and done our best duty with the 'run' up to the Line, supporting the Battalion with the rations they need each night.

Darling, soon leave will be opening and you and I will be together for what will be a blissful time. You see I love you and love you, and will arrive 'home' to devote all my energy to showing you just how much that love means to me.

Meanwhile Girlie Mine I am dead-beat and am falling asleep after two or three days with only a minute or two of rest of any kind.

Good night my love
From your true and devoted
Bubbie xx

A memory flashes through my head about the 'Great Race', and this dreadful morning of 21st March1918. The cloud of gas seems thicker than a mist, and certainly thicker than the 'normal' greenish/yellow fog. It is like riding through a poisonous, waxy and hellish 'soup'. But the gas masks are working quite well, although giving orders wearing a mask is more than a little difficult.

In these last months up near the Hindenburg line, we are ok with the gas, since the new respirators work quite well if you get them on in about twenty seconds from the 'plop' of the shell landing.

My own Dearest Darling,
Whoops Dearie! I was a beautiful yellow today through a wicked gas shell bursting quite near me last night!! But I don't feel any ill effects!! All my clothes are yellow and my hands and hair! But it's coming off nicely in the wash. This place is no health resort!
Please may I have a nice large piece of soap.
I have only a small piece left, and that looks like a chewed piece of toffee!
Goodbye my Love
Your Bubbikins xxxxxxxxxxxxxxx

Gas is damned stuff! And, I've had 'More Than A Whiff!'

I've lost many pals and animals to it in the last 3 years of war, and I've seen the horrors it can deliver. But, right now, all I 'see' is only a yellow haze.

That soap hasn't arrived yet.

Anyway, now it's too late for any soap!

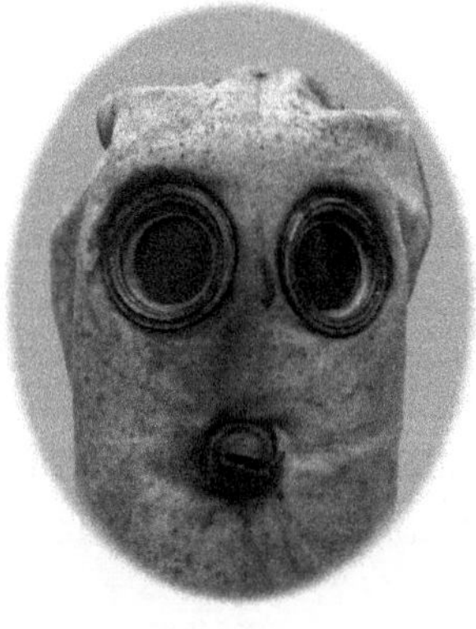

8

TRANSPORT OF DELIGHT

"Sing the joys of a Transport man, who drives along with a gay 'Hallo'!"

Laying in this darkness with life in the balance, I hear the sound of fellow schoolboy choristers singing at King Edward's assemblies all those years ago; 'The King of love My Shepherd is". I flashback to those innocent days, and the words of that hymn come streaming back;

'Thou spreadst a table in my sight;
thy unction grace bestoweth;
and oh, what ***transport of delight***
from thy pure chalice floweth!"

'Oh, what transport of delight', now brings me visions of my job as 1st Battalion Royal Munster Fusiliers Transport Officer; times which are rich, fulfilling, often exciting, and, yes, which are generally full of 'delights'.

I try to describe to Dorice some of the duties in an early letter;

My dearest darlingest Girlie-Girlie,
A long topping letter from you this morn and one from

mother. You are a naughty little girl not to practice singing very, very often. I know how busy you are but you have the voice of an angel and I would love you to continue to sing in public. Poor old mother can't help advising me this, that and the other, but she does want us both to be happy.

I have had a rather worrying evening as I sent a limber out this afternoon and it didn't come back until 11pm. The driver was drunk and the brakeman very nearly, and of course it is jolly dark about here. Fortunately the animals knew their way back. These are not the same men I found having 'parked' their wagon outside a local estaminet last week. They were not there for a 'cup of coffee' as they claimed; 'cos the place had a red lamp outside!

Now, as well as plodding my way up to the trenches and getting back about 3am, I still have to organise a disciplining meeting for early in the morning for the men on report. Generally, all these men are fine chaps, but give them and inch – well you know.

Bad news too; there's talk of all the Transport Officers going back to the Battalion as regular Company officers, and getting the ASC to do the work! 'S awful. 'S enough said!

I don't mind going to the trenches but I do mind losing all my horses and especially DoriceII. It's bad luck, but it may not take place.

Time to go up to the line Dorice darling, and I will write a few more 'tender thoughts' on my return.

Goodnight sweetest little one, all my love to you Girlie mine Take care of your pretty little self

Your own devoted old

Bubbie xxxxxxx

Well, now the War Office have schemes to delete this TO with the amalgamation of the 8th Battalion with our own 1st Battalion There are three of us up for the job, including a Captain sent from the War Office in London. Yet, I've got it! No promotion though, and, I am running two transport lines for my sins. But, I do get a bonus, as I get rid of the rather 'sillier' mules and have the pick of horses from the other transport.

In this job I get a lot of freedom to ride during the day, sometimes up to thirty miles on Jack with my groom riding DoriceII as we go about our business. It gives time to think about the night 'run'. And also my next letter to dear Dorice's Pater:

Dear Mr. Hookway,

I want to thank you and the dear little Mater for putting me up, and putting-up-with-me on my last leave. I am so sorry that I must have caused so many disruptions to life at 1, South Parade! But now, I must say I feel more and more part of your family, and as you know I am committing my life totally to dearest Dorice.

Since I returned, we have moved all over the place - C'est la guerre and c'est the Army! Tonight I have found a 'quiet' spot to write, except for the usual nightly hate going on; we are responding very well and knocking their blocks off.

You did say that if I ever got a moment, to try to drop you a line describing my job here with the good old RMF. So I will have a go (without upsetting the censor of course!).

As you know, this Battalion is part of a Brigade and part again of The 16th (Irish) Division. The logistics of supply are complicated and, by and large, work well, when you consider the tons of men, animals and materials that come to France from across the seas.

Here, up at the Lines, we keep it as simple as possible with the Battalion supply dump up to 8 miles or so behind the front, depending on the nearest railhead. We sometimes use a narrow gauge railway that's easy to build and easy to repair – usually by the ASC. No more about THEM!

The old QM, my friend Baxter, is responsible for making sure the Battalion's main store is filled with all the material requirements needed when we are in or out of the line. Thank heavens Baxter does 80 pc of the paperwork – this being the Army, there is no shortage of that-ever!

The QM on a daily basis, divides the standard rations load between the 4 Companies manning the frontline plus one for the Battalion HQ. In the day, I send my limbers and men to load up for the 'run' later that night, and then return to my own transport line. Often, we have up to 8 limbers and kitchen and water carts as well loaded and drawn by heavy and light horse draughts, and mules.

I have located the Transport with my 50 men and 60 animals a few miles (usually less than 3) behind the lines, but the Hun knows that, and often makes us a target of bombing, shelling and gassing too! – curse him!!

Each night we set out when it is quite dark, after 9 pm, but often much later. My groom has saddled and prepared DoriceII for me, while my Transport Sergeant has lined up our limbers and carts ready for my inspection of the 'Ration Party' as we call it. It's NOT a 'Party', really!!

Of course, there is always a real 'hate' going on with shells whooshing over us, and landing all around and the sound of machine guns chattering from up at the front. Often, the beastly Bosche have their 5.9's targeted on certain roadways and especially crossroads, which makes the trip up to the line very interesting!! Bow Wow!!

As the officer in charge, I ride in front, alongside and sometimes behind the party, depending on the conditions. The pace is quite slow as the wagons are heavily loaded, but when we pass through a 'hot' location (you might have heard of 'Suicide Corner', 'Windy Crossroads', 'Hellblast Corner' and suchlike names), we rush through at a gallop with spaces between each dash of a limber, so as to dodge shells and bullets as best we can.

It is often very eerie when the Huns loose off some flares that illuminate our position! It's a spooky scene, and definitely NOT a pretty sight! Then their machine guns start up in our direction – usually over our heads thank Heavens!

At a certain point there is no road or track left – just muddy, wet or frozen fields with the stench and debris of war all around. We move off for another half a mile or so to reach the trenches. RMF men are waiting from each Company to collect their rations and other supplies.

I most often then walk to the trenches, and chat with my pals, the Company Officers in-the-line, in their primitive dugouts, to share a drink and a smoke. I feel my job is also to cheer up the fellows up there, especially those about to go on a raid. The men are tired but always glad to see us with the hot food, the rum jars, and tobacco and, sometimes, the comfort of extra blankets that QM Baxter has procured from somewhere.

It is strange to think that there is some fellow of a Hun TO doing the same job as me; bringing beer and pumpernickel to the Bosche troops just a few yards away! He's still a swine!

Of course the night is not over for our Ration Party. We collect some 'disposables' from the trenches and set-off back to my Transport lines. All being well we get back at about 3am (through the 'Corner' again! – "Any casualties Sergeant?! " No, all present and correct soarh"). Then we unhitch the animals from the limbers, tie them to their lines, and check if there is any damage to the wagons. I then post 2 guards and I get to turn-in, into my tent or little hut. I usually finish my daily letter to Dorice before falling asleep 'till the post-corporal comes by at 7.30am to take letters away and, hopefully, deliver to me, my post from home.

We do all this often with the nightly 'hate' going on all around with shells landing everywhere, and, tonight, luckily not where I am. Oh, and the Hun bombers fly over and try to bomb us to bits!

As you can see; busy 20-hour-days are normal for a TO! Well, Mr. H. I am getting tired, and duty calls again. That is something of life out here. Did I mention the other jobs I do between running the Transport?

I am often a kind of 'lawyer' for my men on charges, 'scrounger' of animals and fodder, and 'banker' for the officers and men especially when it is payday and loans are brought in!

I am a horse provider to the officers, an accounts officer to the Battalion and often to the Brigade as well. I am 'Sports day organiser' for the Battalion, and more recently have become the Mess president!! That means plenty of paperwork and form-filling in addition to the nightly 'run' up to the trenches.

It is not a 'soft' or 'cushy' job, but generally I am pleased to be still working with animals like I did while I was in the Duke of Lancaster's Own Yeomanry. That seems like a lifetime ago, and those boys are still in Egypt fighting the Turks and some Sennusi tribesmen in a desert to the west of Egypt!

Meanwhile dear 'future father-in-law', if I may be so bold, I look forward to sharing some more stories with you in some more detail over a glass or three of the 'auld stuff' when I next come home.

Please pass on my love to the dear little Mater and of course to 'my Dorice'.

Yours sincerely

George H Annaheim (Herbert)

ps I enclose a part of a poem from a trench newspaper. I think this what is called 'ironic pentameter'!

JE NE LE PENSE PAS

Sing the joys of a transport man,
Who drives along with a gay "Hallo!"
Cracking his whip as he only can,
A smile and a joke as away they go.

His cap is jauntily placed on his head,
His clothes show the care of an old time beau,
He hums to the tune that his mules' hooves tread,
His voice runs in dulcet tones and low.

Driving along on the smooth hard roads,
With never a jolt and never an oath,
Till at Hellfire Corner he drops his loads,
And fondles his mules, for he loves them both.

Then homeward he wends his weary way
To the rose-decked villa, where he may sleep
Till night shall again give place to day,
And the angels above him their vigil keep.

I don't think so! G.H.A

Good days and not-so-good days seem to flash by and I share with Dorice all the delights as well as the frustrations of my life out here:

My dearest darling Girlie,

I received your loving letter today. There were several passages in it that made me homesick such as; "It's 2pm and I am wishing so much for you to come home and longing to be in your dear arms again". Heavens, I wish I was with you now in your old dining room in front of the fire!! Instead I am sitting here alone in my hut. The QM Baxter is away so, I am doing his job as well as all the others that I do.

Yesterday was a terrible day as 3 Generals came round my Lines! whoops dearie! Red Tabs all of 'em. But none could find any faults; 'Course they couldn't!

Today one of my wagons drivers had a smash-up with a car – smashing 2 wheels of the car and the axle. I had to explain the accident in writing – on an Army form of course! The only thing to do was to tell a lot of lies because I want my man to get off.

You do have to be jack-of-all-trades out here; builder, vet, lawyer mechanic, marksman, and the rest!

Talking of being a mechanic, my friend and I drove into the nearest village in a galloping wagon, which belongs to me. It's a delightful French 'wagonette' which was 'found' in Loos some time ago. I've had it painted and 'done-up', so it's the pride of the Regiment.

I wanted to christen it and so put on 2 miles to the village. Halfway back, the bloomin' wheel came off and careered down the road. After an hour of mechanical work we fixed it so the men could take it back to the lines. Then we walked slowly back just as the Bosche started their infernal shelling. If I get any trouble from my fellow officers I will set them up for the wheel to come off 10 miles away!

Now sweetheart mine, I must turn in to dream sweet dreams of the best little girlie in all the world.

So with millions of hugs "comme la peinture"
And thousands of kisses and all my love Baby mine.
Goodnight dearest
Ever your very own most devoted Hubbie
Bubbie xxxxxxx

The old Army tries again to replace me as TO with another War Office 'Johnny'; a Captain of course, and he is under orders to replace me as regimental TO looking after 1st and

2nd Battalions as we are now close together at the Front. I am already doing that job and, by all accounts, pretty well too.

He arrives with a swagger-stick and all, and begins 'Lording-it' over me. I stay quiet and we go off to HQ. The CO takes a dislike to him immediately, and informs Div HQ that this man is not required in the RMF! But the TO job is no 'cushy number'.

Later in a letter to Dorice I am writing:

My dearest little Darling,

We have very busy all week and I am sorry I haven't written to you little Girl quite as much as I ought to have done.

I have lost another one of my very best pals out here. Well he was TO of another Irish Battalion who are nearby. He fell in the line of duty as a Bosche sniper got him on his night 'run'.

C'est La Vie, C'est La Guerre!

I have lost so many pals it is too painful to think about them all.

I count my life as very lucky, having fallen in love and married YOU my Darling. Dorice mine I can't tell you how much I long to be cuddled by you once more. The war can't last very much longer and we will be together forever. I want something Darling!

Can you send me two tins of Keatings!!! There are all sorts of creepy crawlies that are a damned nuisance. S'awful I can't get the stuff out here it must be all bought up!! No mail today but it might come up yet. I dearly hope so.

Goodbye my dearest darling little baby wifie. May God bless you and love you as I do. All the kisses in the world and thousands of hugs.

Ever your own old Hubbie
Bubbie xxxxxx (no kissing Bill!)

Now, it is already months later into 1918, and nearer the front line, which is rolling forwards at quite a pace. We are constantly on the move; so, another daily letter of love and war:

My dearest Darling

Since my last letter of 3 days ago we have been always moving the whole business forward, sometimes miles at a time. After years of moving all the men and all their stuff I am quite used to it! We have now arrived in the 'wilds'. Baxter and I have a tent while the remainder of the Battalion are living out in a nice green field!!! Rain or no Rain!!!

Honestly we are having a pretty thin time of it but I know your letters will be waiting for me in the 'mess', which is just three walls with a tarpaulin thrown over the top! S'nice.

Dear old girl how are you? The only thing I look forward to is a letter from you Darling and the thought of leave.

The animals are all jolly fit and well because I can get grazing out here, but water for them and the men is scarce, and then tastes of the petrol tins it comes in! The 'run' tonight will be a bit easier than usual, as the Bosche have stopped shelling in these parts for the moment. Don't worry darling, I always take care, even when one thinks it's quiet, one knows some 'plane might pop over and try to drop a bomb or two on the transport!

Girlie it is a relief to me you are feeling well and merry and bright. I should worry hopelessly if you were unwell. I'm inclined to think that married life agrees with you!! It certainly does me.

Goodbye dearest darling wifie. I adore you and love you. God bless you and take care of us all.

Ever your true adoring Hubbie
Bubbie xxx

Heavy shelling is incessant, as we move forward, always eastwards, and pushing back the Hun. His artillery, though moving back, continues to give us a bad time.

Darling Girl,

We are moving up everyday and each day seems the same. But this morning we had orders to move and were all packed up and then orders came along cancelling them. So here we are again.

This country round here is dreadful. Although the Battalion is only a mile away from me I have to go five miles round and bring up the rations on pack animals because the country is just all shell holes and barbed wire! S'awful.

My tent is pitched in a shell hole for safety, but it has just started raining so I shall probably be swimming soon!

I was bucked up last evening as I found the two horses which were presumed blown up together with the limber, quite safe and sound in some artillery lines. The driver was blown off his horses and has gone to hospital with the 'wind-up' and perhaps a small wound.

I haven't told you how much I love and adore you. Marriage, my Darling has surpassed anything I imagined it to be – I never thought I could be so happy in this old world. Something to live for and someone to love, and to be loved in turn by you.

You know that don't you Darling ?

It is now well after midnight and I must seal this letter so it goes off early in the morning. Now to bed. Goodnight my own one. God bless you.

From your devoted and true Hubbie
Bubbie xxxxx

The joys and delights of my job now seem rather distant if not onerous as, again, I haven't slept for days as the push moves on-and-on, and deeper into the Hindenburg support Line.

For my section, it is increasingly a struggle to get up the Line with the rations on our nightly run. I try it in daylight when the Bosche can see us, but they only irritate us with light machine gun fire, which goes over our heads. Risky though, but the men in the line have little food and even less water.

They deserve their rations. But we are really in a bad state. My transport lines are just behind me, and rather too exposed on the skyline. I lost four men and six animals to Hun shelling today.

Despite all this savagery and loss, me and my transport (men and animals), have had a whole lot of delights with this job. Only now we seem to be again, going through Hell together. The Bosche are zeroing-in some 'big stuff' and the aeroplanes are battling it out overhead.

And here I am at the end.

For me, now it's getting very dark. Blackness. Nothing.
The sound of that hymn from the school choir plays in my head again:

"In death's dark vale I fear no ill
with thee dear Lord beside me"

In fact, it is Baxter and Nightingale who are beside me.

But I fear no ill.

I only fear for Dorice.

9

DAYS OF LEAVE – AND LOVE

*"I am sitting and thinking of the last leave and blush!!!
I wasn't a very naughty boy was I?"*

Memories of glorious 'Days of Leave' that have all become 'Days of love ' are surging through my fading brain.

In Egypt we have the 'odd' days leave; climbing the Pyramids, sailing on the Nile in a felucca, and maybe a jaunt or three into Cairo to buy some 'exotic ciggies'. It is quite exciting, but it is the hospital recovery times, which are more exotic still.

Memories with real lifetime 'Escapades'.

These are all powerful flashbacks merging into one not-so-long happy memory.

My first leave from France, after twenty-two months away in Egypt, is a hurly-burly of meeting family and friends; the pals from school, those from Bath NP Bank branch, as well as those at the Bath and Avon Rowing Club.

Not all the family are there of course, as Eddy is still away – he is in the Med somewhere. Dais organises everything as usual; the char-a-banc trips to Cheddar and Weston-super-Mare and those 'electric' arranged, 'first meetings' with the pretty young Dorice Hookway.

It is such a whirlwind, that the first leave passes in a flash but with life-changing happenings all the time.

My Darling Child,

Two topping letters from you today. Hooray!!

So you did get my letter, the eight-page one after my leave. You must train your new maid to run down and fetch your letter from me in the morning and bring them up to you double quick time!

I think of our trip to Cheddar so often. You see, I was such a cad wanting to walk you off your feet, and now I find out that you loved me then but didn't show it. Do you know I half thought you did love me then, or I wouldn't have kissed you. I really kissed you a lot in the old char-a-banc didn't I?

So it now comes to this. We simply must get married on my next leave or elope if the folks object at all.

Goodnight Sweetheart mine, be a good little girl until I am able to come back. Rest assured I will come back as soon as I am able.

All my love and hugs and kisses

Ever your devoted Bubbie xxxxx

LEAVE is the lynchpin of my getting through this war. To master the art of going on leave takes some time, and I am good at working the system to maximize the leave-time at home. Getting the old CO (M-M) to sign the warrant or to get my pal, the Adjutant Marsden, to move me up the list (and send me via Boulogne and not Havre) isn't easy, but all things are possible.

Darling dearest Girl,

No letter today but tomorrow might bring two. I can't wait.

Yesterday I went up to HQ with the Battalion Accounts to show the Colonel what a great job I had done in squaring away all the little anomalies. It's the bank training I suppose. It is really a job for the Adj, but as you know old Marsden is away on leave right now, so the 'pleasure is all mine'!

Anyway I was a bit cheeky when up with the Colonel and placed a leave request in front of him – yes right there and then. Well he cussed me and signed it – so when leave opens again I'll be on my way!

Darling Girlie, I have been called away and on my return found my men playing football, so I joined in and scored (to cheers and jeers!) and then retired to my hut to finish this letter.

Goodbye darling little Babs. Lets hope the leave roster opens soon so I may return to kiss and hug you like never before.

All my love
Ever your own
Bubbie xxxxx

This particular leave never happens, due to the big 'stunt' at Ginchy where so many of my pals are 'pipped'.

Later, when leave opens, the warrant is signed off again and a few ration chits collected, I am excited and active, and work for a couple of days to 'clear-the-decks' with my Transport Sergeant and the men. All is now ready to hand over the job to Baxter.

Many of my pals have been killed in the last few days before their leave – some kind of freakish fate befalling them. So I take especial care.

I'm off! Up to the railhead by the gig with my valise, and thank Dan, my groom, for bringing me here. I always ask him to take care of Jack and DoriceII and, of course, himself, while I am away.

The Rail TO is a key man in getting a quick connection. There are about fifty trains a day up to Boulogne, from the main stations, and a good word and a half bottle of the 'auld stuff' is enough to get me on the first one out, and, with a seat on the Pullman at Folkestone.

This time it is a 'hairy' night-time passage across; stormy seas and destroyers escorting us across some mine infested waters. All is well. I am on my way HOME.

Time for a telegram to darling Dorice and my parents stating the eta in Bath. I prefer that she doesn't come to Victoria as the sights of the wounded being taken off the train, is not one for a pretty girl to view. One never really gets used to it oneself. I am just trying not to dwell on all the horror and pain, and keeping such bad thoughts away.

'Home' with Dorice, and the Hookways, is such a treat. They are so understanding of my love for D, and treat me like the son they never had. Nothing is too much trouble, and life is warm and comfortable in so many ways.

I do go up to my Annaheim home up at Belgrave Place and sleep in my boyhood bedroom.

Here there is a certain nostalgic comfort, though the parents seem mystified by all that is going on in the world. I suppose it is their strict upbringings brought together – the strictly Protestant, Irish and the Swiss, views of behaviours in the world of today – totally out of touch. Poor Father. They both look so old and tired.

I am torn about all this too. I have experienced some horrific situations and appalling sights that have made me grow up, and which they never can, never should, and probably never will, experience or comprehend.

Mr. Hookway, in contrast, enjoys a yarn over a good bottle of scotch or brandy and understands a more manly view of life as it really is today.

Awful War an' all

Writing from the Queens Hotel, Folkestone in January 1917, I pour out some of this 'anxiete' about Leaves to dear Dorice.

My Dearest darling little Girlie

The boat doesn't leave for two hours so here's just a little letter whilst I am having a cup of coffee. Well the leave is over now and I love you more, much more than I used to. It nearly broke my heart to leave you. I didn't show how I felt at all 'cos I wanted you to be Darling as bright as possible. I am going to write to your dear little Mater and your dear old Dad. They were both jolly good to me.

I can't be merry and bright in this letter as I am not feeling that way after such a wonderful time this leave. I now know that you really do love me, and, darling Girlie, I love you, and love you and love you.

In a day or two I will write what I omitted to say when I was with you – sometimes it is difficult for me to express my feelings, especially when I know I have to return to this awful war.

It was Heaven to hear you call me "Bubbikins" Nobody has loved me as you do, and nobody ever could have loved you as I do.

I am longing to see you and hug you again although it's only a few hours ago I had my "Goodbye Kiss". It has been a miserable journey back so far. I spent the few hours in London at an officers Club, had a bath and some breakfast there and arrived here at about 9.30am and the boat doesn't leave until midday. If I have to stay in Calais tonight I will try and write from there.

Goodbye my very own sweetheart
Your own loving
Bubbie xxxx

Of course, I am keeping my promise, and write to the Hookways and Dorice as soon as I am back with the Battalion:

Dear Mr Hookway,

Just a line to thank you for the excellent time you gave me during my short leave .You cannot imagine what a difference it made, to be allowed to see so much of Dorice.

I expect your house-keeping bill went up including the wine bill! I drank your jolly good health on the boat coming back. The sailors said it was the roughest crossing for years!! I do not want to waste your time by writing a longer scrawl, but I could not let the opportunity of thanking you slip by.

Best wishes to the "little Mrs." and your dear old self
Yours Sincerely
George Herbert Annaheim

We are 'quietly' engaged now, which allows more 'freedoms' on leaves!

My Darling Little Dorice,

I'm now back at the Battalion just behind the Line again. Not too noisy on this sector other than the roar of the Hun guns and our own artillery giving 'em back fourfold! A Bosche shell landed under one of my water carts and blew it into the air – more paperwork to fill in!

Otherwise I am quite merry tho' with lots of work to do to bring the transport up to the mark after my absence.

I am sitting and thinking of the last leave and blush!!! I wasn't a very naughty boy was I? Well, whatever I did, it was because I loved you really and truly as I do now. Babs I love you with my whole strength and my whole soul and you are mine Sweetheart. Body and Soul!

Poor little you; you aren't frightened of me are you!! Now darling I am going to endeavor to sleep and needless to say dream of you. Goodnight Darling,

All my love and, oooo-er!, all sorts of kisses and hugs.

Ever your own devoted

Bubbie xxxx

But the 'Leave of Leaves' happens unexpectedly as I have gone down with measles, after fighting this dreadful tiredness for many days.

Darling dearest Girlie Mine,

Oh, such a nice long loving letter today Sweetheart. Sorry about all my mad ideas that are worrying you. But I am sincere that we should get married on my next leave. We must do it.

I am far from well and think I have 'Flue' but shall try and stick it out in my little wooden hut, and rest a lot.

Otherwise it will be hospital for 'yours truly'.

Babs, I must admit I am far from well, and may have to go to hospital, which is not what I want at all. John Bosche is shelling over our heads now. S'nice, we can hear the boom of his gun, hear the swoosh of the shell coming through the air and then see the burst.

'S not such a bad war Darling, but I do keep looking at my chest in case a dinky Meazle might have turned up!!

All my love Babs and hug and kisses.

Ever your very own Bubbie xxx

The Docman Bisset, posts a letter from me (in Glasgow apparently):

Darling Babs,

The Docman Bissett (bless his dear old heart!) is going on leave so will post this and it will arrive faster this way. Darling don't have a fit but I fear, at least, I don't fear, but the dear old Doc says I have measles!! I am really rather frightened to write as I don't wish to spread the infection!! But you must just read this scrawl and commit it to the fire!!

The Doc has taken great care of me and he is going home tomorrow. He always enquires after you and is taking great care of me 'till you are able to, darling Doris.

I will see the (other) Doc tomorrow at the hospital so all will be well. I am only getting letters from you twice a week so please write and tell me that you still love me. Just write and tell me as I am a bit 'down' right now. I fear this war will last another three years but we won't wait three years for each other Babs, will we. Next leave – no more waiting! I will try and write a longer letter tomorrow but you will get this first.

All my love and hugs and kisses

Ever your loving infectious

Bubbie xxxxx Good night beloved

Dearest Dorice bucks me up from my poor state. But, her letter has taken eight days to reach me:

Bubbikins, my own Darling,

I was so glad to get a long letter from you but I am so very sorry Sweetheart to hear about the Measles. Your Mother received a telegram from the War Office and she came over to tell me. I feel I could cuss Kaiser Bill and all the bally Germans this afternoon, 'cos if it wasn't for them YOU wouldn't be over there beloved with the 'M'. Poor Darling!

I would give anything to be with you and nurse you, though that's not the 'right thing' I suppose. I should not get fed up of looking after you my Darling and I don't believe you would be a bad patient if I were your nurse. I think you would be quite happy if I were there. Anyway if you weren't, I would smack you! Perhaps if I didn't kiss you!

The only 'good' thing about this is that the Colonel will give you leave, darling, Now! You certainly need ten days leave! Tell the Doc that it's absolutely necessary. Bubbie, my own, I'm longing for more news I shall be waiting for the postman.

I feel so far away from you and horribly helpless. I DO consider you mine, myself, yours, body and soul that I occasionally lose sight of the fact that we are not yet married! It almost feels as though we are. Try to come home soon dear one. May God bless you my Darling and may you get well again soon.

With all my love and kisses and hugs
Your own little 'Baby Wifie'xxxxxxxx

Now we are losing contact, since I am being 'stretchered' to the Base Hospital and then off to Boulogne. From the 14th Stationary Hospital, Boulogne I am writing furiously and daily to Dorice with my news about the 'Measles' and to Dais about how to get a special marriage license if I get back to Bath after this sickness.

Darling Dorice

At last my high temperature is coming down and I am feeling better; yet not allowed out for a few more days. And then a Medical Board and hoping for some serious LEAVE. I am sure this time. The fellows here made up this ditty:

Everbody calls me Winnie-W-I-N-N-Y
Silly ninny in her Red Cross pinny
She's a VAD that's why
All day long she's working hard
Soon she'll drop down dead
Are you there little VA Dear
Come along and make my bed!

These sisters lead a hard life and I am sorry for them. They look after us jolly well here – but there's no nurse as sweet as you dearest. Don't worry! I would love you to nurse me Darling, but one day soon, we will care for each other like only true lovers can.

Darling, I think your prayers will be answered as I expect at least a ten-day leave to be granted very soon. I must warn you I shall look like a tramp as all my kit is back with the Battalion Baby Mine, I am excited because on this leave we shall tie-the-knot. I have written to Dais and to your Pater and Mater about how we can arrange a marriage. Symons too, (by the way, he lost an arm in Macedonia). He will come up from his medical studies in Bristol to be my 'Best man'. Get Kiki to come up from Torquay to be a maid (and a pretty one too!) for you.

We will do this, even against my parents wishes, although I know they love you and will come round in time.
Look out for a letter and telegram about my movements – things will happen fast on Bubbie's next leave!

Sooooon Darling! I am so excited about our future.

All my love Sweetheart. And ooooo-er millions of first kisses as real Hubbie and Wife
Your Very Own Loving
Bubbie xxxxxxxx

ps Darling, please order from Tilley in Cheap Street, a new uniform jacket, light breeches and a pair of puttees. You know my sizes!

Home!

And this most memorable of all my leaves; my wedding to Dorice. April 3rd 1917.

It is a wonderful rush of activity; St Andrews Church, hardly time for photos, lunch at the 'Francis', watching young Kiki flirt with my Best man, and off by train to a glorious honeymoon in Southsea.

Activities in Room 88 at the Royal Beach Hotel, flash across my memory. We make our 'mark' there by disturbing those in the next room with our cries of passion;
"Oh Bubbie, you are hurting me!"
"Whoops!"

This is a glorious leave and a fabulous Honeymoon!

Letters go back and forth from the folks back in Bath, especially the dear Hookways; now they are my REAL in-laws:

My dear Children,
We were glad to get your wire and your cheery letter this morning. Mrs. Martin came in yesterday just after you had

left and was surprised at the suddenness of the doings of you young people. She is coming on Saturday evening to drink your health. Your dear mother called this afternoon (please drop her a line if you haven't already).

The best girl, Kiki, is doing well – grandly – and if we had to make a wish until your return it would be for the Best man to help her to keep the merriment going!

God Bless you both, from Your Loving Father.

Henry Hookway

My darling Dorice,

Just a wee note to thank you both, for your cards and letters from Southsea. I am so glad that you are both Happy and that you are having a good time. Your 'best girl' and I went to the pictures and she is now pen-pushing, but not to you, as she says you don't have time to read letters!!!

Kiki has been a dear kid hasn't she during the exciting times? (I think the Best man is still infatuated with her) Your wedding cards have not arrived yet from the printers in London they probably don't have to print in such haste very often! Please remember me to Dais and Mr. Carpenter. We send our dearest love to you both and fond love from Kiki too xx

Ever your loving Mother

Albertha M Hookway xxxxx

It's later, in December 1917, I am home on Special Leave of twenty four days. Postal contact with the Battalion is still happening during this leave.

A charming letter arrives from the Colonel, staying with his own 'new' wife on leave at the Lansdown Grove Hotel, Bath.

Dear Annaheim,

Will you and Mrs. Annaheim lunch with us here tomorrow at 1.15. I am so sorry to give such short notice but I couldn't fix up anything until we arrived. I hope you will both be able to come. Could you ring us up and let us know, if we are out then let the people on the phone know.

We are so looking forward to lunching with you both.

Yours Sincerely

R. Monck-Mason

Our lunch is rather jolly, as old Monck-Mason is a delightful host, but he looks tired and washed–out. He is the longest serving CO in the Division. Dorice, of course, looks as pretty as a picture with a Munster brooch on her dress which Mrs M-M notices. The Colonel has a 'quiet' word with Dorice about some of the 'bad' things going on at the front and says "To be brave and realistic my Dear". Quietly too, he promises me some kind of medal. Some hopes!

Just now, nearer Christmas 1917, a card from John, my servant in France arrives; *"Very Happy Xmas Sir."* Touching.

Letters also from 'Docman' Bisset and the dear old QM Baxter too:

Dear Anna,

Many thanks for the Xmas card from Mrs. GHA and yourself. We've had a great Battalion Officers Mess Dinner on Xmas night here in Tincourt. The Regimental Band was in attendance and we had the usual high-jinks after the Dinner. Great Fun.

The Division has opened up a variety theatre in a large hall just around the corner and we went to see the kick off. It was quite a good show and set-up, regardless of expense. There were no less than three 'Girls' and they are all wonderfully got up! Their dresses are stunning; costing 150 pounds and would make your dear Mrs. GHA envious! You'll see this when you roll up here again ugh! Horrid thought.

We are looking forward to the cake you will be sending us, and Mrs. George's handiwork would be delicious despite your denials and the awful picture you paint of its subsequent fate on you!

We go into the Line on the 29th for the usual 6 days. Wintry weather is here; Xmasy, Xmas snow all over.

Will close now

Love to Mrs. George

Yours, A. G. Bisset RAMC.

My dear Annaheim

I got your letter of 19th this morning. We had our Christmas dinner last night and the officers all dined together and had a jolly time. Bisset did us in his usual grand style and wound-up quite early.

We have a new CO who has arrived; a Canadian, Goodland who has the Badges of Lt. Col up (and Carrigan those of Major), but apparently they have only the verbal permission of General Hickie to put them up.

The roads are in a bad state and the snow is banked up 8 ft either side, and one of the poor animals had to be destroyed due to a fall.

I am in an unlined hut and absolutely frozen, so don't be surprised if I am not here when you return.

Bisset begs to remind you of the new order that says an HQ officer who goes on leave must send a cake. I sent them one but apparently you and the Colonel have not done so hence the 'Reminders'.

I hope you are having a grand time. Kindest Regards to

your wife and yourself
Yours Sincerely
R T Baxter RMF

So, I am taking a large 'Madeira' cake back with me.

In June 1918, Dorice and I use a letter from her to Marsden, to appeal to his 'chivalrous' nature to move me up the leave list! Cheeky!

Dear Captain Marsden,
I am writing to thank you for the lovely flowers which arrived this morning. They are lovely; carnations which are my favourite flowers. How did you know?
I scarcely expected them – knowing from experience how leaves fly, and one never seems to have time to do all one wants to do! Anyway, I'm afraid Bubbie and I never have time to think of anybody else!
I hope you are having a really good time – but I guess you are – as I know you haven't been home for so long.
When you get back to the old Munsters again, do be sweet and see if you can talk nicely to the Colonel and suggest to him that Bubbie needs a change!!! I'm sure he does! When he is on leave we feel like a 'proper' young married couple; this parting is so hard. And you might buck up and finish off the war, so that you can all come home again! Please do your best for us!
Again, I thank you so much for the flowers.
With kindest regards and best wishes
Yours Sincerely
Dorice Annaheim

My own Dearest darling,

I love you and adore you. Voila. You sent me a sweet little love letter today-enclosing Marsden's letter. Thank you sweetheart mine for enclosing a little letter to him.

He's really a jolly good fellow, and as we went out to Egypt together in 1914 we are the greatest of Palls. He exaggerates a frightful lot and lies like 'ell!!

I am not at the bottom of the leave roster by any means. He knows that jolly well but you see, if I do get away soon in my turn, he will probably say it was all his doing!!!

He is a most frightful flirt and simply hundreds of girls write to him and he, in turn, writes to them all. Before I give him your letter, I shall make him promise to absolutely keep it to himself as he talks a deuce of a lot!!

I must away up to the Battalion now, and it will be hours before I am back. I want you to know that things aren't too bad as regards leave; at least not half as bad as Marsden makes out.

Goodbye I will try and write more tomorrow. My love hugs and cuddles, kisses and Tuddles!

God bless you and love you and take care of us both.

Ever your true and adoring

Bubbie xxxxx

Then later I am writing with good news;

Dearest Darling little Baby wifie,

I am a wicked youth because I have not written 'cept a field pc for two days. But Sweetheart you will forgive me when I tell thee that I have been promised to go on LEAVE on 28th inst!! Whoops dearie c'est bon. Now Baxter who is going tomorrow is looking after this letter for me.

I hope to be in town about 4pm on the 28th, but you had better wait for me at Bath GWR.

I must confess that Marsden HAS helped me to go a little earlier than I ought. It must have been your dear sweet letter!

But we must not talk about leave until it actually happens. I will only believe that I am going 'til I get to Boulogne! I can't wait for fourteen days of Heaven!

It has been months since I last saw you, and I have had such a terrible time of it including the 'Cross Country 'Race'. Poor Boy!!

The old Bosche is overhead. So the lights must go out now.

Goodbye Darling Girlie. God Bless you and love you and take care of you and I.

All my love Darling. All the hugs, kisses and cuddles in the world.

Ever Your loving and Devoted
Bubbie xxxx

A letter arrives, to remind me just how long I have been away from my dear wife. Time passes at different speeds out here; fast, when I am deluged with work and 'stunts', and, slow when I am alone in my tent or hut just thinking loving thoughts:

My beloved Hubbie, Bubbikins,

No loving letter from you today. It's the 'ToM' actually, and I have a little tummy pain. A loving letter would have made me feel much better.

Darling, leave MUST come soon. It's been five long months since we were together and so much and so little has happened in our lives in that time. Yet I am more and more in love with you, the darlingest Hubbie anyone ever had.

Do take care of your dear precious self for me, My darling The newspaper boys are shouting "Big German Defeat", so that's somewhat cheering beloved! I do wish it would end, so that you could come home to me for keeps and we could settle down to our long, long honeymoon – the honeymoon that is going to last all our lives – Oh I am longing for it! But a leave would do just fine!

Bubbikins, I am writing in front of the window and dozens of officers have been coming up from the station – some of 'em seem to snaffle all the leave! There are tons of Red Tabs" – staffs – knocking about. They're more plentiful than gooseberries!

By the way, you told me officers are not allowed to wear primrose gloves – well, I've seen dozens of 'em wearing 'em, and white ones too! I thought how nice they looked for summertime.

Darling you asked me to send some polish, and please tell me if there is any other thing I can send.

I roared when you told me the story of Captain Marsden's parcel arriving with the cake all rotten and 'off'-yuk!

Dear Darling big Hubbie, I'm going to say goodnight now. I'm longing for news of leave, that you are fit and well and that you love your little wife more and more every day and every hour. Our love is the thing beloved.

May God Bless you, and bring you back safe and sound. May He bring you back to me very soon, because I need you so. With all my love and kisses dear Husband.

Ever your own loving and true Baby Wife xxx

Dorice's reply to my announcement about this leave has arrived, and has bucked me up no end. LEAVE; I can't wait!

My very own dearest Darling,

I have just received your letter posted by Baxter in Town for you.

You can hardly believe how gloriously happy & excited I am darling hearing that you are coming home on the 28th! That's next Friday! Oh Bubbie Boy! I am so happy! Too happy to write sensibly, but I must try! So here goes.

Please old pal I do want to meet you at Victoria & Daddy has promised to bring me so may I come? You see I'd rather not go straight down to Southsea and, by the way, Dais has no room to put us up.

(Whoops, we shall have to stay at the "Beach" my Hubbie, and have another Honeymoon!). Another reason is I have your new uniform here with me and I want you seen at your most dashing in that!

If we come home here first by the 6.30 we can manage to fly up to Belgrave Place to see the Mater and Pater before we go away to Southsea the next day. Also Mama is longing to see you again – she loves you as much as she loves me and you know how much that is umps?!

I shall be overnight with Grandma in London and ring up the RTO at Victoria and ask him what time your train is due.

My Darling, I KNEW Capt. Marsden would help us – he's a sport! – Please give him my very bestest thanks, beloved. Perhaps you will let me write to him a teeny weeny little note of thanks when we are together in Southsea – will you? Just for making me so happy.

Boy Mine, a week today I'll be in your arms-telling you how very much I love you!

Goodbye my dear one. I will post this now. May God bless you, dearest of Hubbies and protect you & keep you safe and sound during this next week. May He bring you back to me next Friday and make me the happiest little wife in the world.

With all my love kisses hugs and cuddles. (And Tuddles!)

Ever your very own loving and true adoring Baby Wifie xxxxxxx D

Oh, what a leave this is! Everything is working well, and we are staying for five nights at the Royal Beach Hotel in Southsea. Blissful days on our 'second honeymoon'.

These morning 'tuddles' and the afternoon 'matinees' rather exhaust us and we definitely are prepared for a 'wee kid' to arrive in nine months time. Well, we are trying hard enough!

Back 'home' at South Parade, I get a missive from my very best friend and pal, Marsden. It is so typical of the man I have known for six years. He is irrepressible, as his letter is addressed to:

Lieut G.H.Annaheim
"Mule Racer and Transport Dealer"
1st Bn.Roy.Munster Fus.
1 South Parade
Bath.

My dear old Anna,

I will try to write my very neatest and best as I am sure it must be awfully trying 'having' to read letters in the condition you are in!

Oh! I can picture you when you receive this, laying in the arms of your loving wife (who is this orator? Oh, I am sure he draws five shillings extra a day). Are you very washed-out dearest or only feeling rather limp?

You made a helluva mess of that bet of yours, rather typical though wasn't it? Dear Lechup wrote to Condon and tried to borrow the gig, but oh no!! Oh no!! It was in Marieuse where methinks it will stay.

He said he only made a bet of 500 franc but we said liar, and the Colonel is damned annoyed about it (having had a little on) so I think he will stump up – the ugly bugger.

How is Dorice, is she pleased with me letting you come home? And I think she ought to send me a lovable letter (the sort she writes you) to thank me. Or she could send me a pretty picture.

We are in the same old spot and I am fit and cheerful. Of course the transport has gone to the dogs since you left (look at this Dorice dear) but Condon is doing the 3 jobs better than you and Baxter ever did (don't look at this dear, the rude man).

Young D-N got off his court-Martial – the cheeky pup! Whelan has been shot in Germany as a POW trying to escape I hear! Canary is due up tonight at the hut and is going over to the bombing show tomorrow for two days. Imagine the latter having a bon time and doing no work whatsoever.

I woke up feeling all of a bother this morning with my plank in my hand, and am sure if I don't go on leave soon there will be some more monkeys drowned.

I am sick of writing to you so will cease. 'Suppose your dear old face is redder than ever, and your nose more bulbous than usual?

Anna old boy, have a good time on leave and write me all the news.

Yours with love
Cecil

Good old Marsden and his MC!

What is so good about my Darling Wife, is that I can share such things with her, as *we* are also the best of pals – she is never shocked by the things men say and get up to. Especially, when I am about to go on leave, when I am on leave, and after my leave. Leaves bring such joy to us as Dorice shows in her letters:

Dearest darlingest sweetest rippingest and lovable of Husbands!

I am so happy tonight, and do you guess why my Darling? Because you are coming HOME! Home to the little Wifie who is waiting and living for you, and who is counting the days and hours that must elapse before she is safe in your arms again – hugging your big chest!

It was only a field post card that brought this splendid news to me "Coming home about the 30th". Oh Bubbie darling, how much those four little words mean to us! They mean Love and wonderful happiness and all that makes life worth living. I am so happy that I want to laugh and I want to cry and I am all 'trembly' with joy!

We shall be together again in just a few days. After all the worries, heartaches and disappointments of these past months. This time it will be the best leave ever!

Mama and Daddy send you their love dear Heart, and say they will be ever so glad to see you and hear your cheery laugh again.

Bubby–Boy, do you think you could manage to bring your little Wifie home a box of cigarettes for a present (oooer!!! Get another wife!). You can get them cheaper in France, beloved. Daddy mostly smokes cigars and pipes now, so poor Mrs. George seldom gets a chance of sneaking a cig and she does so like an occasional smoke. I thought if you got me a box of fifty, my Darling, they would last me for ages and I could always have one when I felt inclined.

Goodnight, my own dear Hubbie. May God bless you dear old Boy and keep you safe from all danger and keep you safe and sound, and may He bring me back to you very soon, because I need you so.

With all my love and kisses beloved and all my hugs, cuddles and Tuddles.

Ever your very own loving and true and adoring Baby Wifie xxxxxxxxxxx

On this, the last leave EVER, we may have conceived a wee kiddums. Our baby that will have my pal Marsden as its

Godfather, all being well! That'll make him behave!

These flashbacks of these 'Days of Leave' – actually total less than sixty days – have all been 'Days of Love".

But they have now gone from my mind.

FOREVER.

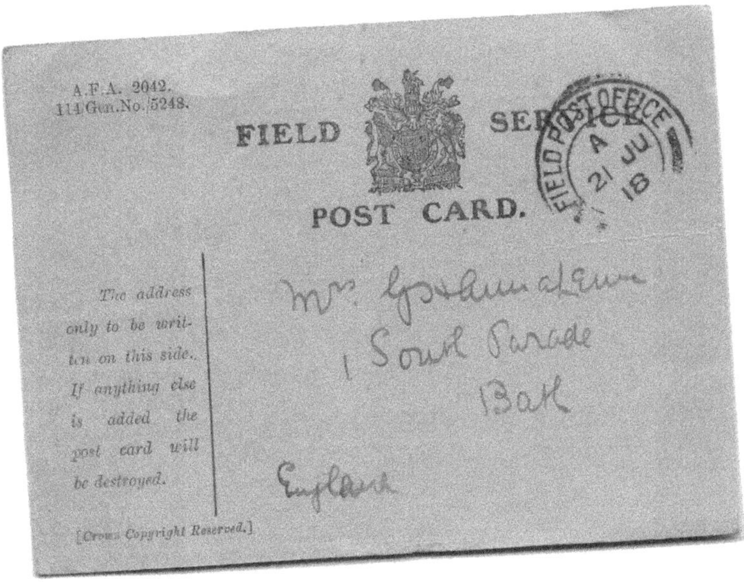

ROYAL MUNSTER FUSILIERS.

A GRAND MATINEE

Under the distinguished Patronage of

Field Marshal H.R.H. The DUKE OF CONNAUGHT, K.G., K.T., K.P., G.C.B., G.C.S.I., G.C.M.G., G.C.I.E., G.C.V.O.
H.R.H. The DUCHESS OF CONNAUGHT.

The Marquis of Lansdowne, K.G., G.C.S.I., G.C.M.G., G.C.T.E.; The Marchioness of Lansdowne; Winifred, Countess of Arran; The Earl of Bandon, K.P., H.M. Lieutenant County of Cork; The Countess of Bandon; The Earl of Kenmare, C.V.O., H.M. Lieutenant County of Kerry; The Countess of Kenmare; The Earl and Countess of Limerick; The Earl of Dunraven, K.P., C.M.G., H.M. Lieutenant County of Limerick; The Lord Wimborne (Lord Lieutenant of Ireland); Lady Wimborne; The Lord and Lady Barrymore; The Lord Shaughnessy, of Montreal; Sir Charles Barrington, Bart.; Lady Barrington; Sir Michael O'Loghlan, Bart., H.M. Lord Lieutenant County of Clare; Sir Morgan O'Connell, Bart.; Lady O'Connell; Lady Fitzgerald; Sara Lady Samuel; The Knight of Glin; The Knight of Kerry; Admiral Sir John Jellicoe, G.C.B., O.M., G.C.V.O.; Lady Jellicoe; Gen. Sir W. R. Robertson, G.C.B., K.C.V.O., D.S.O.; Lady Robertson; Lieut.-Gen. Sir Herbert Miles, G.C.B., G.C.M.G., C.V.O., Colonel Royal Munster Fusiliers; Lady Miles; Lieut.-Gen. Sir Herbert Belfield, K.C.B.; Lieut. Gen. Sir Lawrence Parsons, K.C.B.; Lady Parsons; Sir David Wilson, K.C.M.G.; Lady Wilson; Lieut.-Gen. Sir Bryan Mahon, K.C.V.O., C.B., D.S.O., Command-the Forces in Ireland; Major-Gen. W. B. Hickie, C.B.

will be given at

THE NEW THEATRE,

(Kindly lent by Sir Charles Wyndham, Miss Mary Moore, and Mr. Boucicault.)

— on —

ST. PATRICK'S EVE,

Friday, March 16th, 1917, at 2.30 p.m.

in aid of the

Comforts Funds of the above Regiment at the Front.

Under the auspices of the R.M.F. Old Comrades' Association War Relief Fund.

The following Artists have already consented to appear:

DION BOUCICAULT.
NINA BOUCICAULT.
LEONARD BOYNE.
DONALD CALTHROP.
GLADYS COOPER.
GERALD DU MAURIER.
H. PLUNKETT GREENE.
HELEN HAYE.
CHARLES HAWTREY.
NELSON KEYS.
HARRY LAUDER.
ETHEL LEVEY.
STANLEY LOGAN.
MAIRE O'NEILL.
ARTHUR PLAYFAIR.
MABEL RUSSELL.
IRENE VANBRUGH.
And many others.

Tickets to be had at the New Theatre (Telephone—Regent 4466).

PRICES:—Stalls, £2 2s. and £1 1s.; Dress Circle, 10/6; Upper Circle—Front Row, 7/6, other Rows, 5/-; Unreserved Pit, 4/-; Gallery, 2/6. Boxes by arrangement. All prices include Government Tax.

Any further particulars can be had from the Hon. Sec., 93, Oakley Street, Chelsea, S.W. Tel, 3880 Western.

LEVERIDGE & Co., Harlesden, N.W.

10

TO FLY

"...it's rather bumpy; like riding a boat tossed in a stormy sea swell"

A memory breaks loose. It is the old padre (an R.C. Father!) telling the men that; "When we go, our soul soars through the sky up to heaven. It will be bright and peaceful, as long as you have led good clean lives."

I hate Church Parade. All that preaching, after I've worked half the night, and then I spend the other half dressing for church parade. No sleep, and then marching the men seven miles for a dawn service.

This sky is all dark around me, and is now becoming alight, and I feel I'm floating on air, as I relive my desire to fly.

With Mother and Father and Dais at the Bath County Show in '08, I see my first aeroplane. It looks a flimsy, crackpot device; all wires and string and smelling of dope. It doesn't get off the ground however. Then in 1911, at Alexandra Park, Manchester. on a DLOY training day, I see a 'plane fly. An AV Roe Triplane, and it still looks flimsy!

Another memory; this time two years later, when a chap

called Hucks takes his Avro up to a thousand feet over me and my pals of the 'A Squadron DLOY' in Bellevue Gardens, and makes a sensational triple 'loop-the-loop' over our heads. I decide that, one day, I will become a flyer!

Destiny, or the currents of my life, mean that, so far, I have stuck to horses.

Out in the Egyptian desert, west of the Canal, I see a couple of our chaps flying off eastwards. Apparently, flown by Naval types in Farmans, who are looking for the Turkish Army and seemingly, doing good work in spotting for us.

Here in France things are moving on. The sky above us filling with interesting instruments of war, including many Bosche kite balloons spotting for them, as well as hoards of Hun planes dropping bombs on us from a great height. The Royal Flying Corps are regarded as 'The Cavalry of the Skies', so I am thinking about joining.

To Miss Doris Hookway
1 South Parade,
Bath.

Dearest Little Dorice

No letter today to cheer me up! I blame His Majesty's P.O. not doing their duty.

The boys in the trenches told me last night that they hear the Bosche transport bringing up the beer and a little later they hear me coming up. They still snipe at us but who knows if they will take it in their heads to shell us. Now, in this sector, it's a bit of 'live and let live' but it may become 'die or let die'.

A few weeks ago an aeroplane of ours reported a Bosche transport laying dead on the road opposite our line. They must have been shelled by us by mistake. We are waiting for them to reciprocate!!

I might try to join the RFC. I met a chap from King Edward's, who was in the same year as my brother Eddy, who has convinced me that 'planes are the thing'. I shall go and see the CO about this.

Dais tells me that London is unsafe because of the Zeppelin raids. Well I suppose it's all relative. The Bosche try to bomb my lines, but don't seem very accurate – so far!

Darling, I have just been called away, so will say goodnight darling. I will write again tomorrow.

Sending thousands of hugs and kisses
Your ever loving hubbie-to-be
Bubbie xxx

I count nine Bosche balloons up this evening. They need to be shot down as soon as possible, but our 'Archie' is not as effective as theirs. The 'air war' is clearly heating up.

I meet a couple of RFC flyers in an estaminet ten miles back from Battalion HQ. They are really sporting fellows, so we manage a few 'tinctures' and a lot of laughs. I am invited to dinner in their mess and a flight over the Lines. Today, I can't remember too much about that dinner. What a 'Bash'!

My Dearest Dorice,

I am sorry this letter is more of a scribble than usual. It was a real 'bash' at an aerodrome with my new RFC friends. I am suffering a little from 'bottle ache' today, and am afraid I have taken it out a bit on the men.

I am tempted to change to the RFC. There's lots of leave, a better chance of promotion, and a smarter uniform too. It was an unmemorable night, since I can't remember much! But apparently they've agreed to take me up tomorrow. Don't worry darling Girl it will be a bit of a joy-ride, a kind of test, for the plane, not me!

Girlie we must spend as much time together when I am home, of course with your parent's permiss.

They might get fed up with me because I shall always be with you. I wonder how much difference I may have made to your life. You have given me a reason to live, darling.

Do you know what Dais says?; "Dorice is the sweetest Girl, and you must plan to marry her!!" So there!

Goodbye and good night my sweetheart.

All my love and kisses

Your old Bubbie xxxxx

The man in the RFC is called Keller and is a Captain with an MC from Gallipoli. He is taking me for a ride in his 'bus'. I can' t wait!

Keller gives me a quick briefing about 'Archie': "If it's black its Bosche, if it's white its ours, and oddly, if its pink it comes from an Austrian naval unit!" He adds: "Don't worry about the 'Archie', we will fly above it, but keep your eyes skinned for Hun kites, and wave your hand and point if you see one".

Equipped with the thickest coat I have ever worn, and gloves that go all the way to my elbows, I am placed into the front cockpit. Off we go!

This sector of the line up here near Ypres is quite quiet at the moment, so no action is expected, though I could use the gun if required.

Today there is little sign of 'archie', except beneath us some smoke that looks like a bed of mushroom-shaped puffs. No other 'planes, friendly or otherwise to be seen. The clouds seem far too crisp and dense to fly through, and as we do, it's rather bumpy, like riding a boat tossed in a stormy sea swell.

The land below is an extraordinary sight, grey/brown like the colour of some of my mules, or, the colour of Hun uniforms! Streaks of white chalk bedrock, also cross the landscape

I've seen the 'recce-photos' taken by spotter 'planes of the trenches below, but from up here you can see more clearly the zigzag trench patterns, and remains of farms, villages and steeples. Ypres itself is recognizable, but very much knocked about. The landscape far to the east and west of the Lines have a different look; verdant green fields as far as the eye can see.

The cold is intense, the noise raucous, and the stench of hot Castrol from the motor quite pungent.

Back on the ground I feel chipper. A great ride in a '504'. I thank Keller and invite him over to our own HQ for a mess dinner 'bash'. Riding back to my little hut, I am full of hope for joining the Flying Corps.

Dearest Mother and Father,

All is well here, out of the Line and in a quiet sector for a change. The men and animals are happy with good food and fodder. Plus the old drinks come up regularly which is always good for morale of the men.

I should tell you I've put in for the RFC; a change of job, and a chance to get some serious home leave and training.

Yesterday I had a spin over 'Wprs" in a two-seater. It was jolly sporting; no sign of 'archie' or Hun 'planes but a great

experience. Do you remember seeing a kite at the County Show in '08? They are more powerful in every way and the RFC are nowdays the 'Cavalry of the Skies'.

The request to transfer has to go all the way to Haig himself – so, being the Army, it will take some time! I also have to have an interview and a medical check as well.

The fellows in the Corps are a fine lot of chaps from all over the place, with some Americans pilots thrown in for luck!

So not to worry; the decision won't be made for some time. Meanwhile be assured all is jolly fine with me.

Say hello to Dais and do take care of your Dear selves.

From your loving son

Herbert

They have sent a car over from the airfield at Hazebrouk for an interview and medical. They are not taking pilots directly, but first train you as an observer.

A letter from mother arrives. It's a lecture, and NOT approving. I think she thinks this is a safe job. If only she'd seen me three weeks ago! But I'm glad she thinks I'm safe. I share all my thoughts with Dorice. I really do want to fly, and at least she understands.

Dearest Little Girlie,

Thank you for your dear sweet letters – I got two today.

All is merry and bright with the men and animals out here. I saw ripping sight last night a Bosche balloon came sailing over our lines (with a man in the basket), at a great height. All the 'archies' in the district fired at him until an aeroplane came along and shot him down in flames. The Bosche was collared and turned out to be a young officer about my age. Poor Fellow!!

Still no news of the RFC yet. We can't put much faith in 3 months in England. It's only when they are short of pilots and that was some time ago. Now you have to start as an observer and after 3 months might get your pilots certificate and no chance to go to England.

'C'est la guerre'! Oh, I must go now so, sending all my hugs and kisses as I go up to the trenches, I will try to finish this when I return.

All my love to you sweetheart from your ever devoted
Bubby xxx

But disappointment came today, as I get officially the bad news about the RFC job.

My very own Darling,

I ought to be really down in the dumps today! Cos I haven't received a letter from you today, and, they will not accept me for the RFC. Cos – do you know Girlie? I'm almost too ashamed to admit it. I'm 12 stone 10lbs. 'S awful, I had no idea I was so heavy!! They say in a month or two they may accept me as a pilot. We will see.

I am quite happy now thinking about leave. It will come soon. Perhaps all is for the good as I am near the top of the leave list so we will be together sweetheart – soonest. I can't wait till then, cos I will be able to hold you in my arms and hear you say: "I love you Bubbie". That will be certain bliss.

I am so glad your dear Mater's flue has gone and all is merry and bright at 1 SP, just as it is here.

Sending all my hugs and cuddles and kisses to you, Girlie Mine.

Ever your devoted
Bubbie xxxx

Aeroplane activity is getting to be more than a nuisance nowdays. I probably would have 'gone west' by now if I would have joined the RFC, as the Hun 'planes seem to roam the skies at will.

A Bosche 'plane comes over while I am playing rugger for the Brigade against the next one to our right. (we win; 20 to nil). He must have thought the English funny to be playing football just behind the guns! His bomb misses us by miles!

But, during the big Bosche push and our Great Retreat' in March 1918, it is the worst time for aircraft; when scores of 'em are coming across low, with guns spraying the ground around us, as we hasten out of the salient at great speed. They say the Red Baron is among them. We do finally get him though.

I am rather glad I have stuck with the animals and didn't get to fly, again. Ironically, though, it is a Bosche 'plane that has got ME in the end.

As the light dims, I feel I am beginning to float away – into the sky.

Perhaps the old Padre had a point!

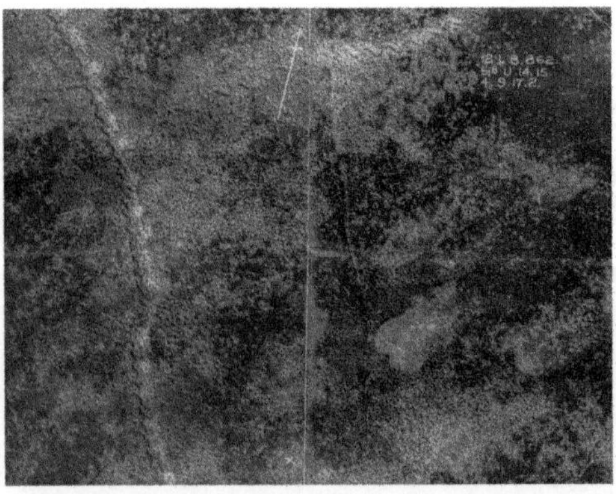

11

PALS, PROSPECTS & PROMOTIONS

"... if I stay in the army, I shall never have any money – if I don't, I might"

Suddenly, it's the unique smell of beeswax and floor polish that is so evocative; triggering vivid flashbacks of my earlier life working in the National Provincial Bank.

Wax, covering the oak flooring and all the dark furniture; desks, chairs and walls-it's a powerful reminder of Wellsway Branch Bath, but more especially, the inside of 41 Spring Gardens, Manchester Branch.

Wellsway Branch is too near to home, but it does serve as a base for an apprenticeship till 1911, and is allowing me to stay in touch with school pals like Symons (at Bristol medical school), as well as Hippesley, Cox and the other rowing pals on the Avon. At the weekends I train with the Royal Gloucestershire Hussars as a yeomanry cadet and nurture my love of horse riding, polo and other mounted 'stunts'.

I work alongside good pals like Brian at the Branch there, until he suddenly goes off to a tea plantation in Ceylon – it's called Rayigam Estate in Padukka. We write to each other:

My dear old 'Anna',

I can't say what joy it gave me to get your letter. I must say I felt like a bit of a shit not writing to you before I sailed, but I did it all in such a hurry, only getting 3 weeks notice rather than 3 months.

This really is indeed 'God's Own Country' and all is serene so far. It would take weeks to tell you all that has happened since I left the old NP Bank and came out by Bibby boat from Liverpool (all first class – about £45).

Well the voyage was ripping; I won a sweep on board and had a 'perfect peach' all to myself as far as Port Said, and very nearly did the silly thing!

My cousin out here has been the chief influence on me to chuck the Bank. My uncle, his father, is intimate with Sir Edward Rosling who is one of the leading men in the Island and owns several 'totums' (plantations). So I had an interview and he offered to send me here to learn planting and rubber tapping. I do have a comfortable billet in a bungalow with good grub and the chance for riding, shooting and fishing (with dynamite actually!)

The work is strenuous and I do need to learn Tamil and Singalese. The lingo is a real bugger, but it is needed as the workers come from both races.

You must not think you are your own boss exactly, tho' much more so than in the National Provincial of course. All I can say is the life appeals to me and I have no desire to see the N.P. again and as you know, I wouldn't advise any man with any guts to stay in that show.

I must stop now, as I must start my home letter. Write again and let me know how ye are.

Cherio old thing. Ever your old pal

Brian

"'Old that bloody 'orse" (signed) Major RM Yorke

D squadron R.G.H.

Brian joined the Ceylon Rifles in 1914, and I hear that he died at Tanga in German East Africa within a year. A good pal, and another one now 'pipped'.

Whatever he says, and to be fair, the Bank is decent to me all along this army stint of mine. Still in 1911, I am applying to the Bank of Montreal, and am feeling that a life abroad could be an adventure! Before I get that offer to go to Canada, the promotion comes through with National Provincial to come up here to the Manchester Branch.

Bank work is good. I am good at it as well. Lots of pals here – we all have proper mahogany desks with electric lamps, and the windows are tall; to let in a lot of light.

Freddie 'He of the "doggy" bow tie, Miles 'The Fairy', Johnny D – always at the back of the room making 'remarks sotto voce', Browning – 'He who is married' and, of course, 'The Rogue". All are special pals.

However, I seem to be the favourite of old Mr. Williams the manager. He often 'disappears' for afternoon 'soirees' or 'matinees' and leaves me in charge of the bank. Effectively, I am the assistant manager. It seems to work out all right. The boys are able to respect me and we are still good pals outside work. I am sure I will keep up with them all into the future.

Now that I am properly away from the stultifying home in Belgrave Place, and no longer living with Mother and Father, it feels like freedom. But how will my friendship with Katherine survive this move? Time, as always, will tell.

In Manchester life is busy; working at the bank with new pals, joining 'A Squadron' Duke of Lancaster's Own Yeomanry and, there, meeting my new best pal, Cecil Marsden. I am able frequently to swim at the Baths in Manchester, and am getting back home to Bath about once-a-month whenever the Yeomanry training allows.

Old Marsden says: "Break it off with Kathy – and play the field!" But I say that I have given her a ring and we have an 'understanding'. Things are good with Katherine and me, but now War is declared, my overseas escapades away from the Bank really start! The 'Love situation' sorts itself out on the voyage to Egypt.

After Egypt, life has changed. I am Transport Officer in the 1st Battalion Royal Munster Fusiliers in France, but I am still only a Temporary 2nd Lieutenant after twenty-two months fighting for King, Country and Empire.

The Bank is actually rather decent, paying officers like me my salary, while in the Army, so money is not such an issue.

It is now all about getting through – or maybe getting a 'blighty' wound, as I just want to live a long and happy life with Dorice after this awful war is over.

Bank or Army? THAT is the Question (as Shakespeare said!).

The decisions on this issue are with me for many months – years actually – even this early in 1916 just after my first meeting with Darling Dorice;

My darling little Dorice,

I have just had grub with my men after being out all day, but must tell you a little news.

I have just heard unofficially that there is little chance of receiving a permanent Commission as they refuse to give it to anybody under the rank of Captain. But my papers have already gone in, but I shall be jolly glad if I was unable to obtain one-cos – well – if I stay in the Army I shall never have any money – if I don't – then I might. Anyway, I've still got a job at home waiting for me, and although it is only in a bank, it's a safe job and I was getting on quite well until the war broke out. I do hope now I don't get a Commiss., as it would mean living abroad (India?), or in Barracks.

I've had enough of foreign countries. And d – – near enough of the Army!

Now dearest, I hope this letter won't make you sad. Would you like me to stay in the Army? Do you only love me because I am a soldier Dorice? Or would you still love me in civilian 'togs'. I don't look too bad in flannels!!! Whoops dearie!!

I hear there is talk of a banking Trade Union – well that would help push the salaries up! The Bank is paying staff bonuses at about 10pc during the war and even paying their income tax. Course, this will come to an end with Peace, so some kind of Trade Union might help us. More later Darling.

I can't wait to reread your last loving letter and receive the next one tomorrow darling Girl.

With all my love and kisses
Ever your own
Bubbie xxx

Dorice is really understanding about this conundrum and seems to be happy with me having a civilian career in the Bank, 'apres la guerre':

Darling Little One ,

I am looking forward to tomorrow as I didn't get a letter from you today – so am hoping for two tomorrow.

I loved it when you wrote that whatever happened after the war we would be together and life would be a long honeymoon. Oh, I wish for our first Honeymoon and being together!

Let's not worry about my future profession until we see if His Majesty wants me in his bally Army.

My papers have gone up the ladder-with a strong recommendation from Colonel Monck-Mason. Then they go on to the Brigadier and then to the General and so on up to Sir D Haig and onto the War Office. Then it will take six months to get Gazetted. If I was in Kitchener's Army I would be a Captain now, but promotion is slower in the Regulars. What! what!!

But I would chuck up the Army if it meant going to India without YOU!

If I came back to the bank I would have leave, then join at Manchester Branch before transferring to a nice small Branch in the South. There are already about 300 Branches across England – so plenty of choice. And then Dorice you could come with me!!

I did think about working up in London, perhaps for the Bank of England, but right now it is probably too early to worry, umps! Let us leave all this talk of professions till much later.

Every night I pray that our love for each other may last, come what may. Surely no one ever loved each other as much as we do, and I pray I will always be worthy of your love. Besides wanting to be your loving Husband I want to be your best pal.

With all my love and millions of kisses
Ever Your Own Devoted and Loving
Bubbie xxx

The war is going on-and-on, and the Line moves backwards and then forwards; especially after the successful Ginchy 'stunt' on the Somme where we, the 16th Irish Division, give it to the Bosche in the neck. Perhaps the war will be short and I can resume a peaceful life 'après'.

My Dearest Darling Little Girlie,

No letter yesterday or today – 's awful! Never mind, better luck tomorrow I hope.

Did you see in the papers the Bosche is retiring in several places. Whoops Dearie! The war will soon be over and then you will have your own Bubbikins with you forever and a day! Well, I might need a job, but we can sort that out when this show ends.

At present my job in this short life is split between the Army and the Bank. I was perfectly contented in the Bank, and am sure I will get on and become a Manager because the work interested me. In the Manchester branch there was only the Manager and me to run the show. He used to leave quite often and let me run the shop, and I was quite capable of doing so.

I left for the War with their blessing and I am getting bank pay now plus my Army pay, so am much better off than others. I now worry that, if and when, the permanent commission comes through the Bank may see my appointment and confiscate £100 or so.

It is true that before we met I promised myself a roving career and life perhaps in Canada, India or even Africa, but now Girlie I see myself settling down in a Bank somewhere nice with you as my darling wife. Well, we will see about all this, but dearest believe me when I tell you; "I ain't wanting to rove no more".

Did you see Erwood's death in the paper? Poor kid, he was with me in the NP branch in Wellsway. His father is a builder in Bath and he was a young apprentice before I went up to Manchester. He joined up without asking the Bank and his salary was stopped. He was a 2nd Lt. in the KRRC and I did meet him briefly once again, waiting for the boat in Boulogne. Everybody seems to be getting pipped – it's bad when your pals go.

Yes, the tummy is better and the throat less sore now. How are you Darling? Is the cold better Babs?

I can't wait for your next loving letter to arrive-apart from that, everything is lovely in the garden here.

Goodbye Darling little Babs I will try and write a more interesting letter tomorrow.

All my love sweetheart Dorice. Sent with all my kisses and hugs.

Ever Your Loving
Bubbie xxxxxxx

April 1917, and my life is fundamentally changed for the better, after our wedding and glorious honeymoon. The job prospects and promotions issue haunts me still. Should I tell the bank that I'm married? I can't afford to lose a big slice of income, yet don't want to spoil my chances in the NP Bank after this war is over.

My Dearest Darling Little Babs,

Many, many thanks for two ripping love letters and a nice fountain pen, which I am using – it's topping. You are my darling sweet pretty little Baby Girlie and I love you and adore you. I love being married!!!

Oooer!! I must tell you this. I had a letter from the new Manager at Manchester branch and he said Head Office had heard I had married and did he (the Manager) know any particulars as the "Directors did not consider it advisable for any officer-of-the-Bank getting married under £150 per annum". And they said; "Undertake the responsibilities of married life" Bow Wow!! Sounds terrible don't it?

Well I wrote a decent letter and said if I came back to the Bank this year my salary would be £140 and my people had promised to make my salary up to £160!!!

Of course they haven't – but I wrote and told Mother to keep the £30 she owes me (that 'loan' she took to try and stop us getting married!).

I also said that I was certainly able "to undertake the responsibilities of married life", now and after the war. I really laid it into them that the Army was paying me £240 p. annum.

As you can imagine it worried me a lot yesterday, but anyway Babs, I feel pretty safe having a job après la guerre. I don't think I'll get the sack and I hope mother will turn up trumps and tell Head Office that she will make up my salary as I said. You might explain to her Sweetheart. I have written to her but a visit to her would help umps! I am so glad you are seeing her occasionally. She's jolly proud of you – they all love you Babs.

I can picture you coming into my hut now. It would be Heaven if you were here we could go out and look at the horses and see all the men and then go and look at the Bosche trenches – oooer! Get another Hubbie!!

Darling, I could go on for ever tonight. I want to be with you and hug you. Oh for PEACE. Goodbye dearest Darling Wife of Mine

Ever Your Loving Hubbie

Bubbie xxxx

The bank salary issue is always in the back of my mind, but out here there are bigger worries – like; will the next Hun shell get me? Still the irritating letters to and from the Bank roll on, and am I keeping my darling wife up with the story:

Dorice My Darling little Wifie,

Just received your letter which was written in the garden. What do you think Babs; The Manager of the Manchester Branch has written to me saying the Directors want to know what job I have in the Army which brings me £240 per annum I say to hell with the whole – lot of them. I can give them particulars if they want it!!! Done! (But in my own good time!!). After all – out here we are trying to win this awful war – not quizzing people by mail.

Sorry, I am in a bit of a mood tonight – just so much work and a lot of shelling. Just back from the Line. I was lucky as usual and the old Bosche shelled every blessed spot except the exact spot I was standing in. The sniping missed, but only just! I should tell that to the Bank Directors!

We are moving in the next few days so writing will be hard Darling. But never fear, I have paper and the pen with me so whenever there is a chance I will write or scribble a few loving words.

Oh, how I miss laying in your dear arms. Darling may God take care of you and bless you till I come home again. All my love and kisses and cuddles and 'tuddles'too!!

Ever Your Own Loving Husband

Bubbie

With this 'Army or Bank conundrum' preying on my mind, the Colonel, meanwhile, is desperately keen I should obtain my Permanent Commission. I am now letting this big issue 'slide'.

But more and more inexperienced chaps come out from England more senior than me. It is hard to swallow. I am the only officer, who has been here since the Battalion landed in France over a year ago, without a medal or promotion of any kind. Especially after the Ginchy 'stunt' on the Somme when I wasn't even 'M in D' – but neither was the Docman, who deserves it more than me. Still, I do get direct praise, and a card, from General Hickie. C'est La Guerre, c'est the Army, I suppose.

And, I have been spared, unlike so many of my pals.

My promotion eventually comes through; Full Lieutenant and the pip goes up! Drinks all round. As for medals, I just don't want to talk about it, as I think they are unfairly dished out!

Meeting a Lt. Creech of the Worcesters in a restaurant in Amiens proves valuable. He was previously with the bank Head Office. I ask him about my 'big issue': about telling the Bank I got married. It still worries me.

He says: " Write to my pal Sitford at Head Office and ask his opinion – the chap is an old-boy of KE's School in Bath, which should help". This was a good idea, and rather reassuring, and I send the letter I get from Sitford on to Dorice:

Dear Annaheim,

I'm glad you met my friend Creech. He is one of the best sort in the Bank.

I was never at Bath Branch, but it is my home, and I think I was at King Edward's School at the same time as you and your brother, probably a year ahead of you. With regard to marrying – the GM's take very little notice of it and the Directors are not aware of a lot of these things.

You are not likely to be penalized on your return in any way, though of course they never do miss a chance of giving a pious opinion and a little cheap advice.

So you can be quite easy on that point – in fact those of us who are constrained to stay behind anticipate the men on military service will be lionized – while we sink into obscurity.

The salary scale has not been altered and I don't think it will be so until after the war. We still get bonuses occasionally to keep things going.

The staff is getting very short and now crowds of girls are working all over, since close to 1600 of our men are serving in the Army and Navy.

The Roll of Honour is assuming big proportions – 130 men have been killed and 15 prisoners of war, so the Bank has done a good 'bit'.

We get an occasional air raid to remind us of the dangers you fellows get everyday and the Huns latest stunt is raiding by moonlight.

But no one is downhearted although we shall of course be glad when we can settle down to a peaceful life again. Try and come in to Head Office when you get leave again.

I hope you are fit and well and have a safe return when this war ends. You may be sure of a good welcome from the Bank with no reservations so don't worry.

Best regards
Yours sincerely
Alex Sitford

Keeping in touch with the Branch, as well as Head Office seems a good idea, and I must say the Bank folks are supportive right up to 1918:

Dear Mr. Annaheim,

I was glad to receive your letter of 13th inst., and enclose your Deposit Account Book written up to date.

I am sorry you are having such a rough time of it, but wish you the best of luck and hope your wish may someday be granted to return to your old civilian duties.

Needless to say we shall be pleased to see you back. All who know you reciprocate your kind regards.

Yours faithfully.
G D Edwards
The Manager
National Provincial Bank of England Limited,
41, Spring Gardens, Manchester

Before the 'Great Race' and my 'Adventures in Retreat' begin, the Bank agrees to leave things as they are salary-wise until after the war and my 'discharge from the Army'. I have stopped worrying about the Bank.

But, on the next leave I will go into Head Office with Dorice to charm the old Directors. They will give me a good job after they meet my dear sweetheart:

My own dear darling little Wife.

I shall be disappointed if the old mail has gone wrong again and you had to go a day without your daily letter from me.

Is your poor wee head better Darling? I hate to think you are unwell and I am not there to care for you.

There is such a lot of peace talk about that I am wondering about 'après'. So much so, I had a dream last night that I had rejoined the Manchester Branch and was fed up they would not give me leave!! Then I saw us in a little country town – like Ringwood or Marlborough where I know the country is very nice. Dreams <u>*will*</u> *come true for us...umps!*

As the NP has amalgamated with the Union Bank, I might get a smaller Branch somewhere nice – but we will have to wait and see.

We will muck along together somehow and we will be jolly

happy too, umps Sweetheart?

All my hugs and cuddles and two long tuddles which leaves us both "spent"

Ever Your Loving and True Hubbie

Bubbie xxx

That smell of wax from the woodwork inside those Banks is fading. Someone said once, that beeswax was meant to signal 'the survival of man in a natural world'. But my world is now absolutely un-natural; limited in senses, limited in space and limited in time.

Dream-like memories of the Bank; and thoughts in my head of Pals, Prospects and Promotions fade, and are gone.

No more smells of beeswax. My sense of smell has gone.

I am gone.

12

THE BOYS FROM ERIN'S ISLE

"... they offered me a hare the other day, but I let them cook it for themselves ".

I now hear the strident sound of the Irish pipes. It is the sound, or noise, that triggers memories of my fearless Irishmen.

I am not fond of the pipes, but they certainly stir the men. I love some of the pretty tunes played on the chanter alone; sweet melodies, while the words seem to contain allusions to a green land full of dreams and fairies.

Oh, politics as well. Joining the 1st. Battalion Royal Munster Fusiliers in Egypt after they had been completely knocked out in Gallipoli is eye-opening.

First the accents – plenty of slurring, 'shoar' for 'sir', 'wesht' for 'west' (then everything seems to 'go wesht' – it's lost, or just a problem, or someone has died). I am getting used to the various accents from north and south very quickly. But I don't reveal my own Irish ancestry from Mother's side

Then there is the drinking. So many of these men have prodigious thirsts for both the hard stuff (rum or German schnapps, if they can get it) and what they call Porter which is a sweet black beer brewed only in Ireland. I do like a 'snifter' myself, but their consumption dwarfs my own capabilities!

This is my first Christmas in France, and I am learning very fast to cope with these situations.
As I write to darling Dorice;

Darling Baby Mine,

I've had a terrible day.

Xmas Day in an Irish Battalion is just about the limit when there's any work to be done. I haven't heard a shot fired all day so between the Huns and ourselves there seems to be for today anyway an armistice.

I am told there were two letters for me this evening, but everything here is such chaos that they seem to have gone astray bl – and d – m!

I am rather fed-up tonight because nearly everyone is drunk, or, as they say in their broad Irish accents, "half seas over".

When you have sixty animals to water and feed it is rather trying, besides which, Irishmen are apt to forget they are in the Army and – well – anything might happen.

I have just been out and it's now 2am and after much trouble I think they are all in bed now. This has been a rotten Xmas, still I didn't expect much more. I hope yours was Happy little Girlie, and may the New Year bring me home to you once more.

Eight more days sweetheart!!! I am tired tonight because I had to do about ten men's work today otherwise it never would have been done!

Still the men are sleeping it off and the animals all fed and watered and my transport lines ready for tomorrow's efforts.

I am a more than a bit homesick with no letters! Better tomorrow!
All my love and kisses
Ever your own devoted Bubbie

As I am in my tent writing to dear darling Dorice I reflect that my men also have darling girls back home. Apparently most of them are married and some of the older men joined-up in Ireland to earn quite a bit more than being just a casual labourer. It is my job to censor their letters, and even occasionally help them write them, as some of these men cannot write. I am not sure they send much of their pay home.

Many of them, like John King my servant, haven't been home for well over a year. He seems to have a nice girl back in Cork, and I copy it and send it to Dorice:

30/1/17
My dearest Molly,

Just a five lines answer to your fond and loving letter. I received it quite early today, Tuesday, and was delighted to hear from you my dear Molly.

I am hoping to get a pass soon so that I may come home to see you as we shall have a Good old time together when we meet and I am longing for that day. When I looks at your photo I think of you in my dreams at night and day. How I will be glad when I come back and we can lock arms together.

My dear Molly we have very cold weather out here with first snow but we hope for better weather to come soon. My dear Molly I must say Goodnight as it is late when I am writing to you, so Goodbye for the time with fondest love from your sincerely

John

Days after, I refer to Dorice's reaction to John's letter which she found very touching

Dorice, my Darling little Pet,

A dinky little love letter from your made me happy today. 'Scuse pencil but I am writing "dans mon petit lit". So, you liked my servant's love letter did you? Girlie. He cannot write, so I helped him with all the endearments – those that I have learned since I met you – umps!!

They tell me Molly is a very sweet little Irish flapper. He will be going home in about a month for his leave – the first for over two years. At present he has a very bad cold and I've told him to stay in bed tomorrow. I will give him an Oxo cube – one of those you sent and I thanked you for.

Because it is so late when I get back from the line there is no hot water, so I normally have my Oxo drink at 11am. John deserves one at least as he is good to me.

Darling it is so late I am going to sleep. I wish you were in my arms, still, I suppose, it wouldn't be 'THE THING". Whoops Dearie!!

Goodbye Darling Child, I love you.

Ever your very own old

Bubbie

Ps its awfully untidy xx (like Dorice's hair January 1917!!)

Payday is a headache for me as my men go wild with joy and excitement, as they now have funds to spend at the 'red-light' houses in the village just a couple of miles away.

How strange are these men – fighting and dishing out to each other bloody noses one minute, going to town for a 'bit of the usual' the next, and then coming back to the lines and showing touching tenderness to 'Jenny' their kid goat and all the animals on the line.

They are marvelous singers of all the patriotic songs while they are working, and are often really comic – even when they are not trying for a laugh.

I write to Father and Mother about this. It should interest him especially, as well as give them both something other than worries-about-me to think about:

Dear Mother and Father,

I am sorry I haven't written for quite sometime, but I do love getting your letters and, of course, the papers you send so regularly.

All is merry and bright out here with me, and the Battalion We are far behind the Line and working hard, mainly training the men. I am living in a small but nice hut with a bench for a bed. It has a coal fire and a table, and I will ask the chaps at a nearby balloon section to wire me across some electricity from their generator so I can write by electric lamp and not as I do now by a candle.

How are you both? Mother, I hope you are getting out from time to time – I know my dear Dorice visits you at least once a week. That's the spirit! And you dear Father; I hope you leg is not so painful and that all is well at old King Edward's.

'S an awful war, but we are giving the Bosche a real bucketful of stuff every night, and we will soon have them running home to the old Kaiser!

The Divisions exploits at Ginchy showed what we really can do. I got a personal commendation from the General, but alas no 'M in D' or medal came my way.

Never mind, my job is safe – don't worry. Of course, I am working 20 hours a day, but I have my 60 men and 70 animals to do the heavy work.

These Irishmen are splendid men and the Colonel is very pleased with my transport lines. The Brigadier and General came on a visit, and I was seen as paragon of all that is good!

There is always the risk that some of the men may say or do something 'odd' on these occasions as these lads often speak more freely and 'out of turn' than an English soldier. Luckily, they do seem to have respect for me.

One of my men, poor fellow, got kicked in the head by a mule and had a few teeth knocked-in. I took him to the hospital or rather had him carried there. I think he's getting on well now, at least I hope so.

To get the best out of them, I am quite sympathetic to their conditions and needs. Remember, I was a ranker myself only a few years ago (it seems like decades ago). I have never told them that of course. Putting their food and comfort before my own, means they are loyal, and protective of me.

They see how I love the animals – we now have Jenny a pet goat, a dog ('Fritz', as he came across from the Hun lines), and a wee kitten. The kitten lives with me, and the goat stays with the men; but he did upset old Baxter the QM when he ate a lot of his papers – the dear old QM had to rewrite many pages of Army bumf!!

Both my servant John and my groom Dan keep me well informed of the mood of the men and any 'issues' to solve.

You see they do like fighting amongst themselves when idle, and especially when the rum ration is allocated. So we do have times of in-discipline. Boy can they drink!

At the same time when given the chance they are some of the bravest men at the Front. Even the Hun knows that. When there is an Irish regiment in the Line, the Bosche go especially quiet with their bombs and shelling.

These men are from the South: Cork, Limerick, Kerry and Co Clare, but we have a few Ulstermen, English and Scots in the section as well.

The humour of these men from Ireland, really keeps me

smiling inside, and their patriotic songs and pipe music stirs the heart. There are some lovely tunes.

Luckily the politics stay in Ireland – there are absolutely no issues here even though the Boschemen shout across the Line about the 'Sinn Feiners' and goings-on in Ireland.

You must have read about the raid by the 2nd Battalion across to the Bosche trenches to capture their offensive sign about; "English soldiers killing your wives and children". The men left a green flag with a harp in its place and another sign with rude remarks about the Kaiser! That captured Hun sign will be a trophy of this war I am sure.

My men of course are almost all Catholics and religion and religious tokens like rosaries play quite a big role in their lives. So the Catholic padre gives blessings and absolution quite frequently, while we don't see much of any Anglican padres (who stay well back behind the Line and rarely venture up).

I think because of these deeper religious needs, the men are more reckless when the Huns are sniping, shelling and gassing us.

I have had to shout at them to put on their gas masks when you can see clouds of it coming over, and have lost some men this way.

The Englishmen seem better at the discipline of Army life, but I know who I would choose to have on my side in a scrap! Munstermen of course!

I am often puzzled by the nature of these fellows, who are quite impulsive and changeable at a moments notice; they are jovial, then fierce; soft with the animals, but not afraid to steal a pig or some hens from a local farm to 'add' to the rations.

I always ask if they got it honestly (knowing full well they didn't). I get a funny reply: "Ah, soarh – it was indeed already asking for the pot!" They offered me a hare the other day – but I let them cook it for themselves.

I can say I am very proud of my men as well as this Battalion and this Regiment and all the men of Munster! We seem to jog along well together.

So all is well with your soldier son and his men and his animals.

I must write now to my dear Dorice and a quick line to Dais. Please send greetings to friends and family when you get this. How is my big brother? I haven't heard from him for ages – last I heard he as up near Salonika shooting duck in the mountains. So much for a life on the ocean wave!

Dais knows roughly where I am, though I am not allowed to say.

I am fit and looking forward to my next leave.

All my love to you both

Your loving son

Herbert

Time enough tonight to write a long loving letter to my Dorice:

Dearest darling naughty lovable Baby Girlie,

Another absolutely topping love letter from you sweetheart. I am truly grateful and it makes my life worthwhile for me. Not only me, but my men too who know they can get away with more when I have received a letter from you!

And then there is the Docman, my pal Bisset, who came in to my hut and wanted me to read little tender thoughts which appeared in your letters!!! Well I told him that Darling-little-you were enquiring about him. He asked to be remembered to you, but he seemed a little depressed because I wouldn't read a few passages. Perhaps he wanted hints for his own letters!

He is a good fellow, though Scotch, and gave me a bottle of whiskey today. Whoops Dearie!!

I have just been round the Line to see if all the boys are happy and have everything they want. Heavens! Some of them are much more comfortable than I!

Later:

There's a deuce of a row going on in the camp tonight; the Corporal who is a fighter, a prize fighter, is taking on everybody else. It's just like the Irish fellows; they are jolly good men; if they are not fighting the Bosche, they are fighting amongst themselves!

Well I must go off and settle all this before I turn in to dream of you. I dream that I will come back to you very soon. God keep you in good spirits; always 'merry and bright'. All my love and all the hugs and different sorts of kisses.

Ever your devoted Hubbie-to-be

Bubbie

Later still:

What a rotten night! I had to put five of my men under arrest and put my little fist under another man's jaw before I could get peace and quiet.

The Regimental QM Sergeant issued my men with rum and they all got tight so I put the RQM Sgt under arrest. Voila!

It really is an extraordinary war umps!!

Goodnight darling Girlie xxxx

Shelling has a big impact on us in the Transport Lines. Most of the men just curse the Kaiser and tend to the animals. And of course the nightly 'run' has its own dangers for us all. Now the shelling disrupts us badly as we are currently the direct target of their 'hate'.

Dearest Darling little Wife,

Dearest, I haven't written for a couple of days, as the fighting has been heavy in these parts. I had two topping letters from you today and one from the Mater. After two nights with no sleep would you believe I fell asleep today with those letters in my hand as I was given them! I am still v tired.

We are going out to 'rest' tomorrow so you can be perfectly happy once more that I am safe. The last month has been terribly hard; we are beating Him, but we are in part of the Line were he is too good for us.

Last night at 11pm he started shelling my transport lines. We ran in all directions as shell after shell rained down on us. All I could find by 2am was ten of my men and eighteen animals instead of sixty animals and fifty men. Just after dawn they all turned up. Great men, and all fit! – and they saved all the animals except the Colonel's two mounts. Never mind I have a couple of nice replacements for him already.

Replacing the men is not easy as there is no conscription in Ireland. They say the politicians are afraid to bring it in there, so we must rely on volunteers from the Island or other British recruits.

One of my men gave me a song or poem-sheet he picked up on leave in Cork, where they still support the Munsters at the Front:

Come pass the call 'round Munster.
Let the notes ring loud and clear.
We want the merchant and the squire,
The peasant and the Peer.
For we mean to whip those Germans,
So away with your paltry affairs
And come join that grand Battalion
Called the Munster Fusiliers

The Kaiser knows each Munster
By the shamrock on his cap

And the famous Bengal tiger
Ever ready for a scrap.
With all his big battalions,
Prussian Guards and Grenadiers,
He feared to face the bayonets
Of the Munster Fusiliers

When marching up through Belgium
Sure we thought of days of old.
The cruel sights that meet your eyes
Would make your blood run cold
To see the ruined convents
And the Holy nuns in tears.
By God on high avenge or die
Cried the Munster Fusiliers.

God rest our fallen comrades,
May they take their long last sleep
On the fields of France and Flanders.
Sure, we have no cause to weep,
For their deeds will live in history
And the youth of future years
Will read with pride
Of the men who died,
The Munster Fusiliers.

Of course I am not sure of the impact, but so far my men are all loyal and when away on leave, tell me they do help with the recruiting.

Leave is opening for officers so I shall be home v soon. John, my servant went on leave today – his first in nearly 3 years. It's a bit too bad isn't it?

He deserves it more than most; especially as he keeps 'yours truly' in good order! I gave him five shillings to spend on his

'Girl Molly', and asked him to post this letter on arriving at Southampton.

Darling I shall not be far behind. Less than three weeks to go before I hold you in my arms sweetheart.

Goodbye my own dearest Darling. Ever Your Own Devoted Hubbie

Bubbie xxxx

As I come back from leave now, my men seem genuinely pleased to see me. The Transport is either in good shape or is a problem depending on who has been the 'caretaker'.

Dorice, my own Darling wee Wifie,

A topping letter today, and merry and bright too!! That's the spirit, and in the right spirit when you look upon me as your protector! I have always looked upon myself as the protector of my forty-five merry men. Heaven knows what they look upon me as. I don't dare to think!!! Still, we get on very well together. When I came back from leave this time, the animals were fit.

The fellow who took over my job when I was away however, had a perfectly rotten time. My men pinched his whiskey, because they didn't like him! I hope they like me as I have a bottle in my dugout!

Tell your Pater that my dear old groom Dan is flourishing and told me last night that he was glad I was back, so I said: "Dan I suppose you didn't like your new foreman?" And he said: "Eigh that was it Mick"!!

They are priceless at times. (But not as priceless as every minute of my leave Darling!)

It is calm and snowing out here, but my hut is quite warm and so are the men. But it makes the nightly run with the limbers quite strenuous for the men as well as the animals. C'est la Guerre darling.

Goodbye my dearest Darling I love you Babs so very much if you write cheery letters like you do each day. They make me so happy.

All my love beloved Girlie.

Ever Your Own true Hubbie

Bubby xx

I often send souvenirs of Army life back to Dorice, including a letter from an Irish wife. It is addressed to me, and written in a large bold hand in black ink but not good on punctuation!

Dear Sir,

Would you let me know any thing about my Husband Private David Condon No.4978 1st Battalion R.M.F. 'Y' Company Transport Section British Expeditionary Force France as I did not hear from him since November as I wrote him 3 letters and got no reply as yet he seems to have forgotten all about his wife and little children as he has got a Good Wife a Better Wife than he is a Husband and a wife he was never deserving of if there is nothing wrong with him he deserves a good showing up.

I know he is not able to write. But that is no excuse any man in his Battalion would do so for him. This is my second time writing to you about him. I am sorry for troubling you so much. Would you kindly let me know anything about him as I will be glad to know. He seems to forget all about them at home it is along time to be waiting for a letter since November

He deserves a good showing up – would you please oblige

Mary Condon

101 Great William O'Brien Street

Blackpool

Cork, Ireland.

My letter tells Dorice what action I am taking:

My very own dear darling wifie,

We have been moving about all day but I want to send a little letter of love because I love you very very dearly my own darling wife.

There was no mail today except one from the wife of one of my men telling me he hasn't written since last November and he had taken to drink!!! I enclose the letter as it is rather funny really but a bit pathetic too!

He, poor fellow cannot write even his name so I don't know how she expects him to write her a letter. Anyway I will have to write to her to make peace!! I have just sent for her husband and I will lecture him. Bow Wow! I can appreciate her feelings being a married man myself!! You won't be jealous, little Girl, if I write to her and tell her that her husband is fit and well. He is really a quite a good man. I have never seen him drunk and never had to scold him before.

I am happy tonight, don't know why! probably because wherever I go everyone who has seen your photos (nearly the whole of the BEF!) says: "Hello Anna, how's the wife"!!

That goes from the General, the Brigadier, the Colonel and, of course, all my pals in the Mess. One of the young officers asked if he could write to you as he had no one to write to and he will send a picture of himself. His name is Morrogh-Bernard and comes from a good family, but is terribly young. (Some days I feel quite 'old' having been in this bally Army since this awful war started – nearly 4 years ago!).

I said yes, that would be alright as I feel so lucky that everybody envies me having such an adorable wife. I know you won't mind, as you are the sweetest Girlie in the world.

I love you so much and worship and adore you and will finish with my prayers for you my very own Darling. May I soon be home with you again.

Ever Your Own true and loving Husband.
Bubbie xx

We are getting a real pounding as we move forward into the Hindenburg Line. There are booby-traps everywhere, and the shelling and bombing are ranged-in very well by the Bosche gunners:

Dorice, my own Darling,

Another weary day without a letter – still only eight days to go before leave. I am longing for it – just think – 14 days leave – BLISS!!

I have just been censoring my men's letters. One of them has been having a little 'vin blanc' because he says in writing to his wife;

"A little gift to tell you Dear
I wish that you were with me here
But still though we may be apart
You are always present in my Heart"

Well, very nice and human. The majority of my men are married and their endearments are truly touching. The men do have a far worse time than officers, as they are not allowed leave unless they have been out here for a year, and often it is more like two.

This Army was designed for officers! Yesterday was Church Parade; the men need it, but YOU know how much I detest it. The men need their blessings and absolutions as often as they can.

Going to bed at 3am and then waking at 4am to inspect the men before setting off on a six-mile march to the nearest Church is not my idea of Heaven! Actually, yesterday, as we marched in the morning light, (and to be fair it was a glorious day), we were filmed by a 'movie camerman' beside the road.

I ordered the men to look tall and smart as they marched by. I would love to see the resulting film at a picture-house one day. You might see your Hubbie on the newsreels marching proudly at the front of his men – walking stick swinging, and with a certain swagger!

That's the 1st Munster's for you. And THAT would also be one for the archives in 100 years time!! (If film material lasts that long).

Lots of my merry men are going on leave – I couldn't stop a man's leave even though I end up doing the work myself!

Tell your Pater that ole Dan Sullivan was born in1868! He tells me he doesn't want to leave the Army! Poor old man – He's old enough to be my father and instead I talk to him like a father!!

As leave approaches closely, life gets pretty nerve-wracking! You imagine the Bosche is going to attack any moment!! Then of course leave would be stopped for all. Let us just hope.

God bless you darling and pray he takes care of us both. All my love to yourself and, if you can spare a little bit, give it to your dear little Mater. Remember me to the dear 'auld man'.

Ever your true and adoring Hubbie
Bubbie xx

Lately, we are constantly on the move with only three hours sleep in the last week; or has it been ten days? I am tired, and I have lost a couple of good men to Hun bombing – the swine come over every night. I write to the next of kin, which is hard for me. Who will do it if my turn comes? Baxter? Marsden?

We have been knocked-about and can find only shell holes to lay-up in – the men and the horses; just to afford a little protection from this bombing and shrapnel. My men seem to appreciate that I am suffering the same discomforts as them, and we do look out for each other.

That sound of the old Band (the pipes) is kicking up a deuce in my head. 'The Wearin of the Green', or is it Brian Boru's March? Both are catchy tunes, although I can do without those damned bagpipes.

That sound is fading fast.

And now, I too, have gone "wesht"

January 26th
1918
C

Dear Sir
Wuld you Let me
know any thing
about my Husband
Pyte David Condon
No. 4978. 1st Batt R.M.F.
Y. Com transport section
Brittish Expeditionary
Force France?
as I did not hear
from him since
November as I

13

COLOURED MIST

"...it sends a cold shiver down my spine when I think of you having gone off to London with anyone else but me"

Laying here on the ground, a dense mist descends over me. My eyes sting like hell and all I see is a green background like a screen above me.

It's not Hun Gas this time. I have been too many times, 'green with envy' in this short life. Pangs of jealousy have swept through my mind over the years, as they seem to be doing now.

My dying thoughts bring back some of these irrational fears. They are personal jealous thoughts, which are probably false, but still make me see green, and occasionally red.

Sudden flashbacks jump out of this mist:

I am five years old and Eddy my brother is ten or eleven. He's a bit of a bully, not a hero, but I am jealous of him. He is at King Edward's Bath where Father teaches, while I am the baby; "Bubbie" to both parents Eddy, and Dais. At seventeen he joins the Navy (eldest son and all that!) and leaves a reputation as both a scholar and sportsman – cricket, rugby, tennis, golf – you name it. I think he is trying to be a hero to me, but it doesn't impress me, since the parents have clearly indulged him with all that education and "extra tuition" that he gets.

Dear sister Dais, two years older than Eddy, understands my jealousy as I go through the school, and tells me not to worry: "It's not a competition with Eddy, just do your best and find yourself". She is right of course, but in these school years, while I am doing well at all the sports and the Cadet Corps, these feelings of envy of Eddy persist.

It seems Eddy has arrived home for some weeks of leave. I last saw him in 1910 when he sailed off to the China station. Now he runs the payments to the trawlermen conscripted for minesweeping duties and is based in Sheerness. One of his very rare letters to me contains a photo of the massive explosion on a minelayer vessel near his base, HMS Actaeon, that killed three hundred; mainly civilians ashore. Even that is just a few words. He is not much of a letter writer even to Mother and Dad, or to sister Dais; from whom I get most family news.

Writing to Dorice, I am trying to introduce Eddy to her with all his foibles, without showing how envious I have been of him:

Dear Darling Dorice,

Thank you for your two topping letters with all the news. I suppose it was time to meet my brother, and I hear he is now on leave. I haven't seen him for five or six years, so I would love to hear about him. I wrote and asked him to visit you with Dais, so I expect that will happen if not already. Would you be jealous if he came over to South Parade once or twice? From what I remember of him he is a dry old stick, and certainly looks older than his years! Anyway I hope you like him. I am sure he will like you as you are the sweetest Girlie in the world.

I bet Eddy has a little girl somewhere in Town. We used to promise each other a week in Town together but it never came off! (and never will!!). Please tell Dais you like me more than my brother! 'Nuff said!!

Poor old Eddy. Dais says he looks old. I always rub it in when I write; asking him what the Navy intends to do concerning the war. Unfortunately he will always be senior to me unless I become a General or something funny like that.

How I wish I was with you all. But this war just has to be won out here. Leave will come round soon, as Baxter has just gone for his. He and his wife live in Scotland and he has been with the Regiment for thirty years! Darling Girl, I am sorry this letter rambles.

I must go now up to the Line and there's a wretched big moon, which is not good for my 'game' but would be very nice if I was with you on the old Avon river.

I am going to say good night Girlie. I wish I could take you in my arms and kiss you. Never mind there's a war to be won. Say hello to Eddy from me. Sent with all the hugs and kisses in the world

Ever your own 'Hubbie-to-Be'
Bubbie xxx

After his home leave Eddy gets sent to the Med on a destroyer based up in Salonika, Greece. I hear from him that: "the duck shooting is good sport up near the British and French lines in Macedonia".

It sounds all right to me; as we are shivering and almost

drowning in mud and slime in this godforsaken country. It must be much warmer and sunnier out there, with only a few U-boats to worry about.

In a letter from darling Dorice, she does comment on my big bro':

Dear Darling Soldier Boy Bubbikins,

I received two dear letters from you today and have read them over and over again and selected bits to read to Mama and Pater.

We are so proud of you and long to see you again as soon as this wretched war allows. I hope you are taking care of yourself for me and not getting into 'scrapes' near the beastly Huns again!

Well darling I finally met your Brother Eddy. His Naval uniform is not so smart as your Munster outfit and I think he is actually smaller and thinner than you, beloved. I think he was a trifle jealous when I said his little brother is bigger than he is!

I told him you were too heavy for the RFC to take you on. And anyway you preferred your animals. Was I right to say that dearest? That's what I said, anyway.

Last night we went to Dais's for supper with Sid and Dais, and your Mater and Pater. Dais persuaded me to sing to the folks present. It made me a bit sad, as I remembered when I sang for you in their house and we fell in love. Oh, and I really wished you were there my Bubbie-boy.

Your brother said nice things and wished us well and then announced he had been called away off his leave, so there was a rather sad parting.

Anyway, sweetheart, there's no doubt to which 'Mister Anna' my heart belongs, and I can't wait for your next leave when we shall be together in each others arms the whole time.

I do wish the Colonel would be sweet and let you come home soon, cos I wants you, Bubbikins.

Goodbye my own Darling .

Ever your only and true 'Baby Wifie'.

Goodnight beloved xxxxx D.

No need to be jealous of Eddy any more.

A flashback from earlier; back in Egypt, it is all so exotic my progression to an officer gives no time for many of these jealous feelings. Only perhaps as Marsden makes a 'pass' at Nurse Callow while I am laying in hospital in Alexandria. The feeling only lasts a couple of seconds, as he really is a good fellow – the best of pals. And, nothing happens there for him anyway.
It does for me though!

But I see 'green' again in these early days of courting my Darling Dorice. We both have 'pasts'! That blasted roller-skate instructor!

Dearest Little Girlie,

Your last letter was 'some' letter and did cheer me up. Don't worry that I will not be home this year for Xmas. We shall be in the Line so the Battalion will be celebrating New Year instead for the festive season. My leave will follow that promptly. All being well.

How could I forget that day at Weston! I haven't forgotten a single moment I spent with you. But on the New Year leave I shan't have to be introduced to you, and you won't tell me you don't allow "just anybody" to hug You and kiss You. This time, I know that you love only big old me.

You are a darling Girl to write to me – it is You who is writing and sending me millions of kisses. I have never in all my life had such topping love letters from a girl, and as you know; before I met you I did have a few letters.

Nobody ever loved me as you do, and certainly nobody loved you as deeply as I do – not anybody else.

I wonder whatever happened to the OTHER – is he alive still? You didn't love him did you Baby Girlie? (the 'roller skater' I mean). It was sweet of you to tell me about yourself and 'the other'. It sends a cold shiver down my spine when I think of your going off to London with anyone but me – chaperone or no chaperone. Don't tell me which.

Now I have a confession to make. Dais tells me you were looking at the photos from Egypt, and among them photos of one girl; 'Sister Callow', the nurse who was looking after me. Now I had scarlet fever, and she was the only nurse allowed to come near. She was very good to me and we took pictures of each other. There was nothing else in it, but I thought you might 'think things'.

I never loved anybody as I love you now, so I can say truthfully YOU are the first and only girl I really love.

I have five little snaps of you all around my bed and space in this billet. I shall read your last letter over and over again.

With all my love and many hugs.
Always your
Bubbie

This 'clears the air' between us, though we don't 'know' each other well enough for me to 'come clean' about the 'Egyptian Affair with Lady D'.

Dorice's cousins cause me a lot of angst. So many of them, but especially those 'boys' who show a lot of "interest" in my Darling – both before and after our marriage.

There are five 'cousies' from the Thomas family in London – all a bit distant. Then, there are three from the Southsea Naval family of Aunt Roy including Dorothy and her soldier husband Bill Adams. Then, Queenie and Kiki; daughters of Aunt Julie from Devonport, and three more from the Croydon-Fowlers in Torquay – Hilgrove (Hillier), Louis and Cecil. These last three, I do resent from time to time as they spend much time with Dorice and write a lot to her, especially young Hillier:

My Darling Dorice,

Your loving letter arrived today. It cheered me up as we have been under terrific shellfire for the last four days. I have lost a lot of my pals during the last week as your will see from the papers soon.

Your letters are like a tonic to me. I wish I could write better and longer as you seem to do. You have such a large family. Just how many cousins do you have? Cos at the last count it seemed like two score, but I may be wrong. Anyway on my next leave I would like to meet them because they are part of your dear family.

That is apart from that cheeky young Hillier who I haven't met yet. Did I say I wasn't feeling so well – just a bit of 'flu. I feel better to hear that you do really love me. You see I was frightfully jealous of young Hillier, because he loves you. But am not now, as you promised to kiss me as often as you kiss my photo and ONLY mine. I did wonder if the 'other fellow' – the skater – wrote to you. I don't mean Hillier – he's a nonentity. The other girl wrote only about once a month and never as loving as you do darling.

I am sorry I must be sounding like a 'green-eyed monster', but I sometimes feel it rather strongly when we are so far apart and with the difference in the daily lives we are leading. Of course it will pass. Especially as I dream of us together on my next leave, being always together, and no sign of the 'so and so' relatives to disturb us.

With that wonderful thought in my head I must say goodnight Darling as I am off up to the Line and not back till 3am

Goodbye my own Darling
With all my hugs and kisses
Your own Bubbie xxx

Dorice is always sensitive to my moods, which seem to go up and down like a yo-yo, when I am here in France, and especially after a 'whiff of gas'. She writes:

My very own Darlingest 'Hubbie-to-be',

I didn't get a letter from you today, darling, but never mind tomorrow two will arrive, so cheerio-ho!

I am being very lazy this afternoon, just sewing as the weather is beastly. It's raining cats and dogs & it's so jolly dark that it gives one the pip!!

So Dais's husband, Sid Carpenter is soon going to be a Captain Sweetheart? Well, what about it. Of course your sister will be pleased. You shouldn't get fed up with the Army just because you can't get promotion. Don't be jealous of those family folk who serve in different ways. Just remember Bubbie mine; I'd much rather have you as you are my dear big Soldier Man. I think 'Transport Officer' is much more swanky, and anyway you are MY 2nd Lieutenant.

It is a jolly sight nicer than anybody else's Capt. or Major, and that's that! Bill is a 2nd Lieut. Bubbikins, and he's 31 now, and one of those 'kissing cousins' you worry about. Don't worry darling as I don't see them very often and then we may kiss like butterflies – not serious lovers like thee and me!

But what about all my aunts and girl cousins? I don't think

I'll let you kiss 'em all! Only special ones and I don't think I'll let you kiss 'em at all until we've been married at least a year!!! You see you'll be one of the family then!

No more worries about this Bubbie, and all this talk of kisses just makes me long to have you here now – with your lips pressed to mine; (not a cousinly kiss!).

Goodbye my own darling Bubbikins. May God Bless you dear Heart and guard you from all danger and may He bring you back to me again VERY SOON. With all my love, my Darling and all my kisses and all my hugs.

Ever your own true "Baby Wifie"

D xxxx

I then hear that the young scoundrel Hillier gets a second pip!

Dear darling Dorice Mine,

No letter today Baby Girlie, expect I shall have one tomorrow though. It is snowing hard and so jolly cold. I have to go out in a minute or two which isn't very nice; probably get snowed up, but that would make a change anyway.

I get horribly 'fed up' sometimes. Jealous, I suppose. The fellow who has come out from England with a commission is also a full Lt, and now you say young Hillier has another pip. Well it is about the limit when he got his commission so quickly. In the New Army, promotion is so much faster than we in a Regular Regiment. I have been waiting no less than 26 months, and nothing!!

I am going up to Battalion HQ my Darling so may feel in a better mood when I get back.

Later:

My own Little Girlie; I'm in a much better spirit now!! The Colonel has written to Brigade HQ saying he is absolutely satisfied with me and my work. He said my work is excellent and always has been excellent!! Whoops Dearie!!

I am overjoyed that he did this, after that so-and-so with 'blue tabs' came over and strafed me, and everything. That 'chap' then wrote a critical report of my stables and transport lines.

Good old Monck-Mason, put that right and he still is pushing for my 2nd pip.

Just write and tell me you still love me, although you have seen another of your cousins. Leave is open so only a few weeks to go before we will be together darling.

All my love and kisses and hugs and cuddles
Ever your own
Bubbie xxxx

Then there is the Prince of Wales. Can I really be jealous of HIM in the middle of this war?

I write to Dorice during the 'Wytschaete' stunt:

My own dearest Darling Girlie,

I have been absolutely unable to write for 2 days perhaps this letter will never reach you. I am out in the open with a vengeance and going through it some – what!!

But nevertheless I am getting your letters everyday and am so cheered to get your loving letters. I got two today.

I have a ripping bivouac here, but it will all cave – in if it starts to rain. The flies are terrible, simply millions of them. Not nice! But just ahead there are momentous things happening as you will read in the papers.

The noise of the barrage (ours and theirs) is absolutely tremendous, like three thunderstorms all at once and continuously, day and night.

Last night our Regimental Band was playing just behind

the Line with all the noise of the barrage still going on. Would you believe it, but HRH The Prince of Wales was with us, helping lift the mood of the men. He's a decent young fellow who was in the Navy as a Lt. but now wears the uniform of the Grenadier Guards as a Captain.

He certainly is in the thick of it out here like everybody else. They say he has an MC for 'gallantry'. (I haven't got one of those, though the Colonel has promised me one). It is usually given to Lts. in charge of a company in the line for raids into 'no mans land'). I am not too jealous, as you can imagine he, unlike me, has privilege and friends in high places!! The Highest!!!

I saw him again this morning, cycling along a very dusty road by himself, and he seemed quite merry and bright. More than I was. I was dog tired and riding Jack on a twenty mile round trip.

I received a topping little letter from you this morning My Darling after I got back. I immediately forgot all about my tiredness as well as my jealous thoughts regarding cousins, princes or medals!!

Poor little Girlie I knew you would be down-hearted 'cos you haven't received a letter from me for so long. But cheer up Darling! C'est La Guerre.

The mail is really going this time so Cheerio Sweetheart Mine.

All my love, many hugs and kisses. Ever your own loving and true love

Goodbye little Girl

Bubbie xxxx

Later, Dorice writes to me about the visit to Bath of the King and Queen with the PoW. She says, she has "fallen in love with the Prince of Wales". It sounds like a title of a song.

There's no need to be jealous of him, because I have her deep and honest love – for Me.

What a waste of my brain, being jealous over the years. Envious of others? I wonder if I *now* have good cause? Too late.

The misty background is getting denser. It's more like a red goo. Blood running into my eyes I suppose...

14

ABOUT A KIDDUMS

"... make sure you write to me if 'IT' happens on 17th next"

Guilt saturates these flickering thoughts, as the sound "waaaa", just like a baby's cry, pierces my ears and head. Is it the cry of the wee "A" kid? No, that's not possible!

I was a fool to make Dorice take those pills in 1917. She lost two kids - one of which was a boy. A son. But I am in the middle of a war; married to my darling wife, and learning the periodic mysteries of 'time-of-the-month', and pregnancies planned and unplanned.

This guilt comes from the thought of leaving her to raise a kid alone. At the same time, isn't it right to give her a 'little Annaheim' to love and to hold, as I may not be going home? Quite a dilemma; and one that has challenged me for nearly two long years of war. There is no one with whom I can share my innermost thoughts - except Dorice herself.

The first scare has come so soon after our wonderful honeymoon. Dorice writes a long loving letter thinking she is with child. She reports sore breasts and stomach pains. I write back:

Dear Darling little Wifie,

I just received your letter written in the garden. It made me think a devil of a lot. It's about the possibility of having a kiddums. You see I know exactly what Mother asked you and I have wondered if your Mater asked you the same question. Has she Babs?

Now, are you happy Babs? You wouldn't talk about anything before we were married, but I knew our marriage would be a risk in wartime!

My idea – Well you knew Babs; I say; "Apres la guerre-Righto!" So for the present let us be selfish and live for only ourselves.

Dearest, it is rotten of me to say 'no' and that I may make you cry and unhappy. That is just the very last thing I want for the dearest and sweetest wife in all the world. Remember we have years to live yet, but you MUST please let me know your innermost thoughts.

I may be in a strange mood tonight. I wish I was with you as we could talk all this through much better than in writing. I shall await your answer jolly eagerly Sweetheart mine.

Perhaps I am a wee bit worried because you weren't able to tell the Mater the answer was in the affirmative and you WANTED to be able to say yes. Write to me Babs, tell me everything.

I love you and adore you and worship you. May God bless you Wifie, all my love and hugs and kisses!!

Goodnight dearheart.
Ever your loving Hubbie
Bubbie xxx

We agree that she should take those pills – antimony pills – that end the anguish and cause our worries to end. They seem to be giving her an even more nasty ache in the tummy. Hot baths and a little drink or two solve it completely.

Dorice opens up with long loving letters talking about this subject, which is always present. As the year unfolds, I am constantly torn between should we have a wee kiddums? Or not? It remains a conundrum for me. I am really annoyed as the family pushes their own opinions, which puts even more worries in her head.

Dais is all for it. She has two of her own and seems fulfilled as a pharmacist and mother, as well as supporting her husband, Carpenter. It works for them all right, but they have been married for five years.

My own Mother upsets Dorice. Her idea about kiddies is all about "Seven Years". I write to say don't listen to her!

Dearest darling Darling,

Three long cheery letters today! I love you and adore you sweetheart. At last we are settled and in the thick of it – you will read all about this 'push' in the papers. I cannot write everyday as you will understand. My darling I do my very best.

The mail is going out this afternoon so this letter might be short, but you will know how happy I am because you love me and I love you. Although there's a devil of a war going on around these parts of Belgium, I am still alive.

I am happy I can say more because you are happy too.

I don't agree with Mother ref the "seven years"!!! She must be thinking of that song; "Seven Years After We Wish You Joy – First a Girl, Then a Boy". Do you remember it? It comes from "Kiss on the Ring". I'm afraid my poor old Mother takes things to heart very much. What on earth she will say to you next – Gawd knows. Don't believe half of what she says!

Don't let any of 'em come between us; even if it's our own

Father and Mother, because we shall both be alive after they've gone!

Your own Mater is a brick and I love her dearly and respect all her thoughts, of course, on all this.

A great pal of mine went home, got married and came out again. The next time he went home he was about to have a little kiddie. He unfortunately had to come to France again before it was born. The next leave the kid was a few months old and he told me he didn't enjoy his leave a little bit as he wanted his wife to himself, but there was always a kiddie crying!! Poor old Fellah!!

Babs, I wonder am I selfish?? I certainly want you and I to enjoy life together a bit and not get tied down too soon. What do you think now, Babs?

So let's not keep these worrying thoughts to ourselves, but share them with each other and our worries will disappear.

I thought you were worrying because we are not going to have a kiddie just yet. But telling each other helps so much. Voila!

Goodbye my dearest darling Pet. May God bless you and keep you smiling

Ever your own loving

Bubbie xx

Goodnight Girl, tonight I am sleeping under the stars.

Now, with two months of intense fighting just south of Ypres; at Messines and Wytschaete, I can only focus on the job at hand. I am really in the middle of all the 'stunts' – and all the mud – and have plenty of other worries – like staying alive!

I am thanked by the Company commanders and the Colonel, for getting the rations and ammo up closer to the fighting than any other Battalion Transport in these parts.

'Passchendaele' they call it. But my passion lays elsewhere-with my Darling Dorice.

My decision regarding a kiddie does seem absolutely justified in my mind; as I have flirted with the closest of encounters; with Bosche gas, snipers and all the whizz-bangs they throw in my direction – missing me, JUST, but, by God, am I tired!

Leave again in autumn 1917, and fourteen glorious days together, mostly in bed. And then; returning to the Front, I have more 'thinking time'.

Darling Wifie mine,

You are an absolute brick to write to me every day. I love you and love you. I adored our leave and am trusting that our sins don't catch up too quickly darling. Make sure you write to me about if "it" happens on the17th next!

All will be well and this war can't last more than a few more months, now the Americans are in.

Didn't we have a wonderful time together wifie mine, tho' we could have done without being interrupted in our afternoon 'matinees' by your Mater and then Kiki! It makes me blush to think of last Sunday afternoon and the bath we had together; who's idea was that?!

I know how much we love each other, but we must finish the war and until that is done my place is over here of course.

Leave may not be for 3 months but never fear I will take it whenever I get it. 'Cos I loves ya. See?

When my pals see your picture they say "God Anna – your wife doesn't know you as I do. What on earth made a pretty thing like that want to marry you?!"

Well Wifie mine, I am proud to be your one and only true 'Hubbie'; knowing that with God's blessing we will have a long life together.

I have to go up to the Line tonight, but as always I carry a picture of you in my pocket and all of you in my heart.

Ever your loving and devoted

Bubbie Boy

Goodnight my Darling Beloved Dorice

The 17th of the month has arrived. Another round of anxiety as I struggle with the thought of being a father while out here, and so far away from Dorice. She again takes the pills but gets very sick.

I am rethinking this whole issue, even as I am in a very hot spot and I am working twenty hours a day or more. 'S an awful war!

After the Christmas and New Year leave, Dorice tells me that again she is missing her period – "it" hasn't come, but we have had a long talk and are ready to let 'what will be, will be':

My dearest Darling,

Well dearest this, I expect, is "the Day!!!" You made me laugh Girlie when you said "the young Annaheim may refuse to come".

Listen Girlie, I want you to promise me you wont take any more of those pills. I agree with you about a wee kiddie making it into the world. One thing is for sure our baby when it comes, will be no ordinary baby! And we will be the very bestest of parents.

Let's keep it our special secret, and surprise all the family in seven months time. I shall adore our youngster if he is pretty or ugly, fair or dark, short or tall. It will be all the same he will be "ours".

I want you please to be merry and bright whatever the

outcome. I shall be happy if he comes or not so we can on the next leave carry on endeavouring to make one!! I quite agree with you Girlie; two or three years between our first effort and second will be an excellent time for "ours" to have a brother or sister. I will make a damn good father don't you think so!! But not half as good a parent as my adorable Wifie!!

I adore and love you with all my heart
Goodbye my Darling Wifie
Ever your Bubbie xx

The news from Dorice is that again a young "A" hasn't arrived. She has had quite a time of it and lost the kid – a boy. This is now affecting me quite deeply, but in my letters I am keeping positive and cheerful for her sake:

My own dear darling Wifie

I have had 3 letters from you darling. Marvellous, and they just keep me merry and bright in this wretched old war. The field pcs I sent were just to let you know I am alive and survived the 'Great Race'.

Now we are at rest and re-equipping with men and material, although at any moment may be on the move. My good news darling is the Colonel has promised to let me go on leave, one of the first – Cheerio!!. My dysentery is cleared up and things are looking merry and bright although the war news isn't too hopeful. There's still plenty of time to have a smack at 'em!

Now to much more important news Darling. I was very happy when you told me about the loss of "Him" not affecting you. Still my heart went out to you when you told me. But again I was glad that all your pains have gone away.

Girlie you say you would like a kiddie when you are still young. Righto old sport, we'll see what can be done next leave!

Only don't blame your old Hubbie if Mrs. George has a little pain in her tummy after I leave you next leave!! I will allez to bed now to dream of you my darling.

All my love and the hugs and kisses in the world and one long tuddle

Ever your adoring Hubbie

Bubbie xxx

This latest leave is the best ever. Was the 'conception deed' done at the Royal Beach Hotel in Southsea, in Aunt Julie's home in Torquay (bed or bath?), or perhaps in my old bed at Belgrave Place (which would be one in the eye for Mother!). Maybe all three. A kid is now on the way and I am at ease with the whole idea.

My own darling little wifie

Your ever welcome letter arrived. It was beautifully long and lovable.

Poor little you; are you being so very sick in the mornings? Never mind umps! Cheer up and laugh and grow fat!! Don't worry so much dearest we are on our way to have our own wee kiddie. Next March will be the time, and the war will be well over by then and PEACE will give us time to be together and introduce a young'un to a quieter world. What! what!!

I, of course, wish I was with ye to cheer you up because, although I have been shelled and strafed unmercifully be the evil Hun – not to mention bombed nearly every night, I am quite merry and bright.

During the last few days I have learned a lot from the QM, dear old Baxter. He is an experienced married man with a daughter, and said how to tell if it will be a HE or a SHE.

Well, listen and you shall learn. If it's a 'HE' your dear wee right breast will grow first. If it's a 'SHE' your dear wee left breast will grow first. Let me know! We cannot take this for gospel darling, but it has just put in mind my love for your 'hand grenades'. When they get larger can I still lay my head on them? Which makes me ask "Can we still have tuddles with you pregnant?"

These are the thoughts and questions that run through my mind as I ride along on DoriceII over this terribly bleak, godforsaken countryside. Yesterday I covered nearly 30 miles. Some thinking time Dearie!!

I am not certain if 25th March next year will be "Der Tag". I hope it will be the beginning of April.

Wouldn't it be grand if 'ours' was born on our 2nd wedding anniversary? But I will find out for certain from our Doc and let you know.

God bless you Sweetheart and love you. All my hugs and cuddles and kisses.

Ever your true adoring Bubbie xx

The war is progressing, and we are advancing steadily so that I can write a bit more freely to Dorice regarding our progress. Our letters remain 'fruity' and I carefully burn hers to me, after reading each about ten times.

Dearest Darling little Girl,

August is so hot. Too hot to do much, but my days work is finished, so I have jumped into pyjamas and reading the dear little love letter you sent me today. I know you are still loving and missing me Girlie, as I am you.

All is well back here out of the line. We are being fattened up for something big I suppose. Even the animals are looking perfectly priceless. They all have nice shiny coats, which reminds me that it is time you buy a winter coat so you may stay warm – 'for two'!

I am glad you went to see 'My Lady Frayle'. I haven't seen that play but have heard of it. I think it's a musical with some very naughty ideas! The Irish papers, which I see sometimes out here, said it was full of immoral jokes and suggestions!! The opening chorus goes something like "We are going into action with a glowing satisfaction, due to knowing our attraction to the wiliest of foes". Quite relevant. What! what!! I must get to see it on my next leave. Bow Wow!!

It does my heart good to read that you are fit and well and merry and bright. That's the stuff, Girlie Mine!! The only thing worrying me is that you like having this child so much, you will want a round dozen!! Oooer, get another Hubbie!!

I cannot quite fathom why you want a 'tuddle' so much. I was under the impression that if one got 'comme ca' the desire wore off! Let me know, as it's rather interesting!!
Personally I should love one!!

The news is ripping tonight. We are nearing Bapaume, so when we go into the line it may well be The Hindenburg Line!! It will all be over by Xmas, though the Bosche are still making a fight of it. Plenty of cacophony from their guns and they still come over to bomb us every night.

Goodbye my Darling I'm off being a busy man; what!! All my love Darling.

Millions of hugs, cuddles and tuddles.

Ever your true and adoring
Bubbikins

The latest news from Dorice is that all the signs (the growing LEFT breast!) are that my little kiddums is going to be a girl. Well that is absolutely great! I am so proud yet have little time to think through all the ramifications as the Battalion moves into the front line:

My own sweet Darling,

Just a wee note tonight as we are busy and on the move again; this time into the Line. The usual hate will be coming our way. What! what!! Don't worry Darling, leave will open in another month, and all will be fine.

You see Girlie, we will have a quieter time next leave. We may have to!! Thanks Girlie for giving up the whiskey. It cannot be good for HER!!

Now darling I must hasten away. I am sending you my deepest loving thoughts with all the kisses, cuddles and tuddles(!) I can muster.

Ever your devoted Bubbikins xxx

I am busier than ever, and some of my pals and a host of other officers and men fall. This great 'stunt' will hopefully, and at last, end this awful business:

Dearest darling little Wifie,

I am just waiting for the post to arrive on a pack mule!! The 'Bataille' is still going on all around as we push on and on, and I am terribly busy as they have made me TO of not just this Battalion, but also the 2nd Battalion RMF, BUT, AS WELL AS the Brigade! I am now Brigade Transport Officer, so 'Yours Truly' has 3 jobs now – of course no medals or official promotions for this Hubbie of yours, but it matters not!

You see Girlie, since you tell me that my little Baby is going to be a Girl! I'm jolly glad, actually thrilled, for us.
I hope and know fully well that she will be as sweet in every way and take absolutely after her pretty little mother.

I am so glad your dear old folks have taken you down to Torquay, because it will be so good for our "wee un".

Let me know Sweetheart when you want to buy anything for "ours" or your dear wee self. So little Girl's clothes will have to be made now Ha Ha – well that's damn good. I will love a little girl – all ours.

I am off to have a drink in the Hindenburg Line. It is a

marvelous piece of work, and now there are souvenirs Galore!! If one wants them.

So for now, Goodbye Darling. All my love and may God bless and protect you, me and "ours".

Ever your Loving Bubbie xxxxxx

The attack into and across the Bosche defensive line continues so that we are all now terribly weary. This is all-out war, but we are moving forward each day, causing me and my section a huge load of work – day and night.

I manage half a letter to Doris that expresses my joy at our success, but I don't share just how 'nervy' I have become, as I lose my pals and my men at a great rate during this latest 'stunt'.

My dearest darling little Girl,

The war will soon be over sweetheart mine and there have been so many officer casualties that means my leave will come before Xmas!!

We have had rather a knocking about in this 'stunt' but I wanted to tell you I am fit and well and 'horribly merry and bright'. Weary of course, and I haven't had my clothes off for about a month. We have pushed across canals and rivers at a furious pace, across land a year ago I used to canter over – but it is not recognizable now. I have lost several more men and have written quite a few letters to their next-of-kin. 'S an awful war.

Darling, I am so pleased that you are feeling in the pink. I am deliriously happy about "our wee'un on the way". Girlie we were made for each other, and made to make a wee kiddums. In our next letters let's discuss what names we hold in our thoughts for HER. WE will decide, not the bally relations!!

Girlie mine I am longing to see you again and I long to

hug you-gently but firmly – to feel your tummy and hold your sweet breasts. It won't be long before I am home again. I couldn't manage a Blighty, although I have been damn near it on many occasions!

Goodbye little Girl. All my love to you, and to "ours". God bless you and take care of you as he has taken care of me. Ever your adoring Hubbie and Father-to-Be.

Goodbye beloved

Bubbie xxx

Today as we hole-up in what is jokingly called 'La Folie Wood' outside Cambrai (no 'follies' and no sign of any trees left here!), I receive two love letters, which cheer me up. I am ever more 'twitchy'; so tired, so filthy, yet I am blessed with life, a darling wife, and a wee child to come. All around me is the paraphernalia and debris of war as well as horrific noise, sacrifice, and death.

Up at HQ, Baxter shows me the casualty list for the last four days. Eleven Officers killed or wounded and scores of the men. So we are down to twelve or so officers and only about 150 men.

Just time to write a short letter and get it to the post corporal.

My own dearest little Darling,

Thank you so much for your cheery, merry and bright love letters. It was sweet of you to say don't worry about me being with you on 'der Tag' in April next year. The war will be over sweetheart and I will be granted Special Leave for the birth of our first wee kiddums.

For a name, lets go for something outside the sphere of our family. For a boy, I like Cecil (Marsden's!), Dennis or David and for a girl, while I do like Sophia (as my Mother's), I'd rather have a Marguerite or a Sybil. What do you prefer Darling? Do share your thoughts with me so I can imagine our kid by name, as we wait for the young'un to arrive. It's not bad luck is it?

We should keep all this to ourselves darling, but I expect by now your own dear Mater is 'fully aware'.

I never seem to tell you how much I adore you Girl. I long and yearn to hold you in my arms again but I shall have to take great care of YOU sweetheart mine shan't I? Perhaps tuddles will be banned!! Oooer get another wife!! Can we risk it umps?!!

I send my love to the dear Mater and I do hope the 'old man' is merry and bright.

Darling I am rather tired having had only three hours sleep in the last week!

Baxter is sharing a tent with me, and is writing to his own wife as I finish this letter to you my own Dearest Darling Wife.

God is taking good care of me for you and I am sure will answer my prayers and take care of you and "ours". I am so happy you are going to be a mother soon. It seems wonderful to me that you and I can produce a wee 'un. Truly wonderful!

Goodbye Dearest most Darlingest Wifie in the World. All my Love, hugs, kisses and one dinky tuddle.

Ever Your Adoring Hubbie
Bubbie x
Goodnight My Love

It is all fading. Just that ear-piercing cry. It isn't a Baby – but I believe it is wailing from dear old Baxter – NOT from a wee kid.

Of course, there are no bawling kids over here!'

I am drifting away.

We never did agree on a name, but whatever happens, it will be a "wee Anna".

Thank God; Dorice will soon get more than a telegram from the King.

25/1/17

My dearest darling Baby "Wifie"

I was jolly glad to get a long loving letter
from you this morning because there was no mail
yesterday. I may have made a mistake in the date
when I wrote on 16th Sweetheart. I only know I have
written every day and on one occasion twice. Anyway
Gorke if its missing, dont spects I said anyfink very
import! I have to go up to the Line tonight and I
dont feel like it a little bit. Its terribly cold and
very slippery and I am very comfy in my hut and I
also want to write you a s'nice long love-letter. Sixty-
nine days are nothing Sweetheart when you realize that
when you work it out I can always deduct four because
your sweet letters take four days to arrive. I shall
certainly feel like getting "Special Leave" in April if all
is stopped. Dove of course I am thinking about you
just as much as you are me. I dream of you every night
and love you more every day. Your Pater sent me a
little letter. Please thank him very much. I wrote to
your little mater last night after I had written to you
'Umps the old sofa at home was very comfy wasnt it?
but we were always being interrupted and your poor
little band round your pretty hair was always getting
lost. However it managed to get underneath the sofa
beats me?!!! Shall I ever forget my old mac around
you? I havnt worn it lately because its too cold.

I want to see you again Girlie too ever so much

15

STUNTS

"It's awful, but out here, you can't dwell on these losses or you would go mad".

A tremendous thunderclap shoots through my head as the sounds of battles-past ring loudly across my shattered brain. These thunderous noises have been with me for all these four years in this army; about a thousand days and nights of the stupendous 'hate', interspersed with major 'stunts'.

The stunt across the Suez Canal is a real 'escapade' and quite fun, as we ride into battle in cavalry formation against the Turks. Somehow war in the desert here is 'clean' (but hot), with just you and the enemy to fight it out. No villages or villagers to worry about. No mud either!

In France, there's never been any let-up from the thunder of guns; whether I am part of a 'stunt' or just at 'rest'. It's a war with all the devilish machinery that it contains. Shells ranging from huge twelve inchers to the lower calibre but no less deadly 'Five nines', mortars, machine guns, bombs from aeroplanes and snipers. They are all out to get you. It often feels 'personal'.

It has been my luck to survive 'till now.

My work as TO is important, though often lonely; with me and my men alone for days at a time, and even more often overlooked by those in command. I sometimes crave to go on a raid, win an MC and get a faster promotion.

I write to darling Dorice during the early days of the Somme battles;

Dearest little Girlie Mine,

Many, many thanks for the latest dear loving letter. It made me so happy to hear again that you really love your 'soldier man'.

I think you and Dais know where I am, but by the time you get this I shall have 'been through it'. It won't worry you will it, because when you get this a lot would have happened, as we go into our first proper 'stunt'. I've had no rest for three whole days as we prepare for the push with many runs up to the line. Shells fall all around, but after a while you block out the noise. All my men and animals are safe, despite all the shells dropping, machine guns spitting and the cursed snipers aiming at us.

Today three shells, no 5, landed on an ammo column of the artiller killing men and animals. It was a dreadful sight of wartime carnage. It's all a matter of luck. If a shell drops 50 yards nearer this way – then it would be the finish of a promising young officer!!!Bow wow!

Now don't be worried darling, as out here we laugh a lot; it seems funny and we don't worry out here. We generally know when the shells are coming near. It's the sound they make. (I think I told you that some months ago).

I often think I would like to go on a raid across to the Bosche wire and lines one night. They are so close in this sector and we have been raiding almost every night. Many of my pals have gone across and been put in for medals and promotion. Some of them have been wounded and rather too many killed.

But then I think if this war is to last years (and some say it is another 100 years war!) then my duty is to do my job and survive, and then to spend the rest of my days with you dearest.

No grumbles from me then, 'cos I am alive and that's the main idea. For the present, don't forget how much I love you and can't wait for this war to end so we may get married and spend the rest of our days together.

For the present Girlie Goodbye from
Your Devoted Bubbie

This first real 'stunt' for us is up near Loos with a large number of casualties from more than just a 'whiff of gas'. This is followed by a march south and a massive effort from the Battalion We are part of the 16th Irish Division; the "The Irish Brigade", and it's great achievement in taking the important village of Ginchy in September 1916. All part of the Somme offensive.

Within the censors' rules, I share these moments with Dorice.

My Darling Dearest Little Dorice,

I wonder if this letter will ever reach you. We are in an almighty battle – one that has been going on for two months, and now we are again in the thick of it, but in another place.

I have just got the rations up to the 'line', which here is really just some shell holes joined by wire.

The Huns are shelling us and their planes are dropping bombs on us from above. Nothing new here then!!

I have sent the animals back to the transport lines and am sitting in a shell hole on a large piece of cheese! It is dry here, but the mud and floods in this place is as if the ground is almost all molten. The noise is terrific all around and there is a huge bombardment going on as we are knocking Hellium into the Huns.

Still, I am safe and happy 'cos I know you are praying for me every night as I am for you. I will write more when I get out of Hellium

Whoops Dearie!!

Always your Bubbie xx

I always obey the censor rules about what I can, and cannot say, and my letters are uncensored and get through on trust. However, The Daily Express of 12th September 1916 carries a glowing headline report of our action;

> "Five days and Nights in Shell Craters. How the Irish took GINCHY. Splendid Daring of the Irish Troops. Men Dirty, Unshaven, Thirsty, Hungry, Weary – but Triumphant".

Well, we are all proud to be recognized in that way, but the cost has been very high in this Battalion; which they don't report. There is the stench of death all around the communication trenches and the village itself is just a heap of smashed stones

We were twenty officers and only five hundred men before this stunt, and five days later, just five officers and three hundred men are left. 'Dead, Wounded or Missing', has the most names.

I can now write to Dorice about all this:

My own darling,

I am alive .The last week has been terrible. There are only five officers left in the Battalion instead of thirty we had just two weeks ago. We have lost many brave men of all ranks and the Irish Division has fought as well as any, I am sure. It's rather splendid what the Munsters, Dublins, Leinsters and Connaughts have done. My best pal died and several other pals are gone, including the Docman.

It's awful, but out here you can't dwell on these losses or you would go mad. The night before last, I thought was MY last, as shells dropped all around me as I took my limbers into the lines and we moved through a captured village, which is an important one. You will read about this 'stunt' in the papers I am sure.

The village is raised to rubble by all the shells from both sides, but I think its name will become quite well known and associated with our success. I feel you can wear that shamrock I sent you with real pride Darling. For you are a Munster too, in the way you love me and write so sweetly through all this.

Needless to say; I haven't had much time to write as the push was so fast into the Bosche held lines, and the work of the TO in such times is all day and all night. The noise has been deafening, literally. We will be relieved soon to a quieter spot, having done great things.

This weeks' 'stunt' was the worse I have ever been in and I never want another one like it, but expect there are lots to come. I have been subject to conditions, experiences and incidents that when I was as a bank clerk, my instincts would have made me cower. Here wounds and deaths seem to be just our daily fare.

Meanwhile, I can tell you that the Germans are surrendering wholesale and the Tommies are delighted we are winning 'sans doubte'. It is great to see hundreds of prisoners coming in; sometimes 200 German prisoners guarded by 2 or 4 Tommies.

They are a most miserable lot of Bosche, and some of the letters they write to their homes are quite pathetic.

Do share this news with your 'dear old Pater', although I expect he reads all the papers.

We will be on the move soon so I will say Goodnight Darling Girlie Mine

I get your letter every morning sweetheart, and it just keeps me going (and alive) during each day of this awful war.

Sent with millions of hugs and kisses and all my love

Ever your own Devoted Bubbie

"Hubbie to Be"

That tremendous noise of mines erupting along a short front brings a vivid flashback of 1917 and the Messines 'stunt'.

Dearest little Darling Wifie,

Thank you sweetheart for your letter, which arrives every day without fail. Right now I will be unable to write so often; but each waking moment I think of you my darling and how it's just two months since we were married and I became the happiest a man could ever be.

Although the weather is gloriously hot, the war in this place is quite unhealthy indeed. The guns, our guns, are making a fantastic row and all is set for a stunt.

A mine or two went up today-the finest thing I have seen in my life though I wouldn't have wanted to be in it!! I still have been worrying for promotions and decorations-well if I come through this without a scratch – 'nuff said. Sorry to be so gloomy, it may to that whiff of gas I got the other night.

I am sorry I forgot to answer you about you going up to see Dorothy and Bill. It is not necessary to ask me if you want to enjoy yourself. I want you to be happy, merry and bright all day long. Darling, just toddle off to see them, and if you want any money just let me know.

Don't worry Darling if you don't hear for a few days, as I may be unable to write.

All my love Darling. May God Bless you and protect me.

Ever your own Hubbie

Bubbie xxx

The ridge at Wytschaete is taken with praise all round – including for ME!!

After five days absolutely in the thick of it, I am sending the award of my deeds in the stunt on a small card, in my letter to Dorice, as well as the special order from The General.

Dearest Darling Wifie,

You will no doubt have read Babs, the "little" events which are happening out here and will fully understand why I have been unable to write much!!

I got the rations right up to the 'new' front line each day and night!! The poor old animals had to go 'through it some' as well. It was impossible to get limbers through so all the grub for the men was in pack saddles. I was hugely delighted because I went further than anybody else with my old 'osses.

Gosh it's been a great stunt and we haven't finished yet. It does your heart good to be standing on a ridge which has been held by the Bosche for two years and which has been staring us in the face since last September. Now the ridge is ours and our guns are in No man's Land and even beyond!! That must have been one of the best stunts of the war because there were so few casualties. We lost a few officers and men, but did have plenty of wounded. But my luck held. Each time I arrived at a place they were shelling, they seemed to stop it as I reached it!!

Darling I know you were unhappy weren't you? Because you hadn't heard from me for five days. But you will understand as soon as you read the papers today umps?!!

I am sending you a card with a personal tribute to ME from the General, as well as the Special Order he sent to all ranks. Our CO, dear old Monck-Mason got a DSO, but he recognizes all his officers did their duty – and more!

Gosh Wifie mine, when is this war going to end. It MUST finish some day I suppose. Goodnight Darling, how I wish I was with you now to hug you and kiss you and perhaps have a little tuddle (though I am dog tired after this stunt!). Gosh I nearly forgot to send you some "spondulicks". Here's a fiver.

Goodbye dearest darling wife. May I soon be home with you. All my love, hugs and thousand of kisses.

Ever your loving and true Hubbie
Bubbie xx

§§§§§§§

THE IRISH BRIGADE
2nd Lieut. G.H. Annaheim
1st Royal Munster Fusiliers
I have read with much pleasure the reports of your Regimental Commander and Brigade Commander regarding your Gallant Conduct and Devotion to Duty in the Field on June 7th and 8th 1917 and have ordered your name and deed to be entered in the record of the Irish Division.
W. B. Hickie
Major-General.
Commanding the 16th Irish Division.

SPECIAL ORDER

The 16th Division has been relieved today. For over eight months we have held our portion of the Line in the SPANBROEK, VIERSTRAAT or DIEPPENDAAL Sectors and we can look back with pride and satisfaction to the record of those months. Neither rain or snow or the heat of the summer has interfered with the constant work.

Long distances, wet roads, cold nights, shortage of fuel, hostile shelling have all failed to dampen the spirits of our men. With gun and howitzer, trench mortar, rifle, machine gun and bomb, and sometimes with bayonet, we have gradually worn down the boasting enemy, and two days ago, with small losses to the Division, we have completed this chapter of our History, by taking from him the wood and Village of WYTSCHAETE, and the crest of the hill which means so much for future operations.

The Divisional Commander, in congratulating all arms and all ranks of the Division on their Victory of June7th thanks all the officers N.C.O.'s and men under his Command for their Loyalty and help, and for their bravery and skill in action.

Whatever new role lies before us, it will be tackled with the same endurance, the same cheerfulness, and the same bravery, and again and again the Division and every man in it will justify our motto;

"EVERYWHERE and ALWAYS FAITHFUL"

W. B. Hickie
Major-General.
Commanding the 16th(Irish) Division
June 9th 1917

The Tunnel Trench stunt comes soon after; at the close of 1917. We are getting ready to go at the Hindenburg Line with its new type of concrete blockhouses, deep bunkers and defenses in depth.

The plans for the attack are rehearsed and received in written form together with trench maps and the latest aerial photos via my pal Marsden (it could have been me taking them if I had been able 'to Fly'). He has returned from leave and now is acting Adjutant:

OPERATION ORDERS
by
Lt Col. R.R. MONCK-MASON DSO Commanding
1st Battalion ROYAL MUNSTER FUS.
In the Field 18/11/1917

1. The 47th Infantry Brigade will capture and consolidate TUNNEL TRENCH from Jove to Sap Blocks.
2. The 6th Connaught Rangers are attacking on the right and the 10th Dublins (48th Brigade) on the left.
The 1st ROYAL MUNSTER FUSILIERS will attack from U.14.d.10.30. to SAP at U.14.a.68.12.
3. The attack will be carried out by "W" & "X" Companies in two waves. Strength of Platoons will be 30 men per Platoon. Each Platoon will be composed as follows:-
4 Riflemen. 2 Bombers. 1 Carrier and 1 Rifle Grenadier.
At Zero hour the artillery bombardment starts.
At Zero plus 2 minutes, the Infantry will advance in Line of Sections, in files at about 25 to 30 yards interval......

(Signed) C.M. MARSDEN, Lieutenant,
A/A Adjutant, 1st. Royal Munster Fusiliers

Well, we've done it, and it is a huge success again for the Battalion. Fierce engagements, terrible bombing, counter-bombing and shelling, but the Bosche are driven from their strongpoints across a wide front. Underground fighting in the deep fortified Bosche trench has been learned at some cost. I am managing through all the noise and hell of shelling to get rations right up to Tunnel Trench using pack mules to haul across what was No man's Land.

What a place! That trench system seems equipped for long-term occupancy, but has been surrendered quite lightly. No time to stay for souvenirs, just to unload the rations and get back for another run. Constant hauling for three days and nights, and neck deep in mud. Nonstop work. Quite a stunt 'though!

Writing before:

Dear Darlingest Sweetheart Dorice,

I will be able to tell you why my letters are not turning up at least for ten days or not at all when I see you. Don't worry Darling, but as you have guessed 'there's plenty doin'. All leave has stopped because of the 'Irish Situation' (re recruiting), and the likelyhood of a 'stunt' sometime soon.

In this great war things are not so cheery and the news seems pretty black; what with Russia, Serbia, Italy, Roumania, but then wait and see when the Americans come over in force!!

They are holding back our letters from arriving and you can guess why, so it may be nearly a week before I get to write and post this letter.

Writing After:

Well my Darling it's been a few days since I got back to this. If you look in the papers you will understand what has been happening. The Battalion reached all of its objectives and the transport section played its full role – and more! It is quiet on this bit of the front now, but oh my word, how noisy it has been.

You should have seen me dodging shells of all calibres – ours, and theirs!! You can pride yourself that your Hubbie did his bit when you hear the ringing of the Bath Abbey bells for the "Battle of Cambrai". It wasn't so much of a stunt, but while it lasted it was fun! Of course, people near me did get pipped, including four young officers. Whoops dearie!! But we came through it and things are quieter now.

I am longing for leave – especially if I get a month of 'special' leave, but even fourteen days will be heaven – away from all this devastation. I saw a tank the other day and it went straight over the shell holes and trenches. I managed to follow in his tracks for a bit. S'marvellous!

Boscheman here is beaten. Beaten, but he puts up a good fight and it's a pity he doesn't play the game. The weather has been terrible which has hindered operations. The men are splendid, especially my own section. They worked and fought like Trojans. I lost no men and only had some light wounds to a few animals, which can be patched up by the Vet.

This isn't exactly a love letter Darling is it? I am too full of a spirit of aggression which is rather unusual but when those B – – – have killed your pals, well.

So for now, my Darling Goodbye. All my love, hugs, cuddles and and kisses.

Ever your tired old Hubbie
Bubbie xxxx
I LUV U
Goodbye Wifie mine x

I get nearly the whole of December 1917 as 'special leave' and get a chance to think about the physicality of my Army work and all the spite and hate I have endured from the Bosche to date. I am finding relief from my fragile nerves, in trips to Torquay and Southsea, and visiting my family and friends in Bath. This is what peace feels like. This time with Dorice is beyond bliss.

Going back to the Front is a struggle, as this war is yet to be won. There are more stunts ahead, I fear.

The Bosche too have their own stunts; so often bombing us from 'planes, firing over hundreds of gas shells and following up with bombing parties and grenade throwers. Not to mention the thousands of 'regular' shells screaming at us most days from their gun lines.

That screaming noise sparks a flashback of the "Spring Offensive", or, as we call it; 'The Great Race'. I am experiencing almost indescribable and really frightening 'Adventures in Retreat' as the Bosche drive us back nearly 40 miles towards Amiens.

Gas, Bombs, Machine Guns, Flamethrowers; the whole dreadful apparatus of war seems to be aimed at me personally, at my men, and at my beloved animals.

I have lost so many pals; too many to think about in these last hellish two weeks. The Huns clearly have run-out-of-steam in this, what must have been their 'stunt of all stunts'.

This autumn in August and September, we are in a 'Grand Assault' from Amiens eastwards, and we definitely now feel the war is won. If only the Bosche would realise it! Our actions are successful, but costly in officer pals and men. The gas shelling again is taking its toll and Hun planes seem to dominate the sky, day and night. Well, that's what it seems like to me as my transport seems to be always getting gassed or bombed.

My dearest Darling,

I am sorry I wasn't able to write for the last two days. Poor little Girl I know you must worry when that happens, but I am quite fit considering our movements, and only snatching half an hour's sleep here and there. The war news is good, but it isn't exactly a walk-over as the papers make out.

The noise of the shelling is so loud it makes one deaf. It's a mixture of ours and theirs.

Girlie Mine, I am sure your prayers are being answered because several times lately I have been within a few feet of being blown off my feet. I can't help thinking God is taking care of me for you. Shells have dumped on the road both just in front of me and behind me, but have not touched me.

So let's pray girl that we shall be spared to live a long life together with our wee 'A' that is coming.

I am sorry this is not cheerier darling, but I am tired and a wee bit gassed, but my love for you is never diminished by all the 'goings-on' during these stunts.

Darling sweetheart, I must go off to the Battalion Goodbye till I write again.

All my love dearest Darling. All my hugs, kisses, cuddles and tuddles that I possess

Ever your adoring Hubbie
Bubbie xxxx

And now, in October, as we move forward towards 'the End', all there is, is this piercing noise through my brain.

We live for each day out here. And we die each day.

I suppose today – this is MY day.

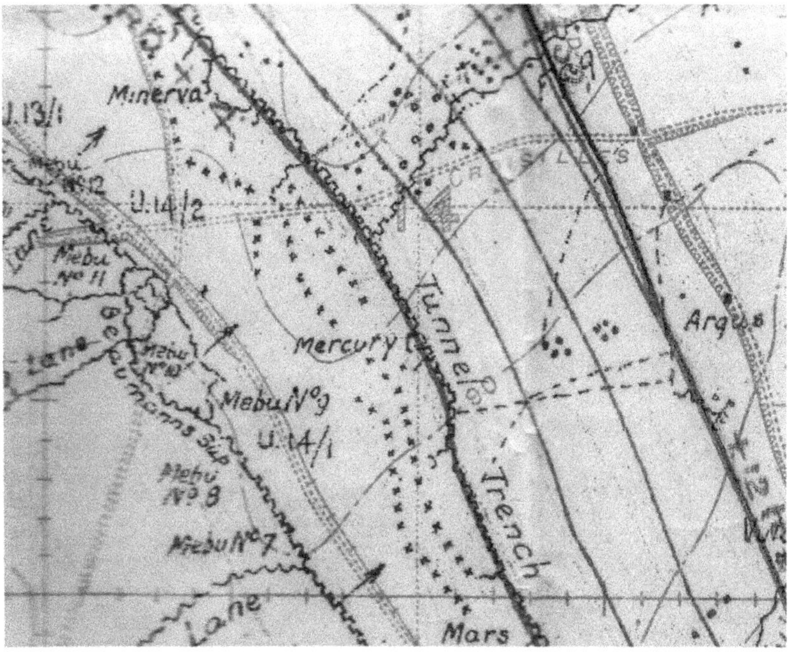

The Irish Brigade

2nd Lieut. G. H. Annaheim
1st Royal Munster Fus.

I HAVE READ WITH MUCH PLEASURE THE REPORTS OF YOUR REGIMENTAL COMMANDER AND BRIGADE COMMANDER REGARDING YOUR GALLANT CONDUCT AND DEVOTION TO DUTY IN THE FIELD ON June 7th & 8th 1917 AND HAVE ORDERED YOUR NAME AND DEED TO BE ENTERED IN THE RECORD OF THE IRISH DIVISION.

W. B. Hickie

Major-General,
Commanding 16th Irish Division.

16

MATINEES AND NIGHTS OF LOVE

"I can imagine a long loving exhausting 'tuddle'... and then falling back totally done-in"

Momentous flashbacks of blissful afternoons and nights spent doing that for which men are designed.

A Man, not a Boy, any longer.

'Egyptian Escapades' are my growing–up opportunities; away from the strict conventions of Bath 'society' and the strictures of a Protestant upbringing. Opportunities for passion come, and it seems, only when I am sick with fever. In fact, each time I have been sick, a passionate affair has resulted. And then a wedding!

That is strange.

Nurse Callow teaches me the fundamentals in Alexandria, while later, 'Lady Dorothy' lets me experience and taste the sweet fragrances of all the sensuous parts of a woman's body. The experiences delight and enthrall me thereafter, and, for the rest of, what has become, an exciting and exhausting life.

These afternoon 'escapades', make me more sensitive – yet bolder, but now seem a world away from the love I hold dearer than my own life.

After Egypt, it seems I am reverting to the 'correct' way; wooing and courting Dorice with a chaperone, and writing letters that may be possibly read by her Mater. I have to behave within all the conventions of English 'polite society'.

Yet, with Dorice, something else is at work. There's an earthy honesty between us that is perfect. There is also a warmth, an empathy, and a sincere welcome from her 'old-man' and the 'little Mater', as well as some of the 'Aunts and Cousins'. This allows more freedom for blissful 'matinees'.

However, on the leave in early 1917 we are still under more 'conventional' rules, but have managed our way around them; both at the Hookways' in South Parade, and in my parents home at Belgrave Place:

My Darling Little Girl,

Two topping long letters from you this morning sweetheart. I thank you and love you. The wretched old war won't last forever; we shall one day be united. Not just being 'allowed to kiss in the daytime' – but do what we want, when we want. Bow wow!!

I am glad you miss your kisses Girlie, and I know how much you enjoyed them!!! We will have thousands of 'first kisses'. I was just beginning to like them when duty called. Bow! wow!

Oh, to be in your little arms again. In one of your last letters you say you did object to me kissing you inside your blouse. If you really did, then why didn't you tell me and I certainly would not have done it. But I can't help thinking you didn't mind. Oooer! I shall never forget the sofa incident. I did forget to strafe my mother about coming in without knocking on the door. But, we did have a jolly good time, Darling.

Your admissions regarding "My Thingee"(let's call it "HIM" in future) – well, do you know they made me blush, only that wasn't noticeable because my face is so red. Not as noticeable as "HIM". Naughty Boy!

I am NOT ashamed of you darling, but am slightly ashamed of myself, but am afraid when I come home I shall (do-it-again!!).

Well sweetheart, I must go up to the Lines with my limbers and men, as they are all ready for me.

Goodnight dearest Girlie in all the world. With all my love, kisses, and hugs. Thousands of 'premier baisers'

Your Devoted 'Hubbie-to-Be-one-day-soon'

Bubbie

Now, thoughts of the 'Honeymoons', first second, and third, come back into my head.

The 'official' one in April 1917; which follows my bout of measles and hospitalization in Boulogne, and after our hurried marriage at St Andrews, Bath, lasts only five days. Each afternoon we disappear back to our room for an afternoon of truly passionate love-making.

We manage to upset the people in the next room with our cries, and with our 'no holds barred'. I do however feel we are both a bit shy, and now, my dear Dorice is starting to come down with the Measles.

C'est la Guerre, and, as they also say in French: "*Nous avons tous assez de force, pour supporter les maux des l'un et l'autres"*. All is calm after these five wonderful days, but the farewell is tough for us both:

My darling little Wifie

God, how great is it to be able to call you "wife". Girlie I can hardly write. I am waiting near Victoria for the train and naturally thinking of my poor baby Wifie.

I am so happy, yet as happy as one can be under the circumstances. I hate leaving you sweetheart. This is the 'rottenest' leave parting I have ever had.

I went off feeling absolutely rotten. Kiki did her utmost to cheer me up – I suppose you heard I nearly missed the train.

Darling wife please write as often as you can, because I shall be worried about you until you are absolutely free from the miserable measles. Let us look forward to my next leave and we will have SOME honeymoon – even more blissful than our 'first'.

I will wire from Boulogne Babs, just in case you think that I am at the bottom of the deep blue sea.

Goodbye dearest darling little baby wifie

Ever your loving and true Hubbie, All the *love I posses is yours*

Bubbikins xxxx

Measles or not, my darling new wife starts writing to me the moment I leave for France making me feel loved and, so proud:

My Dearest Little Wife

I was terribly proud of my first letter from "the wife". Your letter was so cheery that I nearly cried with joy. I am so sorry to have left you with a bout of the 'meesles', but glad to hear the doc says just give it another week only. I know you have the strength to get fully better as soon as possible.

So our 'first' honeymoon is over dearest. It is just the first of many more I promise you. You don't know sweetheart, that I went down on my knees and thanked God I was with you in 'our' room 88 in Southsea. The light was out and I just wanted to thank Him for giving you to me.

But perhaps you did know; just like you know what I like in bed. I thought you would like to undress yourself and, as I wanted you to be happy, I let you. But, next leave – well, 'nuff said!!

I shan't ask permission, but do exactly as I like! Plenty of glorious matinees and loving nighttime's await our second honeymoon Girlie!

I promise to love you and take care of you for the rest of your precious life, and I promise to try and be the best Husband as men go!!

GOODBYE MY DARLING WIFIE
From your loving Hubbie
Bubbikins xx

Now there's plenty of joshing from my pals about coming back to the Battalion as a married man! I am back with pals like Marsden, my men and my 'Four-legged friends'.

My dearest Darling ,

I am writing this in the mess at. HQ trying to concentrate while Marsden is playing the fool nearby. He is clowning around, teasing me unmercifully, though he is my best friend in the Battalion, and I think quite jealous that I found and married 'THE ONE'.

He says that he must meet you as soon as his leave comes. I don't mind, as I am so very proud of you. The pals say things like: "The game is over my lad, and you will be marching from now on; to the dying manhood!"

I still remember that Sunday afternoon and it makes

me blush. Let me see who's idea was that to do it in the bath?!!

I quite remember Kiki flouncing out of the room. Perhaps if I had been there quicker, I would have carried you both upstairs and put you both to bed and then hopped in after you!! Some stunt!!

Next leave I'll undress you and bathe you with no aunts or cousins hanging around! In the winter we'll just have to keep warm with nothing on at all (naughty boy).

Time to go sweetheart. All my love and millions of hugs and kisses, one little tuddle (do you like 'em. I know you do. And, "HIM" does too)

Ever your loving Hubbie
Bubbie xxx
Goodnight beloved xxx

Now, six months after our wedding I am on 'Special Leave' of almost one month. A joyous few weeks for this married officer who has now served over forty long months in this Army. About time I get it too!

And, Christmas at home this time, after three of them away! Time is flying-by so fast; before it starts, it seems it ends.

We are sharing many pleasures; as Dorice and I travel around the relatives in Torquay, London and get another five days at The Beach Hotel, Southsea. Bliss! The outcomes of course are dramatic with a subsequent miscarriage and all the agonies of deciding whether it is a good idea 'To have a Wee Kiddums'. Fate answers that question.

Back again in France in early 1918 we are writing about all the vigorous love-making:

My Own Darling Girl,

Dearest darling I love you and everything about you. Two letters arrived today, and I am quite comfortable here; gosh, about this time of the afternoon in South Parade we would be turning in. Do you know sweetheart why I didn't undress you every night? I'll tell you why. I wanted you to come to bed as quickly as possible and if I started undressing you I was really wasting good time!!!

I blush to think of the matinees! That is true love and as you say; "We do Love well. Darling, we do love VERY well!"

I never thought we could be so happy as we were during those heavenly days. I thought you would be too shocked!! But you stood it jolly well and played the game like a jolly good 'un. I adore you and I know you love me and we are the only ones for each other. Don't worry about the next leave 'cos we will pick-up where we left off!

All my love Girlie. Millions of hugs and kisses, (and what about another tuddle Girlie ?)

Ever your loving and true Hubbie

Bubbie xxx

Our letters get more 'spicy' as I am awaiting the 'Bosche March Offensive', which comes soon after all this correspondence:

Dearest darling Wifie Mine.

Another loving and naughty letter from you sweetheart. Don't worry, I don't share your loving thoughts (and the 'whoar' ones) with anybody. I burn them as it's risky to keep them-especially as we are expecting the Huns to attack soon. What would a Prussian Grenadier think if he found them!?

Girl, you do egg me on to write the most terrible things about what I am going to do on the next leave because you say I'm irresistible when I'm naughty. Oooer!! I yearn for my next leave – only 3 months away.

When I wake up each morning I turn over and wish I could come in!! "Cos I wants yer! And badly too!! 'HIM' gets quite excited. Thank God I can exist till next leave. Some fellows cannot.

I fell asleep between 6pm and 8pm on my bed and dreamt I was with you Dorice Girl. We were having a great tuddle during a very nice afternoon on our old bed!! oooer!! And then, after 'paradise'; to wake up and find oneself in France, lying on my old valise. Well, it's enough to make a fellow take to booze! Don't fret, I'm 'TT' at the moment.

I was quite a good boy till I met you. And now I spend many wistful hours dreaming of naughtiness with my own darling. Dorice my girl; I want, I want, I want a little matinee so very, very badly, umps!!

I want to feel your warm little body next to mine. I want to feel you warming your hands!!

Very often, fellows come into my hut and say; "Anna, your wife is a damned pretty girl". And I say "Looks aren't everything my Boy. It's what's in a girl's heart that makes some of 'em lovable." And I point out your pretty wee face, Darling.

I love it when you said in your naughty letter how much you wish for an imprinting little tuddle – oooer! Gosh our letters are getting absolutely terrible; still, they are jolly nice. Hot baths with my wifie are a great weakness with me. Wait till we have our own bathroom. We'll make it jolly comfy with a sofa – for massage etc!!!! not so much of the
"massage" and a little more of the "etc". Naughty Boy.

I was a good little boy till I met you; and then I think we both took the wrong turning-'twice nightly'!. I love and adore you. All my hugs, kisses and cuddles.

Goodbye Dearest most beloved wifie
Ever your own loving and devoted Hubbie
Bubbikins xxx

It seems that an anticipated leave, is leaving me more than a bit frustrated, and our letters are getting increasingly risqué:

Darling girl,

Two perfectly topping letters today. Cheers, and they were a wee bit naughty, just a soupcon. Bow! wow!

Well Girl, I adore you more and more each day. I have often thought that you may imagine that I only want you for just one thing – you know what that is sweetheart; "Tuddling", because I always seem to be writing about it. But don't forget I loved you for yourself well before our 'matinees' and nighttime love-making were on the cards. Or on the bed! Now of course it is different; 'cos my darling wife is happy and contented with "matinees and nighttimes" with her Hubbie, n'est ce pas?

It does seem ages since we shared the dear old bed. I am so glad your hands are getting better, but even 'gladder' when you wrote that you want your sweet wee paws to be perfectly ok by next leave to do the necessary with 'HIM'.

Gosh, I really love it that you love 'HIM'. I feel like kissing 'IT' tonight and putting some nice powder on it!! Oooer naughty boy!!!

Really, if this letter is censored I shall be court-martialed for sending an 'improper' letter through the post!

It would be good if you come before me next time sweetheart – do you remember a certain afternoon when we came together. You had climbed on me. (Oooer-get another wife!!!) I hope it was as much fun for you. I'll tell you more about that when I come home.

How I wish I was with you right now. It's late, and if I was at 1 SP right now, the little Mater would be saying; "goodnight and be good" but I shouldn't promise!!

By the by, we can certainly start the next leave where we left off last. I was so happy on the last because you acquiesced(?)

to my wonderful idea. At first I thought you would never agree and 'brace yourself' well, you are now so pleased with 'HIM' that he has a fine time. Do you remember I fell asleep in a 'phsycological position', and I nearly kilt my own little wifie. You idea of "economy re clothes" is quite sound. I will fall in with all your desires!!! Oooer!!

It's time finish as the ration party is ready for me to lead it up to the Lines. It's dark and quite quiet for once, thank Heavens.

Goodnight Darling wifie. All my love ,hugs, kisses and cuddles and a matinee tuddle.

Ever your own devoted Hubbie
Bubbikins xxxx

Much later, and we have moved by train and motor lorry to join the 57th Division – a fresh start, with many lads from the Lancashire Battalions, which brings back memories of my time in the Duke of Lancaster's Own Yeomanry, and many northern pals. This Division has a much better staff, so I am happy about the change.

My Transport Lines are in good shape with stables and some green grass for grazing. More importantly, leave has come round but I don't realise this will be the LAST leave – ever.

Ten days with my darling Dorice in July 1918, and to be with her after so many months away, is divine. Another Honeymoon! And, as well as seeing the usual family, and some friends we get away to the bungalow and The Beach Hotel. Just alone; spending days and nights in each other's arms. We are 'throwing-caution-to-the-winds', and dear Dorice will definitely be 'with-child' after all this 'activity'!

Back with the Battalion, Dorice's letters arrive with their usual fits and starts:

My own Darling,

I have just received a perfectly long loving letter from you. It made me so merry and bright.

Of course you were love-sick when I first arrived home and wanted to tempt me to a matinee!! Girlie mine, I didn't need much tempting!!

We were so jolly lucky in getting such good weather. It seems nothing but rain since I returned here. It was simply glorious at Southsea, but I must confess that I was dying for a matinee after the swim!!! I am glad you think I looked after you so well – that's nice to hear, as marriage takes a lot of learning. How am I doing sweetheart? I often think I was a better bachelor than a married man!!

Darling, of course "I'll always be your lover, even if 'it' happens and you start growing fat with a 'little "A".

Always adoring, worshipping and cherishing you with all my heart – both in the afternoons and through the night. What what!!

God bless you and love you. Thousands of kisses and one dinky matinee.

Ever your loving and true Hubbie
Bubbikins xx

Right now, in these very last days of this stressful battle through the Hindenburg Line, I am having a moment to share my deepest thoughts on our love-making. Perhaps it's caused by a premonition of not making it through, that I am writing in this way:

Dearest darling Wife,

I have just come back from the line Sweetheart and am

now in <u>bed</u>. Not being very tired I thought you might like another little letter this evening. My thoughts are ever of you Dorice-Mine. What would I give to be beside you now at home, to pull back your little nightie and kiss your dear little white breasts as I have so often done.

To press my chest against your breast and kiss your sweet little lips and say, "Wifie mine, I adore you"

To feel your little heart beating against mine and feel your wee legs entwined in mine. I would like the gas alight so that I could see you beside me, besides feeling you. I can imagine your dear wee hand wandering all over my body and pressing me to you. I can imagine a long loving exhausting little 'tuddle', which we would both enjoy and then fall back totally done-in, but not too far from each other.

I can imagine falling asleep in each other's arms, but not for long as we just have to go again!

I can imagine taking you out dressed in your pretty summer clothes; everyone looking at you, and envying me. How proud I am because, I thought years ago that no girl would fall in love with me, and now I find myself the adoring Husband of the sweetest prettiest Girlie in the world.

To love is pleasant but to be loved is far more pleasant. I can imagine your cheery little laugh. I can imagine you singing.

It is with these thoughts which come to my mind, that I go to sleep to dream of the times to come when we will never, never part.

Goodnight MY Beloved WIFE
Bubby xx

So, it has been the 'hand of war' that has revealed to me the bliss of both love and sex in their most potent form.

And, as these flashbacks disappear, another thought flashes-by, that at least the devilish Hun didn't get me in the most 'manly' part of me. 'HIM' survived throughout the war and did his job.

While the whole of 'ME' now dies.

A Man – not a Boy.

17

4-LEGGED FRIENDS

"Bubbie-boy, you are not bringing up your animals as you should!"

That sweet smell of horses' steaming bodies comes strongly into my head. Mixed with their hot, rancid breath, this familiar stench is bringing unique and powerful flashing memories of my other 'friends'.

So much of my time has involved riding and working with horses that my life has been shaped by them. And, this, at a time when motorised transport, including tanks, seems to be 'overtaking' everything with hooves. Horses and mules to be specific.

My love of animals has been central to my life, both before, and after I meet darling Dorice. They have helped me triumph in sports; jumping, racing and polo, and they have transported me throughout this war, and yes, taken more than one bullet for me!

While in the Royal Gloucestershire Hussars, I learn the basics; riding, controlling, tacking, grooming, mucking-out and caring for my own mount. In Manchester, in the DLOY with Marsden and the other Lancashire lads, we spend the weekly drill nights, as well as weekends practicing like mad; jumping obstacles with arms outstretched, charging at targets with lances, firing from the saddle, as well as quick dismounts and firing from alongside our mounts. All the tricks we get up to at the DLOY summer camps are of use in war, for sport, and, I believe for just keeping me human, through all these dramatic years.

What fun we have at these summer camps in Greystoke and Knutsford in 1913 and 1914; sleeping under canvas six to a tent, with plenty of stunts and competing for trophies.

True Cavalrymen are we, and with excellent mounts.

Now we are off to War, to Egypt with my Jack; an eventful journey with my superb mount and best-ever '4-legged friend'. He sees me through the Suez stunt right up to my posting to the Officer School in Zeitoun. Writing to Mother from Egypt I am talking a lot about Jack:

Dearest Mother,

How are you and dear Father?

I can tell you I am here in Egypt, well settled with my pals, and exercising and rehearsing for what must be a big stunt against the Turks now we are at war with the Ottomans. The barracks are quite near Cairo and we can see the pyramids and sphinx from here when the sand is not blowing across.

All is well with me and my pals in the squadron and there is a chance I will be made up to L/Corporal quite soon. It is very hot here and there are lots of flies. The food is good for us lads, but not quite so good for the horses.

There is a shortage of oats and typical forage that they are used to, so we substitute chickpeas and a kind of wheat called 'dhurra' a mix of maize and millet. They do suffer quite a bit with this heat and fodder, but be assured, my dear Jack is well and taking good care of me.

He trots with his nose up and his tail perky as we exercise in the desert sand, which here, is covered with hoofprints, as you can imagine.

Dearest Mother, I must stop now as I am on stable guard duty tonight. I wonder how long this letter will take to get to you, but please say hello to Dais and the Carpenter, and if you write to Eddy tell him to drop me a line.

I think in war it is important we all keep in touch, wherever we are in the world.

Meanwhile, I send my fondest love to you and father and all the family. Please keep well and do not worry; this is all rather a fine adventure for me and Jack!

From your loving son
Herbert
Duke of Lancaster's Own Yeomanry
MEF, Cairo, Egypt.

The Australians have brought fine mounts here to Egypt; big powerful horses, mainly black, but Bays and Chestnuts as well. They seem better used to the intense heat, while the Punjabi Regiments have smaller horses that are well conditioned to desert life, as they seem to suffer less from thirst and scouring. These Indians are fine horsemen too!

Jack equips himself superbly in all I ask of him in the Egyptian 'escapades', but now I am sad to say farewell to him.

As Transport Officer to the 1st Battalion RMF in France, I am able to source my animals for my job from the remount centre, about twenty-five miles away from my lines.

I always choose my mounts with care and people say: "The 1st Battalion RMF have the best animals at the Front". And, I believe, better than even some of the Regular Cavalry Regiments! Certainly dear old Monck-Mason, the CO, thinks so, and that's good enough for me.

Mules are quite a different business to horses. The noise they make is a kind of strangulated screeching, that pierces the night and often makes the horses restless. My mules are often more noisy than the nightly hate by the Huns! Yet, as pack animals they carry important parts of the rations for the men; pretty much all the water cans (actually old petrol tins filled with water) and also ammunition boxes, slung on braces on their flanks. They are difficult to handle when pulling a cart, but they do take a lot of the daily burden. They have amazing stamina to endure even the most difficult terrain; especially the soaking mud, goo and slime in this part of France.

I share my love of horses with Dorice from my very earliest letters:

My darling little Sweetheart, (wifie-to-be)

This is the first chance I've had of writing today and I must admit to feeling half dead and nearly asleep. I nearly came home to you this evening – but not of my own design, but by that of some foul Hun machine gunner. I am and have been in a nasty place, and unfortunately one of my horses is a casualty tonight. He, poor fellow saved me absolutely. I was walking on the off side of him and a bullet caught him in his stifle, which corresponds to our thigh. If he hadn't been there at all it would have caught me in the shoulder or neck. So Cheerio Ho!

So far, I am quite well and thanking to my good luck and my four-legged friend for keeping me safe. But it is sad to see the death and wounds of such fine animals.

Did I tell you I have twenty eight horses; a mix of heavy and light draughts, as well as riding horses? I have four dear old draught horses, which are lovely huge animals with such calm temperaments. I love these best of all. They have large heads and lovely eyes.

Then, there are the mules, which are difficult to manage but do a lot of the work out here. So there are about fifty five animals and the same number of men here in the transport section under my command.

Well THAT was a small issue; as I just finished having a row with old Baxter the QM as to 'who is in charge of the horses?' I won!

I am sorry this letter is short, dearest, will you forgive me – with all this 'excitement' tonight I suddenly feel worn out. Tomorrow I will write a long loving letter. Goodnight Girlie, rest assured I am safe and well.

God Bless you sweetheart.
With all my love and many hugs
Ever your loving Bubbie x

DoriceII is the name of my favorite riding mount, which my groom, Dan Sullivan, 'rescues' from outside a French estaminet. Red light, or blue light? He doesn't say. Only, "Well, soarh, she looked so pretty just outside this house, and I thought she would make a perfect mount for ye". What should I say to him? She is a pretty thing, just like the real Dorice. But he did steal her; but then he stole her for me, which is rather flattering I suppose!

No French officer or 'Poilou' has come by to try and retrieve her – yet. So I just frown at Dan and say; "Carry on Dan!" He stains her cannons and fetlocks black, and paints on a few extra dark grey blotches on her flanks for disguise. She is still a pretty horse though!

My darling little Dorice,

Have you forgotten me sweetheart mine? I do hope for a long loving letter from you tomorrow. This is the only moment during the day that I have to myself.

It's Sunday and I have let my men have two hours to themselves as a peace offering because I had a nice loving letter from you yesterday at which I was especially delighted cos you had at last received one of my missives.

I have a new little grey mare as my own riding horse. She is sweet and pretty just like you darling, so I call her DoriceII. We are getting to know each other and although she does her best to chuck me off, we are getting on so well. Does it sound familiar umps??!! (Actually, I think it's only for the love of me). She is a sweet soul.

I do believe such horses have a 'soul' just like people. She shows generosity and a spirit to love and trust me. Horses have intelligence and are able to adapt to new situations and are just sensitive beings, like most people. Anyway, with DoriceII, I feel a bond that will help keep me safe. Especially as so many of my pals have 'left' the Battalion through sickness, wounds and death. Oh I do wish you could see DoriceII. You would love her too.

My great pal the Doc-man came down to the stables the other afternoon. I showed him my new little mare. He admired her and I whispered "Dorice". The dear little animal pricked up her ears and put her nose in my hands.

The Doc-man said it was "a very touching little scene" and if you needed any more proof of my love for YOU; he could easily bring forth evidence if you wished!

He asked if he could write to you to say what good pals we are and how he will endeavor to look after me out here!

Goodbye sweetheart.

All my love, and all my kisses to thee.

Ever your Devoted Bubbie xx

Then there is Jack. 'Black Jack' or 'Mad Jack' as I sometimes call him. If riding has made me fit and heavy (fitter and heavier than my brother, I bet!), then my Jack standing over eighteen hands, is right for me; for my most arduous rides, and especially for my 'Sporting Days':

Dear Dorice dearest,

I missed your letter tremendously today darling – 'spect you miss mine when they don't turn up too.

Dearest I hope you and your dear parents are well; please say hello to the little Mater for me! Tell her I plan to be home for your 21st – so clear the decks. What! what!!

I now have a huge black horse that I call Jack. He is a fine animal and can jump his own height!! I went for a ride on him yesterday and felt so tall in the saddle. I plan to keep him to myself (though not ride him when the Bosche snipers are around).

Of course I haven't forgotten DoriceII, and often ride her up to the trenches. She lifts her feet up so nicely in the dark and never falls into shell holes (touch wood). She is well and 'eating like a horse'!

Darling Baby Girlie I am longing to come back to you. An officer goes on leave every five days and there are three more before me. That means all being well I shall make it back for your birthday. It will be some celebration-whoops dearie!!

Goodnight dearest. I am going to dream of you all night long. All my love

Ever your devoted Bubbie xx

Jack and I are so well matched, though he is rather scared of the nightly Hun bombing and shelling. We get into so many 'scrapes' together that I have to write to my Dorice, but not make them sound as dangerous to life and limb (mine and his), as they really are:

My Dearest Darling Little Girlie,

No letter again, but tomorrow will bring better luck. Did you see in the papers the Bosche are retiring in several places. Whoops dearie!! Maybe this war will be over and we can spend our lives together – forever and a day. Old Bubbikins will want to be hugged and kissed for the remainder of his life!

Hoping this letter finds you "in pinko condition"

Well, I started this letter last evening and was called away, but I am not neglecting you. I am quite merry and well, so you musn't be worried at all. I tell you everything – if I didn't I shouldn't tell you THIS;

I went up to HQ last night and on mounting Jack to come back, I slipped and Jack set off at a canter for the Bosche lines with poor old me. My foot was caught in the stirrup iron and I was dragged merrily along the ground! Not so funny as the devilish Hun started some machine gunning – fortunately over our heads, but not very sporting.

Just before the lines, luckily the stirrup leather tore away from the saddle and Jack carried on by himself. He was obviously frightened by all the noise and excitement! I will send the stirrup and leather to you as a souvenir.

To make matters worse my groom, Dan, was riding DoriceII, and she broke away in all the merriment. The two animals, and you know they are my favourites, were racing all around just about the 'hottest' place they could have chosen.

Luckily Jack came back to me and DoriceII was caught by a sentry shortly afterwards. We started off for home in the dark, and even though the evil Hun had quietened down by now, we got a bit lost and found ourselves VERY close to the Bosche trenches!! Only a couple of yards away – we could hear the 'alte deutsche' chattering beside us. Whoops! S'an awful war!!

However after a swift "about turn" we arrived back none the worse. Then, John, my servant, managed to get some warmish water into a canvas bath for me to clean up. I bet the men had a good laugh when the story got around about "Soarh, and his nighttime excursion into the Hun Lines, and back!"

This morning I was riding another horse when he shied at something and slipped and fell in a ditch leaving me in the mud beside the road. No bones broken after these 'exertions and excursions'. I am just a trifle sore!

Believe me, I am taking care of myself for you Sweetheart, so please don't strafe me in your next letter.

Is your cold better Babs, my throat is quite well again. It only needed a bit of lubricating! And my pal the Doc-man dropped by with a bottle of the auld 'Black and White'. Don't I deserve it after my recent excitements!

I can picture you writing to me on the arm of the chair by the window, or maybe on the little bench underneath that pear tree in your garden, where we sat together there on my last leave. Heaven.

Goodbye darling little Babs. I will try to write a longer more interesting letter tomorrow.

All my love to you Sweetheart

Ever your loving Bubbie xx

I am awaiting Dorice's next letter with some anxiety. But, after all, I did promise to tell her everything within the censor's rules. A gentle 'strafe' has arrived:

My very own darlingest Bubbikins,

I had a ripping long letter from you this morning, Sweetheart, for which I send you a big kiss! I'm glad you received the parcel I sent you and the chocs went down well. One of these days I'm going to send you a cake made with my own fair hands. (Oooer, get another cook!). I am hesitating about it though, as my handmade cakes are usually so rock hard, I am able to throw them along South Parade and back without breaking them!! Pity your poor teeth after trying one of them!

'San awful war! Now listen here soldier-boy, I don't consider you are taking care of yourself for me – you might have hurt yourself very badly the other night when Jack dragged you along. Good Heavens!! He might have killed you Bubbie. Do take more care Darling. I am sure you are too reckless otherwise you wouldn't have had two accidents, one after the other.

I know I shouldn't strafe you, as I guess you are a 'trifle sore'. You can tell Jack from me that I am absolutely ashamed of him! When you slipped he should have stood still! I don't love him a bit now. And DoriceII is in disgrace too! How dare she break away like that. Bubbie-boy you are not bringing up your animals as you should. Do you want me there to teach them manners? Please may I come as your groom?

I do hope the war will end soon because I want my "Hubbie" ever so badly.

I love you and love you and love you! Oh, for après la guerre.

Goodnight my own dear darling. May God Bless You, With all my love and hugs and kisses.

Ever your own little
Baby 'Wifie'

Jack saves my life again and again through his sheer speed at the gallop. I owe my survival during the 'great retreat' to Jack and to DoriceII. We are gassed, shot at, bombed, singed by the Boscheman's flamethrowers and suffer thirst and hunger like never before. My faithful 4-legged friends get me and mine (well most of us anyway) though this punishing hell, lasting two horrific weeks.

Being sniped at is a constant hazard out here, but Jack is too fast. He gets a nick on his back that requires some help from the vet. He is recovering well; especially while we are billeted in this farm, with real grass. It is a wonderful sight to see all the horses rolling in the fields, eating fresh grass, and ignoring the roar of the guns.

All my successes in my 'Sporting Days' are owed to 'Mad Jack' (for both jumping and racing wins) and DoriceII (for polo competitions) at Regiment, Brigade and Divisional sports. They help make me a hero to my men; but 'Jack' and 'DoriceII' also are the heroes of these exciting and memorable events.

It is difficult to love the mules, but even they have individual characters. My favourites are Joe and Stephen. I don't know why – the noisy beasts!

Dearest Darling Little Baby Mine,

I am just off to the Line and the weather is just rotten. I love your letters to me even though they turn up two or three at a time.

Poor little Joe the pet mule has been ordered to be isolated because he is itchy. There's nothing wrong with him I'm sure, but there's a lot of mange about so the vet has ordered him to be separated from the others. He's kicking up an awful row outside in the cold. We've put a large blanket over him, but it must be bitterly cold for him.

I can see the men have rigged up a shelter for Joe so the noise has lessened somewhat.

So now I must be off as it's dark enough now. Goodnight Baby Mine.

I send you all my love and hugs from your own devoted
Bubbie xxx

Jenny the goat comes into my life and joins my 'animal farm'. Where she comes from, I have decided not to ask. But I tell the story to dear Dorice:

Dorice My Love,

I have just received two topping long letters from you. It is extraordinary that you do not get mine more frequently, as I write at least once a day.

It would drive me insane if I had to wait three days for a letter. You are a sweetheart to write to me so regularly, and as you know they just keep me going through this awful war. I will keep writing, even though where we are there's 'plenty doin'. Cos I love you and love you and love you see.

Has your Pater got a goat yet? If not, I have beaten him because I have! Please ask him what to feed it on (there's no grazing to be had in this mud for scores of miles around). At present I am feeding him hay and oats and water. Will he live long! He's a topping little fellow. My Corporal brought him back last night. I didn't ask any questions!

I took him round the stables today just to see what the other animals thought of him. They were all very friendly, including Jack. They kissed each other quite a lot – that is they licked each other's noses.

I suppose that's equivalent to kissing in the animal world. And that was real delight to see in the middle of this awful war. The men say it's a she-goat and call her Jenny.

Talking of kissing; I must tell you that on my next leave, there will be plenty n'est ce pas? Hugs too – millions of them. Not long now Darling

Goodnight my sweet
Ever your own devoted 'Hubbie'
Bubbie xx

The men play with Jenny in the day, and she even sleeps in a tent. Sometimes mine! Old Baxter isn't too pleased when she eats a pile of his paperwork though! She is our 'Mascot', for the 1st Battalion Transport Section, and the saddler-Corporal, Forsyth, has even made a leather collar for her, complete with a Munster's badge.

Back in Ireland, at the Base barracks, there is apparently a massive Irish wolfhound called 'Garry' who is the 'official' Regimental mascot. I've never seen him. I prefer Jenny.

We have a kitten too! She turns up from one of the men who found the mother with five kittens in a barn three months ago. She seems to have taken to me all right, and sleeps on top of me on these freezing winter nights.

After the war Dorice and I will have such a kitten as a pet. But, probably not a dog – too much trouble. The Regimental drummers have one which they call 'Fritz' as he walked into our trenches from the Bosche.

I realise that all these animals have an important part to play in this awful war. The bonds of animal love are tremendously strong. Demanding, but not in the same way as human love, as there is still the element of 'command and control' of these animals. The trust that is built goes both ways – the animals take, and, give as well. They bring something 'almost human'; beautiful and peaceful to our lives. They allow a soft and sentimental side to life out here, in contrast to the squalor and 'hate' that goes on around us.

What a complex mix of emotions I have experienced in these four years of war.

As that reek of animal smells disappears, I recall how:
I love Dorice.
I love all my animals.
I like my men.
I like my job.
I can't stand the 'Red Tabs'.
But I hate the Bosche.

But *they've* just got me.

18

"SOME BASHES!"

"...he also offered me a hundred pounds if I broke his neck on the way over!!"

That's another stupendously loud noise in my head. But this time not the bullet that is 'doing for me' but the sound and sights of raucous laughter; as my mind flashes back to ripping times in the messes.

I recall my first Christmas Dinner as an officer in Heliopolis, Egypt with the 29th Division. I am learning the mess protocols and remain well behaved. The mess rules always include the toast; "The King, God Bless Him", and dining is really regarded as a 'Parade'.

Now, at war in France, certain things are relaxed, including the dress code. But each Regiment and Battalion has its own traditions and practices that may change with the style of the CO as well.

Dear old Monck-Mason makes us feel warm and part of a real family; so different to Colonel Kane with his mad schemes and wild mess nights, with card games with stakes and bets all over.

But, I am remembering my first true 'bender' mess dinner with the Royal Flying Corps at Hazebrouk. Here I am a guest, but I am prepared by taking six bottles of 'Irish' as a gift to their mess president, and am ready to join in the 'post – port' entertainments.

As I formally thank the CO of the RFC squadron for the hospitality of him and his officers, I read my adapted 'Ten Commandments' that I, myself penned, and recently shared with our own mess in the Battalion;

i) *The CO is the boss, thou shalt have no other boss but Him.*
ii) *Thou shalt not make unto thyself any graven images of officers that fly in the heavens above, of staff officers who own the earth and of submarine officers in the waters under the earth. Thou shalt stand up and salute them for the CO Thy boss is a strict boss and will visit thee with Field Punishment in the 1st and 2nd degree of them that salute not, and will shower stripes and decorations on them that salute and obey his commandments.*
iii) *Thou shalt not take the name of the Adjutant in vain for the CO will not hold him guiltless that taketh the Adjutants' name in vain.*
iv) *Remember that thou workest on the Sabbath day. Six days shalt thou labour and do more than thou ought to do, but the seventh day is the Ring of Fatigues. On it thou shalt do all manner of work than thy Officers, thy non commissioned officers, and the Kitchener's Army which is within or near thy trench or airfield.*
v) *Honour the Army Staff that their days may be long in the Regiment; so they can verily send thee on leave.*
vi) *Thou shalt kill only Huns, rats, mice, bugs, beetles and*

other vermin that infect the trenches. And, also the Balloons and 'Fokkers' in the skies above.

vii) *Thou shall not adulterate the men's rum ration or his beer.*

viii) *Thou shalt not look like the Crown Prince does.*

ix) *Thou shalt not bear false witness in the orderly room.*

x) *Thou shalt not covet the ASC's job, nor their pay, nor their motors nor their horses nor their asses, nor any "cushy" thing that is theirs.*

I am certainly a 'hit' with the RFC fellows in their mess but, have an enormous hangover and cannot remember how I returned to my own billet.

'Bashes', as we call Mess nights in the Battalion, sometimes do get spoiled. When the old RC padre living with the 2nd Battalion tries to stop us keeping copies of 'La Vie Parisienne' in the mess there is nearly a mutiny! As far as all the officers here in the 1st are concerned, including the CO, Adjutant, QM, Intel officer, and of course my good self, this periodical is 'required reading' or 'viewing' at least!

The padre; hero, as he is, to the whole Regiment, the Division, and the newspapers of Ireland, has some ideas, which are totally out of order and are rejected with noisy 'ballyhooing'.

We continue to examine the naughty and arousing pictures in 'La Vie' even if our French is not up to much! Pictures tell more than words. For goodness sake, even dear Dorice loves to look at it!

Our new CO; Colonel Rodney Kane – 'the Admiral' to some of us – is full of mad ideas, but I find it easy to get on with him. Apparently he has a famous beknighted naval uncle, a Baronet no less, who did some very brave and daring deeds in the Pacific many years ago; hence the CO's nickname.

He makes me mess president. "Anna, I want a real 'bash' tomorrow night – a mess dinner with my guest. Fix up with Baxter the best 'do' ever". I rope-in Baxter and Marsden, and send some men to the local 'village' and a nearby farm to buy the very best provisions. Marsden orders the Regimental Pipe Band to come over for this mess night. I ask the CO "Sir, who is your guest tonight?" He replies curtly "Never mind Anna, but he is a Major in the Guards and I want a memorable night. Just make it happen!"

It is one of the wildest nights ever experienced and Kane is VERY pleased. I write to Dorice:

My dearest darling little wife,

No mail today so I ain't very cheery. I'll have a drink and cheer up and pray for two tomorrow.

It's rather dull, and dreary out here, quiet actually. Hot and dusty, and I live for leave and 'après la guerre'. I am just carrying on and just dreaming of the time I will come home and be with you for ever and ever.

I am so very proud of my wife. We have tremendous arguments in the mess. Old Baxter and I are the only ones who are married and we get ragged unmercifully. The CO, the 'Admiral', who is quite young and a 'ell of a flirt, tells me he will never get married but will only flirt with every girl he meets, whether married or otherwise!

At least 'Romeo' – our friend Adj. Marsden – only goes for single girls (or so he tells me!).

Last night there was a tremendous "bash" in the mess that the CO had asked me to organise as a 'guest night' As if I don't have enough to do! But then he did relieve me of one of my more tedious duties – squaring the Battalion AND Regimental accounts.

It was a great success as my sergeant managed to purchase twenty pheasants, copious bottles of non–watered down red wine and hunks of cheese from the nearest French farm. The regimental pipe band serenaded outside, playing great Irish music, plus all the old favourites.

So the dinner was splendid; noisy of course, with great food served by the messmen who were looking quite a bit smarter than usual, Six courses in all, starting with oysters, and with port, coffee and Brandy to finish! Toasts all round; "The King, The Regiment (' The Dirty Shirts!') the CO, Fallen Comrades, and, The Guards Regiment".

Our guest was a Guards Major from a nearby Division and apparently well known to the CO.

I have to tell you, in confidence, the most extraordinary story from this 'Bash". The CO quietly asked me to take him back to his billet in the gig. He also offered me a hundred pounds – yes really! – to break his neck on the way over!! Literally!

Of course, I took the fellow safely back and he courteously thanked me for a great 'bash', a fine dinner and the ride back.

When I got back to the HQ mess, the CO told me he frequently wrote to that fellow's wife and always stayed with her when he went home on leave!!!

Apparently the CO was engaged to his wife for twelve months before her marriage, and she married this fellow as it was the wish of her parents, and not because she liked him. Hence the result!!! Pretty awful isn't it? Apparently it's Army life, What! what!!

Darling, sorry this is a short letter, but I will write again after dinner if the CO hasn't got some scheme of cards.

Goodbye wifie mine. I adore you sweetheart and may God

bless you and take care of you so that I may cherish you all my life. All my love, kisses and cuddles

Ever your adoring Hubbie

Bubbie xxxx

Goodnight my love

Some American slang comes through my head and our first 'Bash' with the American Army. I write the story to Dorice:

My own darling wife.

I have just had dinner with some Americans, a General and a few others up at HQ.

Dining avec our Allies is interesting. It was a sober 'bash' as orders were to keep up the prestige of the Regiment – which traces its history back to sixteen fifty something – before America was even founded!

The evening included some rows – which I kept away from, but one of my pals is under arrest for being rude. He was using bad language to our American Allies!! Rather unfortunate as I heard what he said and have to give evidence against him!! Actually he called him a "goddam yank", which is rude, but their chaps do say "goddam" every other word. I hope and think probably we'll get him off. Chap can't take his drink! I will let you know the outcome of the court martial if it takes place.

The Americans seem extra keen on 'attacking on their own across a wide front' (suicide!), and don't seem to want to learn from the experiences of their allies. Probably they are still fighting like in their own Civil War. They will learn, and it is very good they are here.

There's a deuce of a row going on at present, not really many miles away; 'there must be a war on' umps! Yet it doesn't seem the weather is fit for fighting. It's wet and very cold.

Still it's late and I'm off up to the line with the limbers and won't be back till 3am. C'est la vie, c'est la guerre Darling.

I will write a long loving letter tomorrow my darling wifie.

All my love and hugs, cuddles and kisses.

Ever your loving Hubbie. Bubbie

Goodnight beloved

Well my friend gets away with just a reprimand, not a Court Martial – quite right too!

This Conference at Brigade HQ is turning into a 'bash' quickly enough, because my pals are in tremendous form. Morale is high before we go up to the line and play a leading role in the attack at Cambrai. The conference itself isn't the best way to build up the morale of the Battalion officers, but it is all turning out well. Due to myself actually. One of my most vivid and funniest memories, which I share with dear Dorice:

My dearest darling little Babs,

Many thanks for two ripping long love letters I received this morning. How are you Darling?

I am frightfully bucked with life at present. The Brigadier had a 'conference'. with all the officers of the Battalion Food and drink was provided. But instead of the expected 'bash', the Brigadier severely strafed all our officers!

He said "The men are dirty and the officers take no interest in their work". A really heavy strafe!! Then, he spotted me and said "As the Transport Officer is here I may say I have no fault to find with the Transport, and Mr. Annaheim is doing his work very well." Bow Wow!

It was great because all the officers including the CO were there.

'Apres' the 'conference' when the CO and Brigadier had

gone, we all had a drink or three. The other fellows came up and pretended to pin fictious decorations on my breast and kiss me on both cheeks "a la francaise". Then the serious drinking commenced and turned into a good – humoured 'bash' with my comrades in arms!

It is days like this that keep you sane in this Army.

Gosh, I want to go on much longer tonight and tell you loving things about our next leave time together. I want to be with you to hug you and kiss you and love you. Oh for PEACE. Goodbye darling dearest wifie. The bestest wife in the whole wide world.

I must away now Girlie, I will write more of course. Ever your loving Hubbie
Bubbie xxxx

These memories now seem all mixed up with the St. Patrick's Day 'bashes' over the years. Mother reminds me that on her side of the family we are Irish – she being the daughter of some churchman of Drogheda up in Ireland, though I've never met any of that side of the family. I have always kept it quiet from my pals, and the men.

We have a mix of RC's and Protestants in the Battalion and there are no issues as we are all fighting the cause. Right now the politics and strained feelings are showing up in the English papers and the occasional insult of "Fenians" is shouted at us across the lines.

I am proudly English; and if anyone challenges the name, I just say "Dad is naturalized Swiss and, no, we don't speak German at home!" But wherever we come from, in an Irish regiment like this, the St Paddy's Day bashes are 'days to remember'.

In fact there are two that now come flooding into my mind.

1916 on board the Cunarder, HMT Alaunia, and just out of Port Said, on our way to France. The event is a bit subdued in the Officers section, since we are trying to get to know each other, with so many new recruits to the Battalion It was where I get to know dear old Baxter, a Captain QM, who is an 'old hand', having been in India and Burma with the Battalion before the war, and one of the few who has made it back from the horrors of Gallipoli, and the butchery of the landings from the 'River Clyde'.

We become firm friends over several bottles of the 'Irish' and get massive hangovers. The men travelling in the 3rd class are terrifically noisy. Luckily, no one falls overboard! It is an introduction to the huge capacity for drink of the men of Munster! Nobody would care if the ship goes down this night! The Alaunia gets us to France, (but I read she was torpedoed and sunk later).

Of 1917, I have no memories of any 'bash' as I was in Hospital in Boulogne with Measles, and feeling very low. Dorice writes:

My very own dearest Darling Soldier Man,

No letter today beloved and I am really worried about you. Your mother rang at 2pm and said she had a telegram saying you are in hospital with measles. Poor old Bubbikins. Are the measles very horrid? I crave a daily bulletin, please do your best darling and get rest. I hope you are in a proper hospital, and if it was in England, I would be there by your bedside umps! I can't wait for a letter – the last one from you took nine days no less!

Poor Daddy, he is so busy as executor to Mr. Butcher, and has a big case coming up.

Darling, he has promised to take me to London in two days as its St. Patrick's Day. There is a Matinee concert for the 'Comfort Funds' for the good old RMF. He and I will support it, tickets are 10/6 and it starts at 2.30 pm at The New (Wyndam) Theatre. I will wear the shamrock and be a proud Royal Munster 'wife'.

The program says there will be many Lords and Ladies in attendance including the Duke and Duchess of Connaught, the Jellicoes, Lieut-Colonel Sir Herbert Miles etc etc. Famous stars will be performing including Leonard Boyne, Gladys Cooper, Charles Hawtrey, Harry Lauder and many others.

Daddy is so supportive of you my poor sick soldier boy. We are real Munster folk, and will cheer loudly for the Regiment this St. Patrick's Day.

Please, please write or send a card saying you are well as I am horribly unhappy not to have heard from you darling, but I am imagining you are being cared for in hospital. Apparently we captured Bapaume today the papers say. But I can't get interested in war news, only news of you dearest. If only the doc-man wasn't on leave he would have sent a few lines for you.

May God bless you dear Soldier Man and keep you safe and sound, and bring you back to me very soon. All my kisses and millions of hugs

Ever your very own loving and true little
Baby Wife (to be!) xxxxxxx

So much for 1917 St.Paddy's Day – in a hospital ward and miserable, but 1918 becomes a 'bash' in all senses of the word. But this time, for the men. The Regiment is awash with Shamrocks sent from the relatives in Ireland, and has itself, printed a nice card sending 'Best and Truest Wishes' which we are sending to our own loved ones from the Front.

The CO, 'Admiral' Kane, has the Adjutant 'Gestaetner' copies for the men of the poem "Bless the Shamrock".

Lt Colonel R.R. KANE D.S.O and the Officers of the 1st Battalion Royal Munster Fusiliers wish all ranks a very happy St. Patrick's Day.

God's Blessing and his Holy smile
On the emblem leaf of Erin's isle,
Our green immortal Shamrock;
From Irish Hills, though far away,
Through this bright western land we stray,
From every leaf there comes a ray
Of the golden light, of the olden day
While gazing on the Shamrock.

And may our proud and Ancient race,
Uprooted from the dwelling place,
Where grows this votive Shamrock,
Still keep this night, where'er they fly,
Sacred to memories dear and high,
Of the Land where all our kindred lie
In the Green Graves, made beauteous by
Thick verdure of the Shamrock.

God Bless the dear old spot of earth –
God Bless the Green Land of Our Birth,
Where grew this bunch of Shamrock.

Written by MILES O'REILLY in 1800 and is applicable to this date. 17. 3. 18. CO: Lt Col. R R Kane DSO.

St Patrick's Day RC church Parade is at 7am and it's the duty I hate most; marching the men miles along muddy tracks and broken roads to Villiers-Faucon RC Church, just to listen to the sanctimonious old Father going 'on and on'. Still, the men seem to appreciate, and need, their blessings.

The Battalion parade takes place at Saint Emilie at midday. My men are a credit to the Battalion and to myself today. They look smart and the animals all stand to attention and look fit. The CO says, "Well done Anna, fine turnout".

Tonight the men feast on some upgraded food and so much rum that they are almost wild with uncontrolled joy. Singing, falling over, fighting each other, upsetting the animals. It's 4am, and I must go out of my hut and stop the chaos.

It is the 'bash of all bashes' and I stop one of our corporals from slugging the sergeant! My groom is flat out in the hay bales and my servant nowhere to be seen. These Irish boys know how to enjoy themselves!

But I do trust them with my life. What they don't know is that I was one of them only four years ago! A private no less!

I return to my hut alone, and in the morning manage the animal feed myself, while the men sleep off their St Paddy's Day 'Bash'.

All these visions and sounds of laughter disappear.

No more bashes for me.

19

ADVENTURES IN RETREAT

"...we are not worrying about the coming offensive... the 2nd in Command, Nightingale, has sent home for his fly fishing rods"

Everything is misty now. No, foggy. Thick fog. Can't see a thing. I never will again of course.

This fog in my head brings a vivid flashback of times when I am scared, and endure frightening adventures that are too horrific to share with Dorice and the family. Just for my diary only.

Of course everyone expects the offensive to come early this spring; even the British press are anticipating such an onslaught.

Before it starts, I am writing to Dorice every day:

My own darling wifie.

Two ripping letters and very cheery ones too!

Your dinky postcard is exciting for me "Ain't had nobody but you". That's true darling, I like that part the best of the lot 'cause I would, being a bad un!!

We are not worrying about the "coming offensive in the west". If the Hun wants to come let him come, he will only get what it where 'the chicken got the chopper' and where the poor old rabbit will get it. The 2nd in Command, Nightingale, definitely doesn't expect it here, as the ground is so wet and there is nothing but a few desolate villages and devastation from the old Somme battle of 1916, and the blown-up leftovers from the Bosche fall-back of 1917. It is bleak, not the best to fight over again, but with occasional pretty places that seem untouched by all this. Nightingale who is sharing my hut for a few days, has sent home for his fly fishing rods!

We do get to play polo for old times sake, every afternoon – even when the odd Bosche 'plane pays us a flying visit!

It is quiet, and you can look for miles and see no human being – but there are of course thousands hidden.

I am taking no risks at all, so I will be with you shortly. Leave has not been cancelled so we have the exciting prospect of soon-to-come 'matinees' These thoughts help me sleep.

Goodnight dearest darling. May God love you and bless you. All my love, hugs cuddles, kisses and a wee 'tuddle'

Your Bubbie

As usual, the Divisional staff – the red tabs – are running around like headless chickens; sending orders to Brigade and Battalion HQ's and hours later, changing their minds with counter-orders.

All I am doing is trying to stay focused on my job; which is to get the rations, stores and light ammo up to the Line each night.

Remembering from officer school in Zeitoun where we learned about 'how to conduct a fighting withdrawl', I have been scouting-out and planning some reserve positions for dumps and transport lines that will help, should our salient be breached.

My own darling little dearest Wifie,

I had a most rotten day. Moved all my stuff – men, limbers, horses and mules miles away and then had to come back again!! Because orders were cancelled by the staff at Div HQ! Curse 'em!

My last letter to you Darling was posted by a pal in London. But I thought afterwards it might give you a shock, but you see it is much quicker that way, but I won't do it if you don't like it.

Took up the rations to the front at 9pm and got back at about 2am, so it's really been a long tiring day.

Oh yes the Bosche are going to attack all right. It's quite cheery news. We expect them any moment now. Whoops Dearie!! With tanks too!! Oooer – it's an awful war!

There's a 'elluva row going on; a sort of regular evening hate from 'Johnny Hun' but worry thee not – I will take care going up to the lines.

I wish to heavens all the hate was over, still, we are only a few months from Peace and even still closer from Leave and our next trip to Southsea. Then darling Girl we will bathe together. Of course you will look nice in a bathing costume. In fact you would look nice in nothing at all!! Girlie I am so wicked as ever I'm afraid I'm getting worsser and worsser tous-les-jours!!

Girlie I must be gone. Goodnight my beloved. God bless you. All my love, hugs and kisses.

Ever your loving but overworked Hubbie
Bubbie xx

From the forward transport lines and my hut at Villers-Faucon we are supporting our own Battalion at St Emilie. A narrow gauge railway, run by the ASC, is nearby, and the main dump very close.

The Battalion, the Brigade and, yes the 16th Irish Division are short of nothing – except trained fighting men. We have the stores and ammunition and supply dumps well stocked and the ability to resupply the men fast, but the Line is more thinly manned than is ideal.

My own dearest darling,

Cheerio!! Its so jolly cold; snowing, freezing and in the morning there's a sort of freezing mist that covers us with ice. Brrrr!

I'm afraid I missed writing the other night as the CO sent for me; result a five mile ride in pitch darkness and raining like 'ell and my little Girlie doesn't get her daily letter. So voila!

In your last letter you said; "the papers are saying the Bosche had started an offensive". How jolly interesting. I am quite near them and we are giving them 'ell but they are not doing much in reply. We will be in the show when it does start. You see the Bosche may have brought all their troops to this front after the result in Russia, but they are not used to our terrific shellfire. Well, we may have lost an ally in Russia, but of course, have gained one with the Americans.

Meanwhile the new Colonel, 'the Admiral' Kane, is a perfect topper – a bit 'enthusiastic' and has had us drilling for all our worth. He seems to like me; which is good. My men moan and groan a lot about the extra drill, but they are cheery and the animals are getting good fodder and are fit as well.

To be truthful, as I promised always to be to you, everyone does have the 'wind-up' now.

Gosh, let the Bosche attack and get on with it! It can't be much worse than standing-to all day, and nearly all night. We are totally prepared for battle, and my men and I have set up reserve lines and dumps all over the country here. The animals are fit, and DoriceII is such a trooper, she will get me through whatever is about to happen.

Still, I've just been up the line and the feeling is this is the eve of battle. The Bosche are expected to attack tomorrow!! If they do 'Gawd 'elp 'em!' The men are fighting fit, and compare favourably with some of the scrawny Bosche prisoners we've taken in the last few days. Prussian Guards they may be, but are under-fed and afraid of the Irish Regiments in front of them!

Heard that married officers are to be given preference for leave when it reopens – that'll push me up the order!

It is coming up for a year since we were married and I only know I adore you far more now than I did then, Heaven knows, I loved you absolutely then.

Goodbye My Darling Wife. God bless you and love you Girl. I have never been so happy as I have been during the past year and yet unhappy because we are not together.

Ever your adoring Hubbie
Bubbie xxxx

This waiting is frustrating and tiring, as the attack may come at any moment. The Intelligence from the Division is confusing, the orders constantly countermanded, and the staff work generally not at all helpful. Our Battalion, which is part of the 47th Brigade with the 6th Connaught Rangers and 2nd Leinsters, has been on alert since coming out of the Line. The 2nd Battalion RMF is furthest forward near Epehy, at the moment, the sharpest point of this salient.

We, meanwhile, are waiting to go up either in relief or to reinforce the Red Line/Battle Zone where the heaviest fighting is to take place. Not today though; just another round of stand-to and preparing some defences, working with the Hampshires' Pioneers.

Still we wait, so I write a last letter before 'the Race' begins:

Darling Girlie mine,

We are more than halfway through March!! I can't see leave coming much before May. Still the evenings will be quite nice and long and we can go to the Bath Boathouse and take an evening row up the river and then stroll to the bandstand and give the boys a treat!

Girlie Mine, I have been off my head with work lately. Everyone has the 'wind-up' to a frightful extent. There's a Bosche plane coming along right now, but we shan't be bombed, as we are so near their own Line, so; voila, touch wood. But it is unusually quiet – that means something's about to happen umps!

All is well after the St Paddy's Day 'bashes' and the frolics I wrote about. My men are drilled for any eventuality and are armed and alert, but the 'stand-tos' make it very tiring. I am really dozing as I write this because I have had hardly any sleep for more than a week; it's been so noisy. Tonight is quiet for a change. The animals seem restless though.

It may be the dawn of the offensive, whoops dearie!!

Goodbye my very only darling dearest Girl.

All my love, hugs, cuddles and kisses and a most exhausting tuddle

Ever Your Loving Bubbie

There have been so many freezing, misty mornings this cold 'Spring'. But, now, early morning March 21st, this, is the densest fog I have ever seen, as the Hun attacks us in brute strength, and my 'Adventures in Retreat' are just beginning.

The Huns call it 'Michael' or 'Kaiserschlacht'. But our side call it 'The March Offensive' or 'The Great Retreat', while most of us still alive, call it 'The Cross Country Race'. For that's what it has been for us in so many days in retreat. The 'Race' feels like has lasted months.

This is IT! Now it has started! Horrors, greater than I could ever imagine. An onslaught massive in extent and ferocity, aided by the densest, clammiest FOG I have ever experienced. It's thicker than a London 'pea-souper', and far deadlier.

GAS! In such density you can almost swim through it; and they are targeting us in the reserve positions. That is new.

It has started with an earth-shaking rumble. The ground is actually moving under my feet, and, it's like nothing I have come across in this awful war. Between 4.30am, and when it should get light at 9am, the shelling is like no other, just a tremendous, deafening sound, which drowns out anything from our own guns.

High explosive shells and gas shells by the hundred, with a mix of shrapnel, as well as chlorine, phosgene and mustard, are falling all around us.

The fog now is even denser, and greenish-yellow with the men struggling to get gas masks on the animals. We can see only a few yards. It is dark and poisonous. A living Hell on earth!

I make a ration-run up to the men in the daytime. Gosh, we do look thinly spread, but I give the men a few extra jars of rum to keep up spirits. The noise of the barrage is absolutely thunderous, as we calm the animals, which seem unusually restless, as they too are obviously noticing the difference from the regular 'hate'.

Our artillery are replying and our coordinates appear to be good, so the Hun shelling lessens for a while but then soon gets even more intense.

I hear from runners from the Brigades in the line, that the Forward Zone is all but gone. A runner from the 2nd Battalion tells me as he passes through to Div. HQ; "There are thousands of enemy dead in front of the wire, but our prepared redoubts have fallen".

Another reports; "We have lost hundreds today, and the number of bodies all around is worse than after the Somme in 1916. We are falling back to the Red Line".
That is our so-called 'Battle Zone'.

And now I see wounded men streaming back, hundreds of them; a pitiful sight as they are heavily wounded, and gassed to almost extinction; still carrying their rifles, but out of ammunition. They have fought like tigers, but found themselves fired on, by Huns from behind. The Bosche are going for our flanks and rear rather than their usual frontal assault. The fog is still hanging heavily around; visibility is no more than ten yards.

The Red line has fallen to a flank attack. I ride forward to the Brown Line at St Emilie, taking two limbers and eight mules with cans of water and a load of ammo boxes. I cannot risk all the transport in daylight, but understand the needs of the men in the Line. This 'Line' is just a collection of shell holes with a few loops of wire strung between. Good to see our own Artillery giving as good as we've been getting. On the way up, we pass through our own gun line, but this doesn't seem a strong defensive position. I realise this hell of shelling and devastating fire from all sides, will not suit limbers and wagons. All tracks are churned to deep mud. Only mules and the best horses will make it up, and back.

We offload the supplies and I promise more. Machine gun fire sprays us from all sides and I order the men to abandon the limbers and move out on foot from this hellish scene. Leading Dorice*II* and the men leading the other animals by their reins, we are now carrying severely wounded Irishmen slung over the animals' backs. We are trekking westwards towards the casualty clearing station.

The scene there is indescribable with many hundreds, if not thousands of wounded, laid out on the ground waiting to be transported away by ambulances and any transport that may be available. The shells are landing amongst the wounded medical orderlies and stretcher-bearers, all the time.

Arriving back at my transport lines at Villers-Faucon, I find Hun shelling is aimed directly at us here. This is extremely heavy enemy fire and we are taking casualties of men and animals. I now have had eight badly and six less badly wounded men and lost fifteen mules and horses. DoriceII is calm and unhurt, which is some small relief to me.

It's 9pm and the Bosche attacks have diminished as I go up again to the Brown Line. The men were pleased to see us with food, rum and more ammo. They were reduced in numbers and I heard many of my pals were gone. No sleep again tonight, as all is noise and smoke and shells falling all around. That makes at least five sleepless nights in a row.

The 22nd dawns, but again, we are all in a heavy fog. We are alerted to the Bosche outflanking us both left and right. Heavy fighting, but the line is still just about intact. Many more casualties are coming through and now, in the afternoon, orders are for the Division, or what remains of it, to fall back to Tincourt.

With the Huns already behind us in Roisel, I take the transport back via Longavesne to our pre-prepared transport lines, and Baxter's reserve dump at Templeux-la-Fosse. On the way Hun storm-troopers are firing at my detail with flame-throwers – they are only yards away! The nauseous smell of paraffin adds to that of the gas and explosives. And the heat and the flames actually singe us as we ride by. We gallop like never before. A really narrow escape from the flames of hell!

The battalion are digging-in just south of my position. So Baxter and I do a ration run at 7pm for the men in the new line at Tincourt Wood. It is called The Green Line, but there is nothing green here. The few men left get some hot food, as I still can use the one undamaged kitchen wagon that I have left.

I am shocked to find that our Battalion strength is reduced from thirty-four officers and 950 men to twelve officers and 450 men! In two days! The dear old doc-man Bisset has gone as well as the padre and my pals Donnelly, Shea, Boyd, Malone, and so many others killed, wounded, missing, or captured. It is just too awful to think about, as I am tired and exhausted, and gassed to some extent.

It's the 23rd and the start of day three of their Offensive. Yet it seems like a week already, such is the intensity of action. Orders are received to fall back again, to the Line Doignt/ Bussu, east of Peronne. But, as the morning mist clears, the

Bosche aeroplanes come over in force and unleash deadly mg fire on the whole front from very low level.

Flames are starting to appear on the horizon and now a huge explosion erupts as someone blows-up our main ammunition dump in the Salient. The fog has completely lifted now.

Aeroplanes are strafing us – the swine. Relentless ratatattat from their machine guns as they zoom over us at treetop height (of course there are no trees left) but our rifle pot-shots are ineffective. After about twenty minutes of Hun dominance above, our own 'planes have come over at last to drive them off.

A respite, but the intensity of the shelling increases to an ear-shattering crescendo. Shells from both sides are landing on theirs and ours in the confusion of this great battle.

We are pulling back again at the same mad dashing speed as in the old DLOY. We go via Driencourt (or what's left of it) to Clery and cross the Somme just before the bridge is blown.

In the confusion the Battalion has now become split into two different parties; me, with the CO, Adjutant, and QM, and about thirty of my men who are still with me, and the main body who seem to be with the 2nd-in-Command and Captain Nihil.

Staying south of the Somme we reach Cappy, but are still under shellfire and mg fire from behind and from the north. The Huns are streaming through and I am only about half a mile in front of their main assault troops. We hear bridges being blown, aeroplanes bombing troops, and the noise all around is absolutely deafening.

It's the 25th, and we have raced about twenty miles across country, and now find some remnants of our Battalion mixed with a few stragglers from 2nd Battalion and men from other Brigades and Divisions at Mericourt. We manage a short night – very short – as my section and I go and find food and provisions from the 36th Division supply dump at Morcourt. All this time we are under fire and bombardment.

I lose another four men – good men all – Lynch, O'leary, Fisher and Arnott. We are reduced to twenty-five men, two wagons and eighteen horses – the mules are just not fast enough to be in the 'Race' anymore.

The days roll on-no sleep; just racing westwards one step ahead of the remains of the Battalion We are spending daylight hours of the day searching for supplies of rations, and sending them forward in daytime under heavy fire, and then again, to new positions in the night. No fog now, just the confusion of a fighting retreat. Baxter and I work well together supporting the remains of 47th and 48th Brigades which are all mixed together, and are now actually beginning to hold up the Hun advance.

Today is the 27th, and I am proud of the discipline of my men and their willingness to face indescribable enfilading fire as we take up relief supplies to our held positions at Proyart. This enables a counter – attack on the Bosche by our outnumbered forces; and we actually retake two miles at Harbonnieres and Vauvillers to the south. Twenty men of my section provide seventy-five rounds each of rapid rifle fire in support of this counter-attack until we run out of bullets. It feels good to give the Huns something back after these nightmarish days!

Yes, the Transport section 1st Battalion Royal Munster Fusiliers has done well. But we are almost collapsing with fatigue and the effects of gas.

There are orders to withdraw again. This time south to Caix and ever westwards to Demuin and further still to Aubigny, where the Battalion's two groups join-up and the occasional stragglers arrive. I form a new Transport line at Blangy. We now are just five officers and 190 other ranks left of the Battalion

March has ended, and so has this 'Great Retreat', and the greatest adventure of my life. We are in comfortable billets and I can write to my Darling Dorice. How much will I tell her about these adventures in retreat? I promised to tell her everything within the censor's rules, but this has been so harrowing, I am not sure. I will share all of it with my diary, and then with Dorice's Pater when I go back on leave. Oh for leave!

I must write something to my Darling Wife, even though I am exhausted to the point of total collapse:

Darling little Wifie,

As it is the anniversary of the happiest year in my life, I have made a great effort to write a proper line after those field postcards that I tried to send everyday we were in the 'cross country race'. I remember with pride and joy, that day, the 3rd April 1917 when we became Hubbie and Wifie.

Sweetheart mine, I love you so much and adore you to such an extent, I cannot adore you and love you more than

I do at present. I worship you my own dear, dear darling.

We have had a pretty hard time since the 20th and are still roughing it. Honestly I have done my best to send a line whenever it was possible and I only hope you will realise the difficulties with which we had to contend, and love me just the same. Darling the time cannot be far away from when we shall once again be in each other's arms.

I still have the photos of you – I did not leave them in my little hut in which a swine of a Hun officer is now ensconced.

The photos have been with me everywhere and nearly got caught by the Bosche!! Very nearly, but not quite! They kept me alive, I am sure, such is the strength of my love for you.

I will try and write again tomorrow, but at present I am not with the Battalion which has suffered grievously.

I cannot hope to hear from you, but when I join up again, I shall get umpteen dear love letters.

Goodbye my Darling wifie. All my love hugs and kisses and a dinky tuddle

Your ever loving and devoted and rather worn out
Bubbie xxx

Scribbled, and written in red crayon, I find a piece of paper to scrawl another short note before I am called away by the CO, who is a few miles away at Aubigny.

Dearest Darling

Still fit and well and merry and bright. Hellishly busy!! I have had no letters lately, I will write again as soon as I settle down!

All my love Darling Sweetheart . Now for a shave, the first for weeks! And a new uniform as the old tunic was in rags – the first change for over a month!

Ever your loving and true Bubbie xxxx
Goodbye Darling little Girl

By April 6th., it seems we have, at last, held the Bosche in this, their last throw-of-the-dice. In these parts, anyway.

Our brothers in the gallant 2nd Battalion RMF lost thirty six officers and no less than 800 men during these momentous days This was during their steadfast holding of the Battle Zone on that first day, their action in the counter-attack at Proyart, and their nighttime fighting march back to Hamel.

We in the 1st Battalion, have lost nearly thirty officers (many of whom were my good pals) and nearly 600 men; killed, wounded, captured or missing during our rearguard actions, counter-attack and all our other 'Adventures in Retreat'.

Here in Blangy, I have found time to write to dear Dorice, my wife of just one year:

My own dear darling wife

A week into April, and we are AT LAST at rest!! Heavens we have a had a time since the 21st March.

I have only been able to scribble a few short letters since then and goodness knows if you got them. I'm jolly glad you got some of the field pcs, if it was only to let you know I am alive.

The Boschman has got my hut and stables now – curse him, and it was near thing he didn't get me too!! These last weeks have been the most adventurous of my short life. I have experienced nothing so stressful, and frankly, nothing so scary in all my life. But God and my good luck, and most of all, my love for you, darling, has taken care of me. I will have stories to tell you and your dear 'old man' over a quiet drop of the auld stuff! It was a cross country race and I won!

The QM, Col, 2nd in Command and myself are about all

that is left. The dear old Doc was captured with the Padre, but I believe they are both unwounded. I hope the Docman will be able to write soon. I suppose they will be sent to Hamburg or somewhere.

Many, no most, of my pals are gone, but it is not good to dwell on it. I am afraid the Munster's have been hit mighty hard. There is already talk of amalgamating or transferring us. Who knows? Time will tell Darling. The Bosche have 'shot their bolt' and it is back to quieter times, and giving it back to 'em in spades.

I received a dear loving letter today dated 1st April. It was a relief to get a note after the push had started. I will answer all your questions in my next letter.

I was bang in the middle of it all!! When there is anything doing, voila there we are! You can bet your boots. DoriceII is quite well but like all of us rather thin – she got me through it all ok.

Our polo days are over sweetheart. The Bosche used to see us playing and leave us alone until Der Tag (21 March)!! And puis… I do wish the war was over. I long to get back to the old office and then come home to you each night sweetheart mine.

By the way, I was told I looked jolly ill during and especially now, after the stunt. But unfortunately I haven't got the 'worn-out' expression necessitating home-service. In fact I look too dam well altogether! So says Kane; and he's the boss!

I have umpteen jobs to do now including my own which means working hard at clerical jobs during the evening. I ought to be doing some now really, but a letter to my darling little Wifie is much more important umps! My leave is due sweetheart mine – that's something isn't it? Won't be long now. We are in a sweet little village and I have a house to myself – oh for YOU girl!

I love and worship and cherish you Sweetheart mine.

Would that we could cuddle each other tonight. All my love. Ever your own true and loving Hubbie who loves only you
Bubbie xxxx

The 'Kaiserschlacht', has been the most harrowing of all my years in the Army. For much of the last fortnight, I have been inches away from death; having had my 'choice', courtesy of the Bosche, of; gas, shellfire, shrapnel, bombs, machine guns, 'planes gunfire, mortars, tanks and flame throwers. I choose none of these, but choose to live for Dorice, peace, and our future.

That densest of fogs is coming down again, this time it's inside my head.

After the 'Adventures in Retreat'; the end for the Hun was cast.

For me now, the end is cast right here.

Exhaustion then.

Oblivion now.

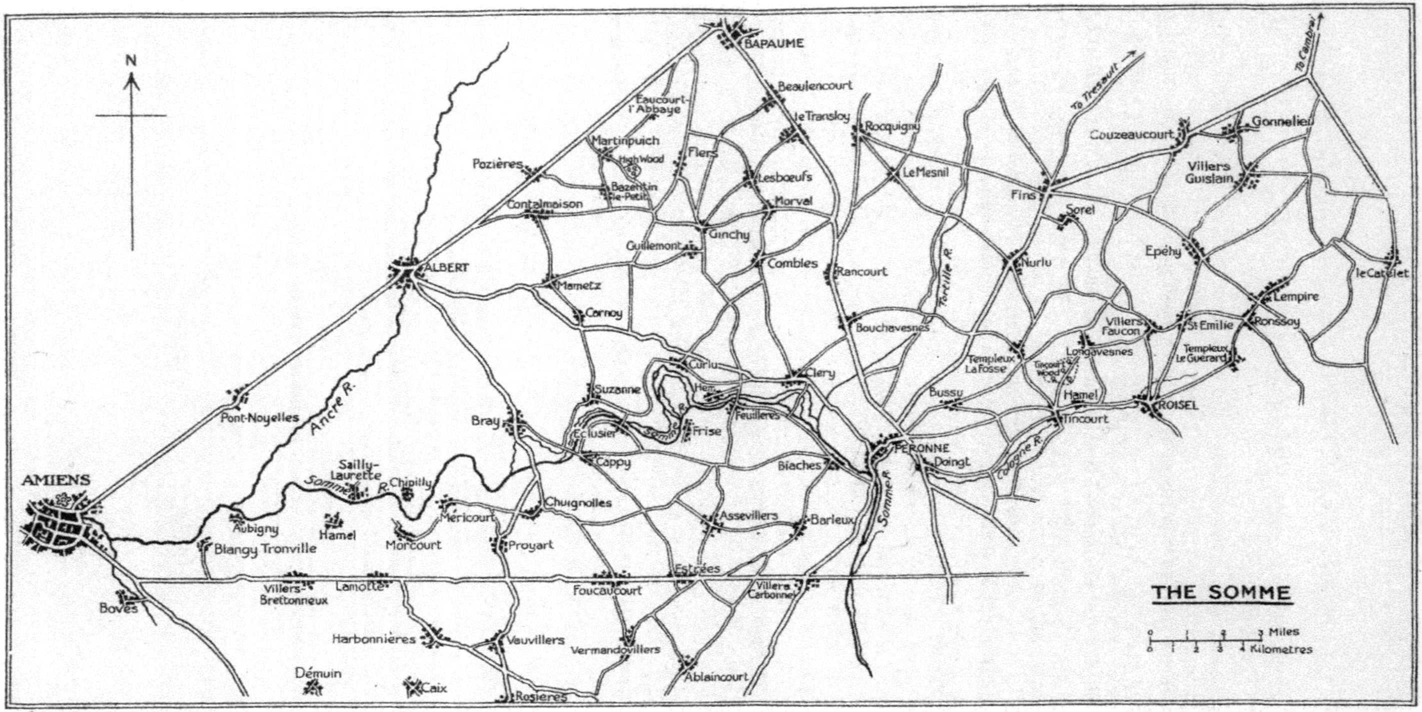
THE SOMME
N
0 1 2 3 Miles
0 1 2 3 4 Kilometres
AMIENS
BAPAUME
ALBERT
PERONNE
ROISEL
Pont-Noyelles
Ancre R.
Somme R.
Tortille R.
Cologne R.
To Cambrai
To Tresault
Pozières
Contalmaison
Martinpuich
Eaucourt-l'Abbaye
High Wood
Bazentin le-Petit
Flers
Beaulencourt
Le Transloy
Lesboeufs
Morval
Ginchy
Guillemont
Combles
Mametz
Carnoy
Rocquigny
Le Mesnil
Rancourt
Bouchavesnes
Curlu
Hem
Clery
Suzanne
Feuillères
Frise
Eclusier
Cappy
Bray
Biaches
Doingt
Bussu
Templeux La Fosse
Tincourt Wood
Tincourt
Hamel
Longavesnes
Villers Faucon
St Emilie
Templeux Le Guerard
Ronssoy
Lempire
Epéhy
le Catelet
Nurlu
Sorel
Fins
Couzeaucourt
Villers Guislain
Gonnelieu
Sailly-Laurette
Chipilly
Aubigny
Hamel
Blangy Tronville
Méricourt
Morcourt
Chuignolles
Proyart
Assevillers
Barleux
Estrées
Villers Carbonnel
Foucaucourt
Villers-Brettonneux
Lamotte
Boves
Harbonnières
Vauvillers
Vermandovillers
Ablaincourt
Démuin
Caix
Rosières
R. Mun. Fus.

20

SPORTING DAYS

"... we all know how well you can ride, but none of us knew how fast you could run"

The sound of loud cheering comes into my head. A real chorus of men shouting wildly. It must be one of those Sporting Days that have peppered my life.

I am good at sport of all kinds starting when I am quite young. At school, it is a welcome release from book learning in the classroom, and particularly those language lessons of my dear Dad!

Cricket is important at school; the boys cheer me as I score 42 as opening bat, and take 5 for 36 against Clifton College – winning play! (And, better than anything done by my big brother Eddy). I realise how sporting success makes one popular with one's pals – male and female.

I meet the lovely Katherine Freeman at the Tennis Club in 1909 where good times are had by all, with plenty of girls and old school pals like Symons. We play tennis, play the fool and generally 'lark around'.

Now, it's the noise of the weir on the Avon that is flooding through my mind, and then sound of applause all round. For me. I have just won the Rowing Challenge Cup, and there are loud cheers for me. Katherine is there, which is a bonus. We get to drink some bubbly from the cup – and I get my first proper kiss! Good Sport this!

Riding for sport is learned in the Yeomanry over the years with the Royal Gloucestershire Hussars and then the DLOY. From summer camps in Badminton to the Heliopolis Racecourse, I win cups, medals and trophies.

Playing polo with Generals, 'red tabs' and other 'staff wallahs' in France over these last three years, is said to be good for promotion prospects. Some hopes!

But it is good for the morale of the Battalion, especially as it counters all the negative stuff in the Papers about 'Fenians' and the recruitment issues in Ireland. The 16th Irish Division, and especially we Munsters, have a great record of winning Army sporting days; from boxing to the tug-o-war, and for my winning contributions with my 'four-legged friends'.

Luckily I am a natural rider, and my lovely horses, especially DoriceII and Jack, are vital to all these wins, and, all these cheers from the crowds.

With all the cheers still in my head, I am writing to my Dorice in July 1916. I am jealous of her cousin Hilgrove, or 'Hillier'. He loves Dorice from afar, but he is in the Worcesters now as a young Lieutenant in the New Army.

Dearest Darling little child,

I wonder if you are getting all my letters. You see they have to go first up to the trenches and the back.

I might get a nice little wound tonight and then some leave – would be good Dearie!

Have you heard from Hillier at all? My Darling of course I trust you and give you full permission to write to anybody or go anywhere. I wonder where young Hillier is? Far from the shells I expect and I don't blame him. There's only one thing I'm 'up against' him for and that is he told Sid Carpenter-according to Dais – that I flunked games at school.

Well I played footer and cricket for the First, and was in the Cadet Corps, but I don't ever remember seeing him on the field. He was probably in the score box marking my batting and bowling averages!

By Jove, if I ever meet him I'd make him swallow his words. Still, I feel sorry for him 'cos perhaps he loves you, but he cannot have you as you are booked! If I come across him I'll tell him so!

I don't often get cross but when I heard this, I was sore for a time.

Now let's talk about something else. I just want to tell you how much I would give to have you in my arms. I would give all I possess which isn't much! But all of it anyway. That's how I feel.

Up to the Lines again tonight, so I will sign off with all my love and waiting impatiently for my next leave.

All my Love to you Darling
Ever your own Hubbie-to-Be
Bubbie

Her cousin Hilgrove Croydon-Fowler, is actually no threat.

The chorus is still ringing in my head, as I recall scoring a try for the 47th Brigade in a match against the 48th Brigade, with hundreds of Irish fellows cheering like mad.

These cheers of the lads at Brigade and Divisional Sports mean a lot. I am popular with my officer pals and the men, because I bring so much sporting success to the Regiment. Cups and trophies add prestige and respect to the 'Dirtyshirts' from Munster. Their reputation as fierce fighters is known widely amongst the Huns, and their reputation as sporting winners is spread widely across the Army.

If I can't win a decoration in this war, then by Jove, I'm doing the best I can at all the sports.

Father doesn't really understand this need for sporting success, (because he was born in a tiny Swiss village), while the rest of the family; (Eddy, Dais, old Carpenter and of course my dear Dorice) all understand how sport plays an important role in my life.

Memories are streaking back; through cheers and hullabaloo from the thousands of men at the 'big' sporting occasions. My sporting achievements definitely 'blow away' big brother Eddy with his golf and 'what-not' in the Navy!

I have a lot of news for my young wife, Darling Dorice;

My dearest Darling little Wife,

I haven't been able to write for two days because we have been running sports. They are a great bother to get up. All the horse jumps have to be made out of absolutely nothing – "tres Difficile!!"

Well I hope to be able to send you the little cup which

the colonel gave me because I managed to win the horse jumping. The Battalion got on jolly well in all events, which were open to the whole Brigade. Both my mules came in a ½ mile race 1st and 2nd respectively. The one I call Joe was the winner.

I just lost the 100 yards for officers by 1/4yard. Really, only by a nose! Fancy me being able to run!!

Well dearest, that was very pleasing, but like all things in time of war, there was a sad side to it too.

I have lost my best pall out here. Do you remember telling you about a fellow named Male who came out from the War Office to take my job – or part of it. The fellow who gave me measles and the chap I met at Victoria on my return to France? Well, he fell off his horse at the sports and landed on his head, became unconscious and died! The chap came from Esher in Surrey apparently. Poor man, that's not a glorious end to a life, in war or peace.

The day before, his Colonel fell off his horse and broke two ribs. That was in the jumping competition that I won. So we are all rather cut up about it.

Sports are on again tomorrow, and, if you please, I have to ride twenty-four miles before the sports begin to buy the Colonel a gig.

I am jolly proud of you Girl you are the prettiest little creature under the sun, and I do love you.

Do take care on the 'osses, cos although you can ride, sometimes falls cannot be prevented and I don't want anything to happen to my precious little Baby Wife.

I was jumping all day yesterday on my old big black horse Jack. He is a perfect devil – he goes like mad at a fence and then checks and you wonder (and all the crowd watching) if he's going over at all. But he does.

I must be off now to get this to the post and perhaps your letter has arrived!

Goodbye dearest Darling All my love Sweetheart. Tons of kisses hugs and cuddles
Ever your true loving and devoted
Bubbie xxxxx

I get the cup from CO Monck-Mason at a mess dinner. He says he is proud of the Battalion's success in the Brigade sports "...and Mr. Annaheim has been exemplary in his preparations for such a successful sports" He then goes on "Well TO, we all know how well you can ride, but none of us knew how fast you can run!" The pals laugh and cheer as the CO presents me with the silver cup that has been engraved:

"Zonnebecke July1917
1st Battalion Royal Munster Fusiliers
First Prize Jumping
Lt G H Annaheim"

I send it home to Dorice for safekeeping. I wonder who will be looking at it in 100 years time?

Contact with the Divisional Staff is infrequent; as they are so far back from my Lines, and rarely visit. I do recall a real highlight of this sporting war service:

My Darling Slave and mistress!!

In answer to your last missive when you strafed me unmercifully, I must ask for your complete forgiveness. I love you and adore you, and I am so sorry I must have been in a bad mood in my last to you. I was a wee bit worried, but I can't remember why-I dunno! Could have been the gas, What what! Still it does us both good to have a little attack without a barrage occasionally umps?

Please don't get another husband. Meanwhile you shall have some chocs. I will send them to you in Torquay.

Now if I tell you what I have been doing this afternoon please don't strafe me, but rather be proud of your dear old Hubby! Bow! Wow!

Well, I was asked to play polo for the Division this afternoon. It was an honour because there are only four to a team. A General, a Colonel, a Staff Captain, and 'your 'umble' composed our team, and we won 3 goals to 1. We all played a perfectly rotten game because it was so hot and the animals were rather sluggish. DoriceII was a real star of the proceedings, lifting her feet so well and turning inside our opponents all the time. But it is rather a great thing to be invited to a team of such exalted 'red-tabs'! On the field they called me 'George' and at the end of the match we each had a swig of the General's flask of the hard stuff. Quite some memory of this awful war, and one that has made my pals quite envious, and my groom and my servant quite proud, I am sure.

I haven't forgotten sweetheart that I must take care of you, my little wife, on the next leave. I suggest we bathe together, by force if necessary. I won't lift a finger in self-defence; so voila! Not long now, sweetheart.

Don't you wish you were here now as I am about to get undressed and get into my little'bed'. Don't you wish you were here to undress me umps?!!

Goodbye dearest Darling. All my love, hugs, cuddles, kisses and tuddles are yours and only yours.God bless you and take care of us and ours

Ever your adoring Hubbie
Bubbie xxx

Dorice has written back to the last missives about my sports:

My own Dearest Darling,

Ever so many thanks for your dear love letter received this morning. I was so glad to get it Hubbie mine. Dear old Boy you say there's no real news about leave. Oh I do wish they would let you come home, cos I want you so. I have been thinking of you all day long. I love you so much that I want you frantically tonight.

My dear pal, I'm glad you played for the Divisional Polo team – Dear me! We are getting swanky to be sure. But it is also good that you can get a moments relief from all the 'doings' that go on out there, darling. I am totally proud of all your sporting achievements soldier-boy. I pray that you will keep safe and God will bring you home to me very soon.

Sent with all the love in the world and all my hugs and cuddles and tuddles.

Ever your own loving and true and adoring Wifie xxxxxxxxxx D

Exactly a year later, down in the Somme and well to the west of Arras; at St. Leger-les-Authie, we have some more Brigade and Divisional Sports Days and Horse Shows. Now, we are in the 172nd Brigade of the 57th Division – and out of the 16th Irish Division, which was smashed to pieces in the March 'Race'.

My own darling little Darling,

I am writing to you in a beautiful wood. All my transport is here and I am living in a tent, which isn't too bad. I haven't received a letter from you yet, but am dying for one to arrive soon and to know you are merry and cheery and bright. We are having Brigade sports tomorrow and Divisional sports later. I don't expect to do very much as I have been away from the preparation, but the men have worked jolly hard during my absence and we ought not to do too badly.

The Colonel has gone on leave and we are having a great time. Out of the Line of course and not caring a damn if the Bosche attacks. That's the Spirit Girlie? What what!

Everyone said how thin I looked after my leave but then it was only to be expected!! What did they mean?

Everyone here is merry and bright, as the CO is on leave – not quite so much work done, What! what!!

Oooer – there are a lot of insects crawling over me as I am writing in a wood. Girlie Mine I must be off and try and do things.

All my love darling Girl I adore you. All the hugs and kisses and one little tuddle!

Ever your loving and adoring Hubbie

Bubbie xxxxx

These sports are especially memorable as I become a bit of a hero to my men, the Battalion and literally thousands of troops.

Dear darling Wifie mine,

I have just received your dear sweet love letter which you wrote on the train. Thank you so much sweetheart. I also received the tunic and spurs OK.

We had some sports for the Brigade yesterday. Everyone thought I had won the jumping, but it turned out the Brigadier had instead. So I was second. 'Rank' and all that! No prize cup for me this year!

Of all the events which included wrestling on mules, jumping bareback with mules etc etc, our Battalion won 56 events and the other two Battalions in our Brigade, 21 and 41 respectively – not bad umps?

Oh, I did win the scurry race and my best mule the Mule jumping competition! Pity the Colonel was away. But I expect he was having some 'fun' too!

Today, in the 57th Division Sports Day, we did well again. No cup for me, BUT our Battalion got the first prize again. The Divisional General presented ME with the horse racing trophy which I won (but can't keep), and my men came third in the 'animal' race. They entered a rabbit that was beaten by a cow and a fox!! (no 'Regular' animals allowed in that race!).

With one event left (which we had to win to get the Division Trophy), it was very tense and lots of noise from the thousands of men in the crowd. It was riding a mule barebacked while leading another one over a jump and back!

You can guess how high the excitement was. Just before the start all the officers came up to me and cussed me and told me I had to win for the honour of the Battalion eh eh!! – Well, the long and short of it was I WON this last event, and we won the Divisional Cup, which the acting Colonel filled with champagne umpteen times this evening. Hence my poor attempt at a letter. I will send the Division Horse Show programme to you, as a souvenir of your Hubbie's success at the sports!

Well my own Darling, your dear photos are on my old soapbox as I write. I adore and love you with all my heart. It is raining like hell today but my tent is quite dry here inside.

God bless you Girlie mine. I send you all the love kisses and cuddles I possess.

Ever your adoring Hubbie
Goodnight my love xxx Bubbie

Two whole days before CO Kane gets back, and we are allowed a 'day-off' to celebrate the win at sports. I sleep till 12, midday. Bliss.

Probably the last sports for a year and by then the war will be over.

The cheers subside.

And now have gone.

The sports are over.

And I am gone.

57th Division

PROGRAMME

HORSE SHOW

July 21 and 22, 1918

(I.6.c. central.)

PATRON:
Lieut.-Gen. Sir G. M. Harper, K.C.B., D.S.O.

PRESIDENT:
Major-General R. W. R. Barnes, C.B., M.V.O.

VICE-PRESIDENTS:
Brig.-General J. C. Wray, C.M.G., D.S.O.
Brig.-General F. G. G. Guggisberg, C.M.G., D.S.O., R.E.
Brig.-General G. C. B. Paynter, D.S.O., S. Guards
Brig.-General F. C. Longbourne, D.S.O., R.W. Surrey Regt.

HON. SECRETARY:
Captain I. B. Jarmay, Ches. Yeo.

21

LINES AND RHYMES

"...a pair of little hearts that beat, a little effort and then – repeat!"

Crowding into my dissolving mind is a memory from eons ago. A nursery rhyme from my very earliest childhood, with Dais reciting:

"Who killed Cock Robin?"
I said the sparrow,
With my bow and arrow,
I killed Cock Robin."

Except this hit was not done with a bow and arrow!
It is a Bosche bullet flying out of the sky.

It forces an instant recall of the importance of all these rhymes, ditties, poems and songs, as well as sketches and photos, that darling Dorice and I share.

This first night at Dais and Sid Carpenter's house, she sings so many songs, with her sweet voice, and accompanies herself on the piano. Dear memories of songs and ditties;

Dearest Little Girl,
Thank you for sending me such a loving letter which arrived while I am sitting in a shell hole trying to find some shelter from the gusts of hate coming over from the Bosche.

Your sweet voice that first evening at the Carpenters' touched my heart, especially when you sang 'Because'. The words mean so much now we are in love:

"Because you come to me,
with naught save love,
and hold my hand and lift mine eyes above,
a wider world of hope and joy I see,
because you come to me!"

Darling, those words make me tearful, because at that moment I fell in love so deeply with you. I feel even more certain now, and as the other verse says:

"Because God made thee mine,
I'll cherish thee,
through light and darkness through all time to be,
and pray His love may make our love divine,
because God made thee mine!"

Be under no doubt, if I come through this awful war, I promise to 'cherish thee' because you are truly 'mine'.

You were a dear child to send me the two photos of you, but sad to tell they are only black pieces of paper, 'tho I have been peeking at them all day.

Do send me two more toned ones. Dais has the negatives of snaps of me. I will send some more 'Munster' buttons and some shamrocks in my next letter.

I cannot believe you really love me but I know that when I hear you say "I love You Bubbie", it will be absolute Heaven.

I am beginning to get very homesick.
Goodbye little darling Girlie,
I am ever your own Bubbie

Snaps and photos are of huge importance throughout this conflict;

My own darling little Girlie,

I cannot understand why you are not receiving my letters. They will turn up all together perhaps cos I have written every bloomin' day. I have read all the letters you have written to me over and over. Your last letter was short but most sweet, and jolly good of you to write to me at all.

Your snaps are simply tophole. I love them, but how I wish I was sitting beside you and not your Pater. I am going to stick them all up with the exception of the "strictly pwoah!" one. I do not see quite why it should be private, but I will respect your wishes. The doctor-man is my best pal in the Battalion and I have shown him your photo. He said as everybody says, you are much too good for me. You see Dorice, he knows me; you don't!!! I have asked him to write to you if anything happens to me – bow! wow!!

Do you know I would like you to sing in public, darling. I should be very proud of you and I don't think your voice needs 'improving' as your singing master said – he just wants more money! Your voice is so lovely that it made me cry as I have told you.

I am just off on the nightly 'run' up to the Line. If I get back early I will try and write again when I get back, but I's so tired when I get back.

All my love and one big long hug and kiss
Your very own
Bubbie

We send each other cuttings from magazines – like 'the first kiss';

Dear darling Girlie,

No trenches tonight, so a nice loving letter instead if possible, if I am not disturbed – either by a rumpus in my men, or in my animals, or by the HQ! I am so lucky that you write to me every day. It makes me realise how much I am in love with you, and also makes me homesick.

My servant comes along and says "Only one letter, shoar". But that's quite enough for me 'cos it's from my own Girlie and wifie-to-be. Don't you like the little picture I sent 'cos the Hero isn't in Khaki!! It's called "First Kiss". I am longing for the day when I shall be allowed to wear "mufti" I haven't worn it for two whole years. 'S awful dearie!

I am going to finish now darling. I love you more and more, and may the Good Lord spare me as he has done in the past, so I may cherish and love you all the rest of my life.

All my love hugs and kisses to you and you only
Ever your devoted and true 'Hubbie-to-be'
Bubbie

Dorice's drawings are often naughty (and I keep those private), and sometimes just charming;

My darling little Wifie,

No letter today!! But then two arrived yesterday so musn't grumble. Will you send me some more drawings and pictures to put up in my little hut when it is finished.

I love the dinky drawing of the ducks and the caption saying "Look Ma, I've captured a Bosche Aeroplane!" They are truly the devils in the sky; bombing us each day, and now they are over London too. 'S an awful war! But I especially love the latest picture you sent of you, Sweetheart. I think the whole of the British Army has seen it including the Brigadier and the old Colonel.

I am enclosing a cheeky picture from 'La Vie'. Would you like a black nightie like that shown Darling? I can perhaps buy one when I get back to one of the larger French towns like those starting with an "A". Marsden is an expert on this kind of shopping so no doubt will offer me his 'expertise'!! Naughty Boy!

How is the only girl in the world getting on? I am awfully busy. A friend of mine has a gramophone. He's playing 'High Jinks' now. The words I like;

"They yield their radiant bloom,
and all the balmy air is laden with rich and rare perfume.
One very little drop placed so
One tiny little whiff and – Lo!"

Gosh, fond memories of Torquay umps!? Goodbye my own sweet precious dearest darling Dorice. Girl, all my love, hugs, kisses and tuddles

From your own devoted and true
Bubbie xxxx

There is often 'entertainment' for the troops that makes them laugh but also very homesick:

My own dearest darling little Baby Wifie,

The letter I received today only took three days to come Babs. That's topping isn't it. It makes me feel that we really aren't so very away from each other after all. So sweetheart, my letters are turning up by degrees umps?! And, about time too.

I am glad you are choosing a list of songs for me. I could never understand why the 'Johnny' who wrote, "Till the Sands of the Desert turn Cold", because there's no sense in it. I was never as cold in my life as I was laying on the sand at night in Egypt. It was colder than ice.

Still, I like the words "Hot sands burning, Fire my veins with passion bold, Love, I love thee". Well, Sweetheart, That's True!

I heard "Some Night" for the first time this evening. One fellow sang it and the other was dressed as a girl, with quite a passable imitation! The men call him "Busty". The previous "Busty Murphy" was 'pipped' last year, but this 'Girl' still did a good job. Made the men laugh a lot, but probably made all of us homesick.

I was dining out tonight actually, but like a good boy came away at 10pm to write to my dear little darling Baby Wife. I want a kiss for that please!

I penned this poem some days ago, while dreaming of home and peace, and you;

"The Confession" by GHA

I have never cared for fashion
Or indulged abnormal passion,
In the hue of socks the cuts of coats and such,
I have paid scant adherence
To the ethics of appearance,
And what I've known of manners wasn't much.

But now a new horizon
Is before me; I've my eyes on
Broader, better, higher, deeper ways;
I'm reading ads for clothing
(Which till lately I'd be loathing)
And I'm shaving now at nights as well as days

I am growing quite a dandy
And am getting very handy
Finding shops where gloves and hats can be bought;
It has dawned on me that living
Has made me happier by giving
More attention to these details than I thought

You may think some Maud or Mabel
Is the reason why I'm so able
To get but 2 hours sleep each blessed night,
You may smile and say it's cupid
Makes this versifier stupid –
Well, I'm so happy to inform you that you're right!

I love you darling and adore you and worship you. Ever your own devoted and loving Hubbie
Bubbie xxxx

With all these flashbacks, I am glad there's never been a question of a "Funk":

My dearest darling Baby Girlie,

No letter for me today, better luck tomorrow. I am sitting by the fire this evening and laughing to myself over one or two funny episodes which happened on the least leave. Heaven knows, these thoughts keep me happy on such a 'quiet' evening.

How's the little Mater, and the old Pater too? I should think I absolutely remember going home from the station 'avec vous' and Dais and the children and all the "First Kisses" we had and – – oooer!! I wish I was with you again Sweetheart.

I owe Symons a retaliation for what he told you about me. Wait till I meet HIS wife! Poor Symons!

"Though I've belted him and flayed him, by the living

Gods that made him. He's a better man than I am" Do you remember that little piece in Kipling?

I love Kipling and Robert Service. The latter has written a lot of poems about this war one I like called 'Funk'. He says" There ain't no bloomin' funk funk funk" Quite right!

Later:

Girlie, I thought I had the evening to myself, but I haven't. I have just come in after being out for four hours. It's bitterly cold and my fire is out and my servant gone to bed. So do you mind if I creep into bed and try to get warm. Oh, what if you were here; we'd be warm together – fire or no fire! Well 'nuff said'

Goodnight Baby Mine. All my hugs and kisses to you Darling

Your own loving
Bubbie xxx

I steal magazines like "La Vie Parisienne, from the mess on occasions to cut out pictures and cartoons to send to Dorice. I know she wonders in awe at the fashions from 'La Vie'. They are so *'French'* and I am often sending them across in a letter. Some are quite risque, with plenty of stocking tops on display (which is why the Padre objects).

The prettiest picture is "Une Montmartroise". I pin them to the wall of my hut when there is room. Naughty! We have "The Bystander" in the Mess, and I sent Dorice one of Leutentant Oakley's famous cut outs – this one of the Transport Lines (though I take exception to the silhouette of the TO himself! Too fat!!):

Darling Little Wife of mine,

I like the sound of that! Darling I am so sorry the post is getting delayed again and they are apparently taking up to twelve days to get across. I could only write a few lines last night as there was a strafe on, and the noise was terrific and we had a 'stand to' in the early hours in case the Huns tried to attack our line. There is still a row going on – morning, noon, and night. C'est la Guerre, Darling. And yet there are lighter sides to it all.

The Brigade Lt-Colonel was riding by today and stopped me and asked "How's your wife Annaheim?" and I said "Very well thank you, Sir."

He stayed a while and looked over my horse lines in some detail. Seemed he is a good judge of 'horse-flesh', because he then praised the condition of the mounts on my lines. I was so glad the men at least were looking busy while he was with us! Bow wow!!

That reminds me; I enclosed some time ago the silhouette that Oakley did for the Bystander called "Supply". Quite good really except for the overweight TO! But the shape of old Baxter the QM is quite accurate! What! what!!

Goodbye dearest Darling and bestest wifie in the wide world. May God bless you and protect you as He is protecting me.

All my love kisses, hugs, and TUDDLES!!!
Ever your own loving Husband
Bubbie xx

In this last year, we exchange more and more poems and sketches sending them both ways:

My Own Dear Darling Wifie,

One nice long letter today. I didn't expect any to tell the truth because I had two yesterday, ooer!

Mac was perfectly right when he said you were a perfect wifie. You are, and I am always thanking God for giving you to me, and praying I may be the best husband in the world.

I have thought of a pretty little French love-song; do you know it, Sweetheart? It's quite easy to translate;

"O toi que j'ai tant aimee
Longes-tu que je t'aime encor
Et dans ton ame alarmee
Ne sens-tu pas quelque reord
Viens avec moi,si tu m'aimes
Habite dans ces deserts
Nous y vivrons pour nous memes
Oublies de tout l'univers"

C'est bon n'est ce pas ma Cherie?

I have forgotten the tune, but yes, Sweetheart, as I lie in my little hut day-dreaming of a future at Peace with just you and me a perhaps a wee 'A' to be together. Always "We will live for ourselves and forget the whole universe".

That's the spirit, and that's how I feel tonight. Goodbye my darling Baby Wife. God bless you. All my love and love, hugs, kisses, cuddles and a wee little tuddle. Ever your own true and loving

Bubbie xx

I write a poem about this last leave; every moment of which I remember with just the greatest intensity of love. I wonder if she likes it:

Dearest darling girlie and Wifie Mine,

Back with the Battalion after a sad, but smooth journey over. Sad at leaving you again. It gets harder for both of us, doesn't it umps! At the rest house in Boulogne, I had a nice cooked chicken and some vino Blanco and retired to bed to think of you Darling.

I then made up this poem about you and I on our last leave together and send with all my love.

A little kiss, a little smile, a handclasp every little while.
A little whisper in the ear, that no one else can hear.
A scribbled note, a little date to meet you when the hour
is late.
A little room in some hotel – a little promise not to tell.
A little dinner first for two, a little drink when we are through.

A little squeezing in a chair, a little toying with her hair.
A little bedroom all in white, a curtain to shut out the light.
A little blouse that's laid aside, a little breast that tries
to hide.
A little skirt laid on a chair, a little scent of underwear that
comes off with a little teasing, and shows a noble form
most pleasing.

A little form of youthful grace, a little blush that floods
her face.
A little bed all cool and white, a little shading of the light.
A little nightie mostly lace, more kisses and a slight embrace.
A little wrestling in the gloom, a deep sigh – – – in a
quiet room.
A pair of little hearts that beat, a little effort and – – repeat!

A little bite or maybe two, a little snuggling up to you.
A little sleep till half past four, a little yearning for
some more.
Another little sleep and then in bed till nine or ten.
A little kissing whilst we dress, a cigarette and a caress.
A little stealing down the stair, a little secret we can share.

(Some girl is mine!)

Darling do you think it is as you remember us at Parkfield in Torquay? We were more gentle there. No more; "you're hurting me Bubbie". Just the warmest times of a couple making love, Sweetheart.

Every time we have to say Goodbye at GWR Bath Station, it gets harder to say what I think and I feel. But this time it was especially so. But it was a loving leave Girlie wasn't it? The war will be over before long and then we shall be together forever. And with a wee "A" or two. What! what!!

All my love Sweetheart. I will write again when I get back to the Battalion

All my love, kisses and hugs and cuddles and tuddles too.

Ever your devoted and true Hubbie
Your Bubbie xxx

Right now as all these 'lines and rhymes' dissolve in the mists of a time so short, I remember Dais reading "Who killed Cock Robin?" to me in the nursery. Except it's now so different:

Who killed George Annaheim?
It was I said the Bosche
Flying my Albatros.
"I did it with my machine gun"
Said that damned Hun in the sun.

Who saw him die?
"I" said Major Guy.
"Me too", said the old QM
Not just a pal; he was a gem.
"We saw him die".

Where will he rest?
Near Cambrai – to the west.
Then poor Dorice will hear
It's the end of the line,
For her own 'Bubbie'; George Annaheim.

That is ME.

D.A.
Heard at the
Ma, I've
a German

22

LAST DAYS

"In this stunt, I am afraid that we have had a bad knocking about"

Talk about time going-by, really fast!

Flashbacks of my life have come and gone in an instant. Yet these memories of last days of my life seem as fresh as ever. I am completely 'worn out'! I feel absolutely shredded of most thoughts and feelings – other than those for my Darling Dorice.

It is early September 1918, and we are starting an attack on the Drocourt-Queant line, west of Hendecourt. We are moving eastwards towards Cambrai, and for the next thirty days the 1st Battalion Royal Munster Fusiliers as part of the 57th Division keep advancing. Staying right in the thick of it. But, losing pals, men and animals.

Now Me.

Now, I am writing to Dorice from my tent near Riencourt:

Darling little sweetheart,
It's perfectly topping as we have a real war at last and we

are advancing – that's the spirit! We today caught Bosche dismounted cavalry, which shows just hard up he must be. As a former cavalryman myself, I relate of course to these prisoners, but found them hungry and disillusioned with Kaiser Bill, the Crown Prince and all their officers. Bow wow! I used a bit of my 'deutsch sprechen', taught by Dad at old King Eddie's, and they said they were short of decent horses after this long war.

With more open warfare coming along, cavalry might be needed, but today tanks are the thing, (though they were late in arriving as we started this stunt).

We are now into the Hindenburg Line and have orders to proceed forward, which will be the stuff to give 'em!

Major Nightingale and I are together in a tent, which we have dug down a few feet as the Bosche have a habit of bombing transport lines these days. But a foot or two below the ground level and we are perfectly safe.

Well darling we're winning. To cut a long story short; by Xmas I will be home in your arms.

Just now I am called away but here's a fiver to get going with the cot and things. I am going slow with the "spondulex" so will send more for you to buy a winter coat to make you happy darling.

Goodbye dearest sweetheart I'm off to work.

I love U

Bubbie xxx

And now:

My own dearest darling,

I had to finish my last letter in a hurry as the Bosche were dropping bombs nearby and then some orders came along that kept me up all night. Thus the letter ended abruptly!! A battle is in progress, so please forgive me dearest.

I was up at Battalion last night, and unfortunately we have lost several officers including my Pals Carrigan and Shaw, and I have lost one man and four horses. The Battalion is again right up front where we are pushing the Bosche and their artillery eastwards at quite a rate, but we, once more, have suffered many losses in our men. The evil Huns are losing more though. We are moving forward still, through the H Line and ever closer to the END!

Right now I am literally dead-beat, but things are going to get better umps. And leave will come soon. We go back for rest and training and reequipping tomorrow.

Goodbye dearest Darling little wifie. I adore you and love you. God Bless you and take care of us all – you, me, and the wee one to come.

Ever your adoring Hubbie
Bubbie xx Goodnight my love

Back for refitting at 'Tunnel Trench' behind Hendecourt, which the Battalion took in the attack over a year ago, and which then was soon lost to the Bosche. This is a godforsaken country, bleak and like nothing can possibly live here.

As I go for a long ride with Baxter, we reach the Transport lines we built in November 1917. My little hut is still here but the QM's is blown-up, as are all the stables. Total devastation of what must have been once peaceful countryside.

I feel quite fit again in this 'rest' period and I tell Dorice:

My darling Wifie,

I have two dear letters from you to answer. I try to write my letters during the day now as the accursed Bosche comes over every night and tries to blow us sky high! I had a terrible nightmare last night – I was home on leave and as evening came on I had to go away and wasn't allowed to sleep with my little Wifie!!! It was terrible!

I almost always seem to be in the middle of everything that's going on out here. Still I suppose it's the right spirit. Gosh, we do see life. What! what!!

The Colonel and Marsden have been having a rest behind my wagon lines. They have gone off together today. I couldn't go, as I am much too busy. Well, the jolly old 'ossies are all looking very well in spite of the fact that water is so scarce. I feel much better since it has been practically impossible to obtain whiskey. I am 'TT' again. Quite a new man in fact!!

Leave for officers, is going rather slowly – there are so few officers left, but the men are going, some after more than a year out here. Marsden says he won't be home till December, but the Colonel says it doesn't matter; in fact it will be much nicer because the nights will be longer!!!?!! What on earth does he mean??!!

It's jolly cold now; I was up this morning at 2.30 to watch a Bosche plane bang over my tent. Whoops Dearie!! No bombing tonight luckily, 'cos it's too windy. Well little Girl this isn't a very good attempt at a letter. Umps?

Keep fit and well Darling. God Bless you and may he take care of us all.

All my love, hugs and cuddles and kisses
Ever your adoring Hubbie
Bubbie xx

Late September, and we have moved up to Lagnicourt, where I am working like a slave; day and night for days on end. With many of my men still on leave, I am getting help from the Pioneers, and we have built a new line for my animals and limbers.

Something big is about to happen in front of me and the Colonel is thirsting for more action now we are deep into the Hindenburg Line:

Dearest Darling Wifie,

We have moved forward again and we are again under 24 hours notice to move. We are about twenty officers and strength in men of about 500, which is quite good at this stage of the 'proceedings'. Soon the Bosche will be going home and Peace will come.

I have really forgotten what a peaceful life will be like. Only that I live for it, with you and 'ours' perhaps in a quiet place. I dream of us and our kiddums, living in a cottage near my bank branch, somewhere very pretty and rural.

I haven't heard from Dais since they returned to Bath. I hope Girlie you will go round occasionally because Dais is really a jolly good Pal when you know her properly. It is sweet of you to send any letter you may write to Marsden via me. I can trust you Sweetheart Mine as you can trust me.

I wrote a sympathy letter to cousin Dorothy telling her how grieved I was on hearing of Bill's Death.

I must tell you though that if I grieved over all the fellows who have gone west in this Battalion since I have been with them, then life would not be worth living. I was only two miles away from where Bill met his end. I will endeavor to ride over there and take a picture of his resting place, and send it to cousin Dorothy.

Darling Girlie, it is only because of you and our wee-one-to-be, that I am spared.

Your sweet little photo is on my table in front of me, but now it's time to bundle everything up as we will be moving forward – out of this very damp shell hole and tent!

Well my Darling it's time to be off and do my work. I

promise I will take care of myself. God Bless you and take care of all of us

Ever your adoring Hubbie

Your Bubbie xx Goodnight my LOVE

In front of us is the Canal-du-Nord; which is in fact a trench about fifty feet deep with steep banks. It is nearly a hundred feet wide, and has no water. A good defensive part of the Hindenburg Line, yet, even though it is full of wire and obstacles, it has to be crossed.

Colonel Kane with a few men from Z Company, go across near Moeuvres, where there is a rudimentary wooden lock still intact. Kane is as brave as his famous uncle. He returns to Battalion HQ with twenty German prisoners caught cowering in a dugout. He orders the Battalion across the Canal towards Graincourt, using the same wooden 'bridge'. Difficult for me and my men, the animals and limbers – causing great exertions!

All this is another brave chapter in the Royal Munster Fusiliers' history. It will, as usual, go unreported, since any 'Irish stunts and deeds' seem to be left out of all newspaper reports, while those of the Guards and Canadian Divisions seem to win all the praise. I am proud of the 'Admiral' and later I share a brandy with him.

As we move forward towards Cantaing, we in the 57th Division, are sharing the advance with the 63rd Naval Division, fighting through the Bosche lines under murderous shellfire – Huns', as well as from our own artillery. Again, we sustain severe casualties in officers and men including three more of my pals.

We are now approaching the next Canal – the St Quentin. So I set up my transport lines behind a rise to the west of the village of Proville and this water-filled canal. This is definitely not a great spot, as the Bosche shells are targetting us directly, with shrapnel and gas. But then nowhere around here is really 'safe' from the constant strafing by day and bombing by night.

Finding the Companies to bring them up their rations, is the most difficult and even more dangerous for me and my men than it was in the 'Great Race' back in March. And I am tired; dog-tired; having not slept for what seems like a month or more. Oh for peace!

My own dearest darling little wifie,

On the field of battle I write to thee!! What what! Sweetheart a letter arrived for me this morning and cheered me up no end. Thank you darling for being so constant with your letters – they just keep me alive and cheery.

A battle is raging all around me, and the auld Bosche are certainly getting it in the neck. You can understand how dead-beat I am, only having had about two hours sleep during – Heavens – the last 15 days at least. Forgive me darling for not writing for a few days and for such a short one today.

Did you hear from Dais or Mother that brother Eddy has been sent to the North America & West Indies Station as a Paymaster Captain – lucky for some!!

I am well and happy Girlie but-oh-so-dead-tired.

I will try and write again this evening, but it is rather difficult out here.

All my love, hugs cuddles and kisses.

Ever your true adoring Hubbie

Bubbie xxxx

With the mess now made-up in the grandstand (or what's left of it) of the old Cambrai Racecourse, there is now some sanctuary from the hell that is taking place all around. I have found a little time to sit and read three letters that arrive from my darling Dorice, even though they have taken up to eight days to reach me.

Scribbling a reply on this, the last day of September, I try to stay positive, despite my tiredness, and the rage that is this war:

My own Dearest Darling,

Your letters are wonderful and make me long for leave, and I'm probably due six months leave after these 4 years of war. Six months leave however in our Battalion seems jolly unlucky.

Only three officers have had six months leave and they have all "gone west". One fellow was accidentally run over by a motor lorry. So little Girl let us just hope for a month when you want me, and when the wee kiddums arrives, and everything in the garden will be lovely umps?!

Isn't it cheery news about the Bulgarians? It must be jolly nice out there now. A little Peace all on their 'ownio'.

I am jolly proud of you 'little misses' for being so merry and bright during these troublesome times.

I have seen the list of officer casualties tonight. We have had four killed and nine wounded during the last four days. The 'stunts' just go on each day and night, whether we are in the line or at 'rest'. We are now sure it will be Peace by Xmas – Bonski.

On a different note; Marsden is due back today. I had a letter from him. He said he had better things to do than write to me!! Rita is the name of his girl and he says she is feeling rather tired and looking a bit pale at present!! It was certainly jolly good of him to worry about sending you flowers.

Girlie mine you musn't worry to send me long letters, at any rate when you are tired and have a cold. Just write a line to say you still love me!! (as if I didn't know!).

Take care of your dear wee self as I am trying to do. May God take care of us and ours.

I adore you my dearest sweetest darling wife.

Ever your own true and adoring Hubbie

Bubbie xx

Goodbye my dearest Beloved

On this day, I hear the news that the Colonel has been badly wounded while up with the men hand-to-hand fighting, in the outskirts of Cambrai. Other officers and pals are wounded and we are losing many men to strong concrete machine gun emplacements around the town.

My transport line is suffering heavy shelling, with some casualties to the animals, but, thank heavens, at least today, my men have come through it all. Ration 'runs' are now almost constant; up to the remains of the Companies in La Folie Wood, where there is no shelter from the strafing coming from the east. The Bosche machine gunners never seem to run out of fight, or ammo, even though they are being constantly blasted by our artillery.

The end MUST be near.

I start a letter to my mother and father on Army issue notebook paper, but I get no further than:

Dearest Mother and Dad,

It seems I am running out of time. But enough time now to write to Dorice, just as I feel my own time is running out:

Dearest darling little girl,

Apparently, it's now October, and a month nearer the end of this war sweetheart mine. There have been so many officer casualties that Baxter's and my turn for leave will soon be round again. I certainly ought to be home before Christmas!!!

I'm sorry to say the Colonel was wounded rather badly, and I have now just seen a telegram saying that he died at the clearing station. What a man! He inspired us all with his attitude to this war, and always supported me in my duties. It's a great pity, but it is to be expected in a great war like this. S'an awful war!

Marsden arrived back, and is in temporary command until the Major Nightingale comes up from Div. HQ. In this 'stunt', that will probably be called the "Battle of the Canals", I am afraid that, while all our objectives have been achieved, we have had a bad knocking about.

Everyone has worked magnificently. We had canals to cross and rivers too, and the Engineers worked day and night on bridges, which were blown up as soon as they were completed. I used to canter over those ruddy bridges!!

Girlie mine I am longing to see you again. It certainly won't be long before I am home again. I couldn't manage a 'Blighty', although I was dam near it sometimes. Also my place is here for the victory, and supporting my pal Marsden right now.

Goodbye little Girl. All my love, hugs and cuddles and kisses. God Bless you and take care of you as he has taken care of me.

Ever your adoring Hubbie
Bubbie xxxxxx
Goodbye Beloved

Resting in 'La Folie Wood', the Battalion now is reduced to only ten officers and about two hundred men. For the men, finding shelter from falling shells is difficult, if not virtually impossible. There is no 'wood'; just shell holes, wire, remains of Bosche defenses, and dead bodies of ours and theirs, laying in grotesque juxtapositions. This is no 'Folly'!

Water is very scarce, gas is all around, and we are about as knocked-about as we have ever been. I am up at the 'mess' with Nightingale, Marsden, Baxter and the few officers left, as I write this; the LAST letter it seems I will ever write in my life:

3-10-18
Darling Girl,

Thanks so much for the dear old letter received today. You were clearly very cheery Girlie mine in spite of that bad cold Are you really feeling better now my darling. It is sweet of you to say "never mind about March, we'll trust to luck if you will be home then". That's the spirit Girlie. The war will be over by then. I'm sure. Really and truly. Sweetheart, I'll soon be home because there are only about a dozen officers in the Battalion and several of these have been home on leave later than I, so cheerio Dorice Girl. I'll do my best to get home about Xmas and try for a month.

My Darling I don't mind if the whole world knows that my little wife is soon to be a wee mother, but I am not going to tell anyone, and especially not my mother, Dais or any other relation.

I'm very, VERY happy Girlie because we are going to have a wee kiddie. HE or SHE – I shall love it. Any day the wee cot will turn up. Hooray!!

Marsden was very pleased that you wrote to him. He had a perfectly glorious leave despite the rain, perhaps he was studying the colour of the ceiling!!

One thing sweetheart; I would like you to send me some

baccy from the place in the corridor in Bath – 8/9 ozs per month. Please try to tell them it should be duty free. I don't want any flannels just yet. I'll wait till the weather gets colder still. Thank you Sweetheart.

We seem to be at a standstill where we are at present. My transport is bang on the skyline but thank heavens the Bosche hasn't got many shells in this area to waste on transport lines. Let me know if you if you want any more cash Girlie.

I never seem to tell you how much I love you and adore you Girl. I long and yearn to hold you in my arms again, but I shall have to take great care of YOU Sweetheart mine on this leave shan't I?

I am thrilled you said your 'Docman' Williams told you that all is well with you and the wee 'A' on the way. We shall make great parents won't we?! March is only just over five short months away.

How's the wee Mater? I would so like to write a little line, will you give her a wee portion of my great love for you, and I do hope the Auld Man is merry and bright. Tell him that I was asking if he sings, "pack up your troubles etc" every morning. And he should "Smile, smile, smile". He will be a marvelous 'grandpapa'!

Girlie, I must be off now to try and get a little sleep. I haven't had my clothes off for over a month, but as long as I have a bath before I come home, there won't be any harm done, will there Girl?

Goodnight my dearest darling little wifie. I adore you and worship you. God Bless you and love you and take care of YOU, I and OURS, so that we may be happy when this war is over.

All my love Darling Girl. All the hugs, cuddles, kisses and "tuddles" I possess.

Ever your own true and adoring Hubbie.

Bubbikins xxx

Goodnight Dearest I wish I was with you right now!!
Good morning Girlie Mine. I will write again later
XXXX

This morning, the fourth of October, so the men tell me, I am up at the 'mess' again, with Nightingale and Baxter, watching a lively aerial battle, right overhead. We are just west of Cambrai, which we can see burning just a couple of miles away to the east.

There are about forty planes zooming around each other with the chatter of their machine guns the dominant noise all around our heads.

Suddenly; silence. Just blackness.

The end.

MY end.

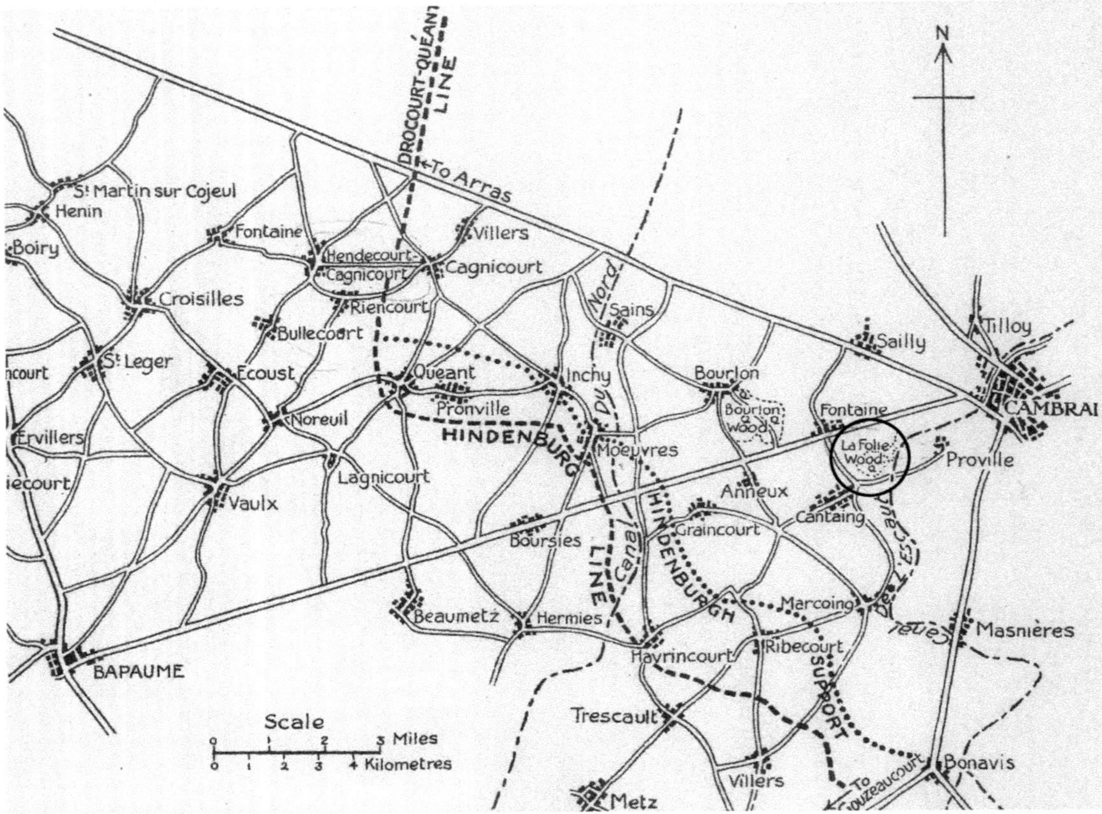
N
DROCOURT-QUÉANT LINE
←To Arras
St Martin sur Cojeul
Henin
Boiry
Fontaine
Hendecourt-Cagnicourt
Cagnicourt
Villers
Croisilles
Riencourt
Bullecourt
St Leger
Ecoust
Queant
Pronville
Noreuil
Ervillers
Lagnicourt
Vaulx
BAPAUME
Beaumetz
Hermies
Boursies
HINDENBURG LINE
Inchy
Sains
Nord
Du
Canal
Moeuvres
Bourlon
Bourlon Wood
Anneux
Graincourt
HINDENBURGH
SUPPORT
Havrincourt
Ribecourt
Marcoing
Trescault
Villers
Metz
Fontaine
La Folie Wood
Cantaing
De L'Escaut
Canal
Sailly
Tilloy
CAMBRAI
Proville
Masnières
Bonavis
To Gouzeaucourt
Scale
0 1 2 3 Miles
0 1 2 3 4 Kilometres

23

LOVE, NOT WAR

"Oh, Dorice, where are you now?"

Suddenly, I am tasting the unique sweetness of kisses. Is that possible after such an explosion in my head?

Was this life worth it all? So much for the sacrifice of all my future prospects, to a war that never seems to end.

Except, it is ending for me now.

Another sudden flashback of how it all started; such an adventure. Off to Egypt; with bands playing and with my pals, like Marsden. We are privates and WAR is THE thing. NOT LOVE.

Life is changing, and so gradually, are my life's priorities.

'Escapades' are fun, and may possibly last for years out here in Egypt. So on the journey out, I write to Katherine Freeman telling her "au revoir", as "WAR comes BEFORE LOVE".

I really do believe it.

Four years later, with these last thoughts, I realise that 'LOVE, NOT WAR' has become THE most important thing of all in my life. A life, which like for so many of my pals, is over.

Too soon.

What is left for Darling Dorice? A box of letters and photos, a few poems, a wee 'A' of course, and, hopefully, some eternal memories of a deep and true love.

Powerful flashbacks again.

We have just met, and the realization is dawning:

My own little darling Girl.

So you are not feeling bright and cheery sweetheart mine. You musn't get "fed-up" Girlie it's not the best spirit although I confess I often get fed up out here.

Last night I was awake all the time. My old hut was nearly blown down; first by a Bosche 12inch shell and then by a huge gust of cold wind. C'est la Guerre sweetheart!

I need to add a few tender thoughts, as the old Docman would say to me. Well Dearie I am still hopelessly and helplessly in love with you and long for the day when we will fall into each other's arms. Although it may be "unbecoming", for an officer and a gentleman.

Still LOVE FIRST, and EVERYTHING ELSE LATER.

That's the spirit from now on. Since I first met you I have had to rethink what is and what is not important to me. And, although this bloomin' War needs to be won, my place is here. My priorities for my life are now; you, you, you!!

Goodnight Sweetest Little one.

After our wedding the feeling of love is ever stronger:

My own precious little Darling.

Just a teeny weeny little note tonight because I have been busy for the last two days. It's only 11.30pm but I am jolly tired and fearfully cold when I turn-in, but I shall soon get warm. I wish I could turn in with you, Sweeetheart Mine. Après la guerre (you must be sick of that phrase), we will never part even for one single night and we'll always sleep together. Always Dearest!

There was no mail for me today. Your dear letters turn up two at a time and it is simply great when they do arrive.

The blooming war never ceases; with plenty of 'hate' going on outside so and I'm now off to my 'sanctum'. Well it's a hut – s'nice. Bow Wow!

I read your cheery letters with great joy and love in the 'quietness' of the hut. And of course, at least I have 16 pictures of you darling to keep me company here.

Tonight I muse on my dear dear love for you and so the 'job' can go to H–!

Girlie I do so want a decoration. Hundreds of fellows have all sorts of medals and distinctions and your own old Hubbie has nix.

If there was no YOU Girlie, I would volunteer for a raid which is about to take place. But I want to come back safe and sound to you my sweetheart, so I won't do it.

Tonight I am a bit 'down'. It might be the little 'gassing' I got the other night. So I asked Baxter to do the run with the rations tonight.

That's the wrong spirit I suppose but 'LOVE COMES BEFORE WAR!' Especially after three long years of it!

Goodbye my own dearest sweetest prettiest Darling. May God Bless you and take care of both of us so that we may share the rest of our days in Peace and happiness.

With my deepest love to you Sweetheart, and Kind regards to the little Mater and Pater.
Ever your loving Husband
Bubbie
Goodnight my Darling
(Oh, I'm half asleep)

In this, the last year of the war, I am starting to think about all this, much more deeply; as I lose so many pals and suffer the horrors and hate in the 'adventures' that are the 'Great Retreat'.

While we hold-on during the 'last-gasp' of the Bosche, I have time to reflect. So, I have decided to write some 'final' letters and give them to Baxter 'just in case'.

'S an awful war'; a kind of ugly comedy at times, but with plenty of tragedy included. I realise that human life is the most precious thing of all. But out here, it seems the war takes the best; as the casualty lists show.

For me it's not so much the fear of death – I'm still not afraid for myself to die – I am afraid of the sadness I will leave behind.

Out here; I am twenty six, look like forty, and sometimes feel, well; sixty! To have survived out here for so long, I have always worked on the principal that 'discretion is sometimes the better part of valour', but often it's about ninety percent. The other ten percent might be sheer luck; whatever steps you may take to stay alive. What has changed for me in this time?

Dorice, of course. I live to be with her, as I write and try and express this:

My dearest darling precious wifie,

Such a nice long loving letter today. I did love it because there was no mail yesterday.

So you love my letters when I write as if I'm talking to you. Well darling I really don't know what sort of letters those are. Sometimes I don't feel in the right sort of mood for writing at all – I worked out that it is usually after a 'stunt', or when I have lost a pal, or when I have been gassed. THAT seems to depress me, and others too.

Anyway, at other times I open the writing pad and just go into a kind of dream. Then, consequently you get a very short love letter.

Tonight like so often, I am alone in my hut ready to brave the 'run' up to the Line. It's rather unhealthy up here with shells flying over us – in both directions.

And there's a strong whiff of gas in the air. To top it all there's quite a bright moon so it will all be quite exciting when the Transport Sergeant tells me; 'Time to go soarh".

Don't worry Darling, 'cos I feel God has looked after me all this time; and our destiny, Girlie mine, is to be together when peace comes. I take especial care these days for you, and for US.

I have worked out that life must have a reason, but Darling YOU are my reason.

Dearest, I must finish now. Back to this WAR, but it's never beaten by my LOVE.

All my hugs, kisses, cuddles and one long tuddle
Ever your own
Bubbie
Goodnight Dearest xx

My letters now contain more and more, about the joys of my LOVE, and less about this damned WAR, which just rolls on and on, month after month; beyond it's fourth year.

In this time, love has taken many forms for me.

Firstly; for my parents, whom, of course, I have loved throughout my whole life. It was not an easy childhood, as I was always in the shadow of big brother Eddy and all his successes

Dais has been my confidante during all these years, and 'kept-the-peace' between Mother and Dad and I. Father was strict; I suppose because until 1900 he was still a Swiss citizen.' I admire him for studying hard, becoming a Professor, and bringing-up his children in England with decent schooling. He is a good and honourable teacher, if rather stern. I think that the presence of LOVE defines a good teacher, and I have realised, maybe a bit late, that in his rather formal way, he loves me too.

My dear Mother always has treated me like a baby, I suppose because I am the youngest, and turned-up quite late for her. Her attitude to Dorice has been remarkably inconsistent since we met in those 'first meetings'. She has never been hostile, but often has said the most inappropriate of things to Dorice, which has upset her several times in the last three years.

For all that, they are my only parents, and have put up with me all these years. Love does seem enduring, despite all the forces that might have opposed it.

So, in my 'what if' letter, that Baxter will soon send, I tried to show my love for them both. It is the best I can do, after these hellish times that I am having during my most grueling weeks of 'this awful war'.

It's all finished for me, but my love will last, as it overrides everything, including this war.

My darling Dorice will get this 'what if" letter very soon, and also that poem I wrote to her back in April, when I felt death's hand on my shoulder:

20/4/1918 BEF France
My only dearest darling wifie Dorice,

I hope you will never get to see this letter, but I have given it to Baxter to get to you if anything bad has happened to me.

I have always been an optimist – things have always worked out for me. This is 'just in case'.

I am writing this 'at rest', miles behind the lines after one of the most difficult times of my life. 'S an awful war.

I am having a quiet time, and feeling deeply loving and thoughtful too. You see, despite my optimistic nature, the last couple of weeks have brought me as close as I've felt to despair, and possibly death.

Yet, I did come through; as only one of five officers and about two hundred men who today are left from the Battalion

I lost many pals including the doc-man and others of whom you would have heard. It has been very hard.

We have known each other since May 1916 and have been married for just over one year, and I must tell you these have been the happiest times of my life. I utterly adore you. And, if you do get to read this letter, you must NEVER EVER have any doubts about that.

We've only spent less than a month actually in each other's arms, but your loving letters have kept me going through some of the most difficult of times-especially the last few weeks. You and God, and good luck have looked after me up to now. But if you are reading this, then my luck has just run out.

Darling, I know how desperately sad you will be after all

the hopes and dreams we have made together. But do not spend too long grieving. Cherish all the wonderful days we have spent together – just as I do.

All my memories are cheery darling Dorice; memories of our meeting, courting and our marriage, and our 'first time' in Torquay as well as our special loving 'matinees' in SP and BP. I carry with me glorious memories of our passionate honeymoons in Southsea. Our exquisite love-making in the afternoons often come to mind. It was always perfection.

I am not writing this to be remembered by the world at large, but by my only truest love in all the world; you, Darling Wife.

Memories flow backwards, like a river in reverse. But, I pray that you will you hold on to the memories of us together, and never let them dry-up completely.

I also know that time will dim the pain of it all; since time is like a bullet out here; it travels forwards, and in one direction only.

So I also pray that you will move forwards with your life, keep singing; your voice is enchanting. You are a beautiful caring little girl and deserve only the best that life can bring after this awful war is over.

So now 'what if' has happened, and I am gone, then your wonderful parents – the little Mater and the dear 'old man' – will never let you down in your time of need.

I am sure my dear sister Dais, old Eddy and my parents will carry on loving you.

Now look here darling; if 'the deed has been done', and a miracle has happened, so that a wee kiddums has, or is, arriving for you, then I want you to know that all the love we share will also be transferred to a 'wee A'. I desperately want you to be a happy and fulfilled Girlie, so be in no doubt at all dearest, that I did always want a wee family to bring up as another 'Anna'. It would make me so proud of you, and us, darling.

It makes me cry writing this, but I wanted, however poorly, to share my deepest thoughts with you and hope this letter will help you remember your own devoted husband and 'soldier-boy', Bubbie.

Over this last year I have realised that LOVE, NOT WAR is the thing.

Darling, you and I have loved each other as deeply as it is possible for two people to love. God brought us together and allowed us to share something very sacred and holy. I believe He will care for you just as I have tried to do.

We WILL meet again as it is God's will.

I am so sorry to go.

Goodbye Darling Dorice Mine

Your Own Bubbie xxxxxxxxxxxxx

In this melancholy mood, I penned this poem, which contains these very last thoughts to you darling. I also sorry for all this, and I hope you never see all these words in this 'what if' letter or read this poem.

(Written 20/4/18 and enclosed with 'what-if' letter via Baxter)

OH DORICE – WHERE ARE YOU NOW??

I heard your charming laughter, on that brief warm summer night,
And loved your sweet singing, your eyes were ever bright.
We motored around with family, oh what blissful summer days,
And kissed in the seaside shelter, where you set my heart ablaze.
I journeyed back to war, to do my duty at the time,
My thoughts of your dear sweetness, helped dismiss the mud and grime.

My leaves were just so topping, as we deeply fell in love,
Two hearts entwined together, with all the mysteries from above.

Oh Dorice – where are you now??

We went upstairs together, your hand inside my own.
And started on a journey that meant we'd never be alone.
I explored the contours your body, while you lay upon my lap.
Your curves and trenches seemed just like the lines upon my map.
Your ease of surrender, towards my yearning lips,
As our bodies came together, around our aching hips.
The sweetness of your kisses, remain with me so long,
The burning of our passion, that has become so deep and strong.

Oh Dorice – where are you now??

It seems like only yesterday we swore that we'd be true,
Our wedding day was joyful, at the Beach Hotel we knew,
Life together would always be filled with greatest joy and cheer,
We were shy with our matinees, but love just overcame our fear.
Two hearts loudly beating, so perfectly in synch,
Our very first honeymoon, just seemed to go in a blink.
The journey back to France, gave me time to dream and reflect,
On each and every moment, that I adored, and was so perfect.

Oh Dorice – where are you now ??

Your letters have filled my evenings, I have savoured every one,
Your words of love and comfort, were always shining like the sun.
The Boscheman couldn't catch me, as I rode towards the Line,
As the shells fell around me, I believed all the luck was mine.
The gas and bullets crossed our path, but my animals kept their tread.
Yet I've seen so many horrors, so many pals just falling dead,
The thoughts of all your kisses, just kept me getting through,
The stresses of the battles, and the strains of missing you.

Oh Dorice – where are you now??

'Tis after the savagery of the Retreat, and oh so many misses,
I realise a time might come, when there will be no more of our kisses.
The intensity of my love for you Dorice, will never ever die,
If you ever get to read this, then I know that you will surely cry.
Be brave my love and hold onto all that came to you,
In our life together, we were the happiest – just we two.
Sharing so many dreams of a lifetime, that are now all in the past,
So remember Dearest, our LOVE is one that will never be surpassed.

Oh Dorice – where are you now??

From your adoring Husband, Bubbie if he should fall.

That taste is back in my mouth. It seems that it is that magical, honeyed taste of that fragrance that only comes with kissing my Dorice.

It finally proves to me that LOVE, definitely, has outlived WAR.

24

AFTERWARDS

"Our Transport Officer was killed this morning. Awful bad luck – got a bullet from an air fight clean through his head".

After such a brief interval, called Life, death brings a host of complex legacies including pain, tears, remorse, sadness, and many other heartfelt emotions.

'Afterwards' fast-forwarded all this, and spanned hours, days, months, years, and now, a full century.

Hours Afterwards: 11am 4/10/18 – 8 am 5/10/18

Baxter arranges for the men to take Anna on two stretchers adapted to cover above and below his body. Then back to the transport line where a burial party of eight of his men is organised. The party includes his servant, King, his groom, Sullivan, and the Transport Serjeant, Hoey.

Under continuous shellfire, the makeshift coffin is placed on a limber, and taken back several miles to Anneux. Sullivan leads Jack, Anna's successful 'jumper' and rides DoriceII, his favourite mount.

A simple ceremony with two officers in attendance, a wooden cross and a last check of his pockets by Baxter and then his body is lowered into the large grave pit. The padre says a brief prayer, as shells land nearby.

Back at the transport line, and before Baxter takes the rations up to the line, he talks to 'Anna's men' of the transport section, and gives each of them a tot of rum to toast their deceased officer. Meanwhile, the war goes on across the Hindenburg Line; more men are lost that night in the 'open' area in La Folie Wood.

Later, Marsden is informed and is visibly shaken. He is asked by the acting CO, Major Guy. W. Nightingale, to write to the next-of-kin; father James Annaheim and wife Dorice Annaheim:

4/10/18 BEF
Dear Mr Annaheim,

It is with great personal sadness that I am writing to you as the official next of kin to Lt George Herbert Annaheim to inform you that he was killed in action earlier today.

It is particularly hard to write this letter, as you probably aware, George, or 'Anna' as he was known out here, was one of my greatest friends, as we have been together ever since Yeomanry days. He was beloved by the Colonel, who was killed a couple of days before, and by us all. Always so full of fun and cheery, when we were up in the Line very tired and depressed, he was like a tonic and livened us all up. He was an excellent soldier, devoted to his duties and praised by the Colonel and all in Command.

During the last great fighting days he had done magnificent work and had been recommended for the Military Cross, which, if he had lived, I am sure he would have received.

We buried him this afternoon, with Military Honours, in the Military Cemetery at Anneux, near Cambrai. Some of his men and two of his favourite horses were in attendance, together with the padre and several Officers.

Be assured, that he met his end bravely, close to the enemy, and he died instantly from a German bullet, and would have felt no pain.

I send to you and Mrs. Annaheim and to his wife, Dorice, my deepest sympathy at this tragic time for all George's family.

I remain sir, your obedient servant,

Sincerely,

Captain C W Marsden

Adjutant, 1st Royal Munster Fusiliers

§§§§§§§

4/10/18 BEF

My dear Dorice, (if you will excuse me addressing you in this familiar manner)

It is with the greatest sadness and deep personal sorrow, that I write to you to 'officially' inform you of the death of your beloved husband Lt. George H Annaheim.

I cannot tell you as to on hearing this news, just how shocked I was for, as you know, your 'Bubbie' was my great friend of more than six years.

I know how much you and 'Bubbie' loved each other during your short time together in this terrible war. He was so proud and happy to be married to his 'Girl' throughout all our difficult times fighting the Huns. His end was swift, within sight of the enemy, and I can confirm it was an instant end. He felt no pain, and we buried him earlier today with military honours at a cemetery near Anneux, just behind the lines.

At this time, I am so devastated by this sad news and

having to write to you in this way, that I will have to stop.

Forgive me if I finish, and, write again in the next days with some more information and, of course, more of my sincerest condolences for the loss of such a fine man and such a good friend.

My deepest sympathy to you and your family at this time, and may God Bless you and give you the strength to bear this awful loss.

With my sincere and deepest sympathy.

Cecil W Marsden

Captain 1st RMF BEF France

Brigade and Division HQs are informed, and the latest officer casualty list, and information is forwarded to both GHQ B.E.F and the War Office, London by telegraph. Acting CO, Major Guy Nightingale, writes to his own mother that same evening:

4. 10. 18 B. E. F.

Dear Mother,

Not much news as the war goes on as usual. We have heard unofficially that Ostend and Douai have fallen, but know nothing for certain. It will clear up the position here at any rate. We are in rather a state of chaos. I have taken over the Battalion with the CO just knocked out, the Signalling officer gone, the P.R.I. (who keeps all the cash and funds and pay of the men of the Bn.) killed, and the Transport Officer killed.

The Brigadier and Brigade Major were both badly wounded about an hour ago and I have one company commander left!... I have such a lot to do I don't know which way to turn, taking over the Battalion with no Hdqtrs. staff, hardly! Thank goodness I have Baxter still. Cambrai is still burning like anything. Have Battalion H.Q. in the grandstand of the racecourse and get a fine view! Jerry is beginning to bring some guns up, or ammunition and has begun shelling us. He nearly blew my orderly room up about midnight last night.

Our Transport Officer (Annaheim) was killed this morning. Awful bad luck – got a bullet from an air fight clean through his head. He and Baxter were just outside the mess looking at an air fight. Baxter frightfully upset and wept like a child. He doesn't see fellows killed much and then it was in cold blood.

The Colonel was buried this morning at Boyelles. I am having a cross made for him. I'm fed up with writing to deceased officer's next-of-kin…

Baxter and I are the only two Gallipoli officers left now. It is quite cheery seeing anyone alive now, but all the same we are winning which is the chief thing, and if our own casualties are heavy, the Boche must have many more. We give him Hell with our Guns and he poor devil can't fire anything back. No more now

Lots of love from your
Loving Son, Guy

Marsden's next-of-kin letters to Mr. James Annaheim and Mrs. Dorice Annaheim are posted, while Telegrams are sent from the War Office, the first of which reaches the Annaheim home on the morning of 5/10/18:

POST OFFICE TELEGRAPHS
5th October 1918 OHMS War Office, London.
Mr J. Annaheim 8, Belgrave Place BATH
Deeply regret to inform you that Lieut. G.H. Annaheim Munster Fusiliers was killed in action fourth October. The Army Council express sympathy.
Secretary War Office

Days Afterwards 5/10/18 – 31/10/18

Early on the 5th, on receiving the telegram, Anna's mother, Sophia, collapses with deep distress, tears and wails. The death of her youngest child is a cruel shock, and she falls down on her knees and prays for his soul.

Mr. James Annaheim says that he must visit the Hookway residence at South Parade, and waits until Dais Carpenter arrives, to comfort her mother.

At 11am, Mr Annaheim is invited into the parlour at 1, South Parade, Bath by their maid Kate. He shows the telegram to Henry Hookway and Mrs. Hookway. The latter falls onto the chaise and remained dumb with shock. She was always the 'Dear little Mater' to Anna; the boy she never had, yet, whom she has treated with love as her own son.

Henry Hookway goes upstairs to break the news to his daughter, Dorice, who was just finishing dressing in her bedroom, and still suffering from morning sickness.

She collapses onto her bed in tears, her father comforting her as best he can, while he valiantly holds back his own heartfelt tears. George was like a son to him, and he too, takes the news badly, but shows stoicism in the face of such tears, all around.

Dorice, with remarkable strength, raises herself, goes downstairs rather unsteadily, passes-by her mother and her father-in-law, and walks quietly into the garden.

She sits alone on the garden bench she had shared so often with her husband, lover and 'best pal'. The bruised and rotting pears laying all around her from their favourite tree, seemed, at that very moment, to be an allegory for her own life.

She holds 'Bubbie's' last letter to her breast with her hands clenched white, with the tightest grip possible. As if she is holding-on to 'Bubbie' himself.

Only a few days ago, she had sent a letter to 'Bubbie' telling him she was his excited and healthy, four months pregnant and Doctor Williams had said all was well with her and that their child was due to be born in April 1919.

She wonders if he had read it, and if there are more letters to come from him.

Henry Hookway pours them all a brandy and includes a glass for Kate, their maid, who attends to the shocked Dorice. There is no toast, no words; only disbelief and sadness, and questions that will need answering. Where, when, how, is it true?

Bad news travels fast, so later, both fathers inform family members by telegram, and letters.

That evening, Dais rushed across Bath to see her friend Dorice and be with her, despite her own desperate feelings of loss. Telegrams are sent to Bubbie's brother Eddy, and to Dorice's aunts and cousins including Dorothy, Kiki, Louis and the wider family.

A night of sadness and mourning at both homes ensued.

The morning of the 6th October brings another official telegram confirming to Dorice that, she is now, like scores of thousands of others, a war widow:

POST OFFICE TELEGRAPHS
6th October 1918 OHMS War Office, London
Mrs. Annaheim 1, South Parade BATH
Deeply regret to inform you that Lieut. G.H. Annaheim Munster Fusiliers was killed in action fourth October. The Army Council express sympathy.
Secretary War Office

Days pass in a weeping daze for Dorice, as if time itself has stopped. This is not made any easier for her, by receiving Bubbie's final letter and poem that arrived, that had been posted by Baxter in France. Letters from Marsden, and Baxter arrive a few days later still. The Battalion is now at rest behind the Lines:

10/10/18 BEF
My dear Dorice,

It is still with the greatest sorrow I write this longer letter to you, to offer my sincerest condolences again to you on the passing of your husband – my best friend – dear Bubbie.

I know how devastated you must be at this sad time, but I urge you to try to be brave and just remember all the good things about such a fine man.

These last few weeks have been some of the hardest to endure out here and we are moving through the Hun defences very fast. Although we are winning and peace cannot be too far away, we have suffered many grievous losses; including many officer pals – but none so dear to me as 'Anna', as most called him.

Our CO, Colonel Kane, died just a few days before, and I do know what respect and fondness Kane had for Bubbie and that he felt he had earned an MC for his most recent brave actions in supporting the Battalion, particularly during this very difficult year.

You probably know that he and I shared so much of our lives together over at least six years; including our times in the Duke of Lancaster's Own Yeomanry in Manchester, fighting the Turks on the Suez Canal, riding together to GHQ in Cairo, and passing-out with our Commissions, from Officer School in Zeitoun.

I have to admit that Bubbie was better than me at musketry as well as all the sports, and his horsemanship was renowned even in those 'old' days.

He loved his sports, and seemed to win them all and earn the respect of the whole Divisional and Regimental staff, as well as all the Munster men, the 'Dirty Shirts', at our sports days.

Dorice, I can tell you that you can be immensely proud of your Bubbie, because despite every evil thing this war and the Huns could throw at us, he was a brave and steadfast model officer. His sense of humour was a boost to the men in the line each night, as he brought up the rations under fire. He did his difficult job with lots of verve, great courage and a sense of optimism that always lifted our spirits in difficult times.

We are in the Hindenburg Line, and he fell quite suddenly; standing next to dear old Baxter the QM, and near Major Nightingale, when his last moment came.

I absolutely know how much Bubbie loved you Dorice; how he loved being a proud and true husband and father-to-be. (Yes, he did tell me that in confidence).

I now do wish you all the strength that God and your family will give to you in the coming days and months. Please write if you can find it in you, to ask anything more about the man with whom we shared such times, and such love.

My deepest sympathy to you and your and his family.

With sincerest thoughts

Cecil W Marsden

Captain

1st Battalion Royal Munster Fusiliers
BEF

p.s. Baxter has arranged for George's personal effects to be sent via Cox's. We have recovered most if not all of his things safely. Perhaps you will let me visit you on my next leave?

15/10/18 BEF
Dear Mrs Annaheim,

I was pleased to get your letter of the 12th, and to know that you are bearing your great loss like a brave soldier's wife.

I am sure that you can hardly realise your great loss. I know poor Anna (as we called him) would not have died happy had he known he was leaving you. It seemed so cruel that his end came as we were together just watching an aerial battle in the sky above. It was a stray Hun bullet from one of their planes that hit him in the head and he fell knowing nothing, dying instantly beside me.

His death is an awful blow to me. I really did not know how much I loved him until I saw him dead at my feet. I wept by his side and I was so thankful there was no one near to see me. He looked so peaceful that it was hard to believe he had gone from me. I have returned your last letter to him, which I found in his tunic pocket.

I was also proud he entrusted me with his 'what if' letters to send if he was to fall, but I had prayed I would never have to send them. I posted them to you and to Mr. J. Annaheim in special Army secure postal packages.

God's ways are sometimes strange. I have lost many comrades in this terrible war, but I have missed none more than your dear husband. We were everything to each other and such confidential friends. I could tell him everything and I knew he would never breathe a word to anybody else, and I think he was the same with me. He was so manly, there are few like he was indeed.

I miss him every hour of the day and I do not know when I shall get over his loss. I know one thing is for certain, and that is that I can never again hope to have such a good friend as your dear Husband.

It was especially hard for me to inform his servant, his groom and all of his men in the transport section of his death. To a man, they were saddened, as he had brought them through so many dangerous times together for almost three years. They drank to him with some 'extra' rum I issued to them, like only Irish soldiers would do – in great respect for their 'own' officer.

If you have a photograph of him I should love to have one and I am sure my wife would like it too.

The small button I am sending with this letter, I cut from his cap. The other must have been shot away. All his possessions will be sent on in a large box in the coming days

I saw his grave for the last time a few days ago. A cross marks it. The following is painted on it;

"Lieut. G.H.A. Annaheim, 1st Royal Munster Fusiliers, killed in action October 4th 1918".

The place is Anneux a small village (or it was a village at one time but is now only a heap of debris) about 6 miles west of Cambrai, just a few hundred yards from a cross roads on the Baupame to Cambrai road. Bourlon Wood is just opposite the military cemetery.

I am enclosing a duplicate list of his kit, which I at once collected, it is the usual official thing, which I have to send to officer's relatives when an officer is killed. I packed up a shell-case he had, although it is against orders to do so, but I know he was keeping it for you, and I disobeyed the order. I think you will like the thing, it is a German one.

If at any time you want to know anything concerning your dear husband and you think I can help you, please write to me dear Mrs. Annaheim. I shall be only too glad to do anything for the wife of the best comrade I ever had in the whole of my 33 years service in the Army.

I have given Captain Marsden your message, and he quite understands that you will write to him later.

I am so pleased that I was such a friend to one of the best soldiers I have ever met and that soldier was your dear husband.

May God give you strength to bear your great loss and keep you well and strong.

Believe me
Dear Mrs. Annaheim
Yours very sincerely
R. T. Baxter

PS If you write to Cox and Co, 16 Charing Cross Road, they will send George's kit to you, in a box and in his valise, I believe. R.T.B.

Dorice's letter found by Baxter on Bubbie's body and returned to her by him, gives her some relief. Thank God he had read it:

My very own darlingest Hubbie,

Your letters from the old H Line are turning up together so I expect the post is upset due to the stunts out there.

I am so glad that you are taking care darling soldier-boy 'cos we will need all our energy to bring up our wee one.

I went with Mama to doctor Williams for a check and he said I (we) were doing well. Blood pressure and all the signs are good. My breasts that you so fondly call my little hand grenades have swollen darling. Now you have two mortar bombs to hold dearest!!

The cot has arrived from London and has pride of place here at SP. The likely date for the 'happening' will be in early

April '19 maybe on our 2nd wedding anniversary umps!

You sounded very tired in your last letter darling, so, I hope John is looking after you properly. I might have to write again to Captain Marsden about getting leave sooner. Let me know if that would help. A month together would be sheer Heaven.

The news seems to be very good on all fronts, but all I care about is what's happening with the 1st Munsters.

Mama and Daddy are excited by our news, and of course, I can't keep it a secret from them, as I seem to be getting a bit plump already. Will you still love me darling in this 'condition'.

Poor old boy are you missing our cuddles and tuddles very much? Well, patience is a virtue and the wait will be worthwhile. I promise.

I went to the corridor to order up the tobacco for your pipe and am wondering if I should send your 'winter warm' to you yet.

I am enclosing another picture since the one of me you said got soaked must be replaced!

Goodbye, my own darling Bubbikins. May God bless you dear heart and keep you from all dangers and keep you safe and sound until you come marching home dearest.

With all my love my Darling, and all my kisses and all of my hugs.

Ever your very own loving and true little, but growing, 'Baby Wifie'

Goodnight beloved.

Good morning Sweetheart xxxxxxxxxxx

A letter from some of his men, obviously encouraged by Baxter, arrives, and causes more tears for Dorice, her tears scented with pride:

10/10/18 BEF
Dear Mrs. Annaheim,
It is a sad thing to write such a letter.

Lt Annaheim was 'our' officer and we served him in the Transport section of the 1st Battalion Royal Munster Fusiliers for many of these wartime months and years.

We wish to send our condolences and our prayers to you for your loss.

Mr. Annaheim was a fair officer who supported all his men, and cared for his animals. We came through many difficult times with him and have respect for his memory.

Mrs. Annaheim, we in the transport section will pray for you, and all our thoughts and blessings go with ye.

Yours Sincerely, with honour to him and with condolences for your sad loss.
Serj. T. Hoey
Cpl. D. Sullivan
Pte. J. King
The Transport Section 1st Batt. Royal Munster Fusiliers

Please excuse our writing to you in this way, but Major Baxter did give us your address.

On the 16th, a telegram arrives from Buckingham Palace:

POST OFFICE TELEGRAPHS
16th October 1918 OHMS Buckingham Palace
Mrs. Annaheim 1, South Parade BATH

The King and Queen deeply regret the loss you and the Army have sustained by the death of your husband in the service of his country.
Their Majesties truly sympathize with you in your sorrow.
Keeper of the Privy Purse

Soon after, a letter arrives from Eddy on HMS Southampton based in Rosyth:

My Dear Dorice,

I don't know what to say in writing to you. I simply can't express in a letter how much I feel for you now at this terrible time. It is always the people at home who have the hardest lot, but I know how well you loved poor old Bubby, and I was glad, though I may have seemed rather reserved about it.

He has done the noblest and finest thing a man could do. I know whatever I say; this will be hardly any consolation to you. I do feel terribly proud of him and almost envy him his glorious departure.

Try and help Mother, will you. She too will need every help to support her, as Bubby was always more at home than I was.

Oh, I am so sorry for you, but do try and be brave – he would like you to be – he was brave enough when it came to the great test. He fell with his face to the enemy. You must think of him now, as happy now. He did his duty for England and for Peace, and for all that is coming soon. I can't say how deeply proud I am of him.

Will you write to me if you can and do try and cheer up Mother and Dad and your own Mother and Dad too. I know my writing can't give you relief from your unhappiness, but be brave for his sake and look forward to meeting him in a happier place.

Yours in deepest sympathy
Eddy

The desperately sad days of October 1918 end with more letters arriving, and there were more to be written; one of which, Dorice wrote in reply to Eddy her brother-in-law, Paymaster on the cruiser HMS Southampton:

My dear Eddy.

Thank you for your kind letter – I am sorry not to have answered it sooner, but since the shock of my Darling Husband's death I seem to have been stunned and have been unable to do anything except think of him – I don't seem able to realise it yet.

God had answered my prayers and spared him for so long that I thought he was going to keep him safe and bring him home to me at the end of this ghastly war. I loved him so! He was just everything to me and I worshipped him and he did me.

We were more than husband and wife – we were the best and truest of pals, and every leave we loved each other more, and it got harder and harder for us to part. I only lived for his home-coming and no one knows how I longed for him during the long weary months we were apart.

Life seems very cruel and it is very hard to be brave when one's happiness is vanished and all one's dreams and hopes are lying shattered at one's feet.

My Darling Bubbie gave me the happiest days of my life and now I have only memories of happiness. God knows our married life was very short, but it was gloriously happy.

My only comfort is that my poor dear Darling was killed instantly and suffered no pain, and didn't know that he was being taken from me. I thank God for that; it would have broken his poor dear heart if he had known that he was going to leave me.

He is buried in the Military Cemetery in the village of Anneux, six miles west of Cambrai on the Baupaume-Cambrai Road.

I don't think I can ever go to see his grave, as I should never want to leave it again. I should want to spend the rest of my life near the resting place of the darling Husband I loved so passionately.

I can't write any more, Eddy, my heart is broken and if it weren't for my darling Mama and Daddy and my little baby that is coming to me, I should ask God to take me too.

May God protect you and keep you safe is the prayer of your affectionate sister.

Dorice

These hours and days afterward, of the life of George Herbert Annaheim, leave much pain at home, and are followed by more months, years, and now a full century of events and memories.

Legacies happened 'in due course' and are the final recorded chapters of an Edwardian young man; a schoolboy, a bank clerk, a sportsman, a soldier, a lover, a husband, a father-to-be, and a grandfather.

Surely, a memory worthy of recording.

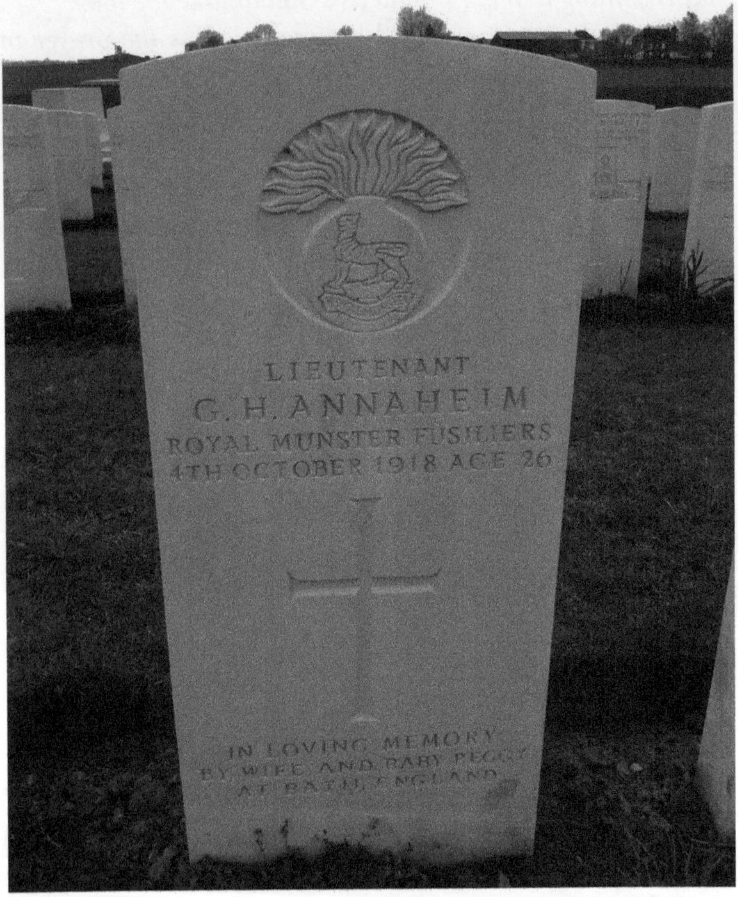
LIEUTENANT
G. H. ANNAHEIM
ROYAL MUNSTER FUSILIERS
4TH OCTOBER 1918 AGE 26
IN LOVING MEMORY
BY WIFE AND BABY PEGGY
AT BATH, ENGLAND

25

IN DUE COURSE

"... he served continuously on the Western Front, his duties affording him many perilous and exciting experiences".

The aftermath of this life snubbed out, like so many others, had a formal 'administrative tail' and many tributes, as well as a significant birth.

6/11/1918

CERTIFICATE OF DEATH

Certified that, according to the records of this Office, Lieutenant GEORGE HERBERT ANNAHEIM, Royal Muster Fusiliers, was killed in action in France, on the 4th day of October, 1918.

Percy Taylor

For the Secretary, War Office.

Dated at the War Office, London this 6th day of November, 1918

§§§§§§§

December 1918
King Edward's School Bath
The EDWARDIAN school magazine
Vol. 10 no 28

LIEUT. GEORGE HERBERT ANNAHEIM
1st Royal Munster Fusiliers
Killed in Action, near Cambrai, October 4th, 1918

Though it is nearly ten years since G. H. Annaheim left the school, he will be remembered by his own generation alike in the classroom and in the playing-field; and the long continued service of his father, Mr. James Annaheim, on the school staff, has kept his connection with the school more closely knit than is usually possible.

He was a member of the school for seven and a half years, and he played both Cricket and Football for the First Elevens.

He was a member of the old Cadet Corps and of the O.T.C., and he was later an enthusiastic member of the Avon Rowing Club, and held the Challenge Cup for one year. When he left school at Christmas, 1908, to join the National Provincial Bank, he became a Volunteer in the Royal Gloucestershire Hussars, and in August 1914, directly war broke out, he enlisted in the Duke of Lancaster's Own Yeomanry.

September 1914 saw him in his regiment in Egypt, where he took part in the engagement, which resulted in the defeat of the Turks when they attempted to capture the Suez Canal. Shortly after this engagement he was given a commission in the 1st Royal Munster Fusiliers, and in early 1916, left Egypt with his Battalion for France.

From that time he served continuously on the Western Front, his duties as Transport Officer affording him many perilous and exciting experiences.

He earned the admiration and affection of his brother officers, and his death by shell-fire on the morning of October 4th, caused general sorrow in the Regiment as well as at home.

During a brief leave in April, 1917, Lieutenant Annaheim married Miss Dorice Hookway, of Bath, and his lamentable death, so near to the conclusion of hostilities, calls forth most profound sympathy both for his parents and his young widow.

§§§§§§§

20/12/1918 extract from CITY PRESS

Bank Heroes

A Memorial Service for members of the National Provincial and Union Bank of England was held at St. Helen's, Bishopsgate last Saturday.

In his address to the crowded, overflowing Church, The Bishop of Stepney enlarged upon a theme of; 'building a better world upon the foundation so solemnly consecrated by the blood of the fallen'.

He commenced by reminding the congregation that; "We have come here to discharge what we believe to be a real duty to those who died for us. The dear lads are in the hands of God, they are in peace. Thank God for all this".

Directors of the bank were present as the last post was sounded to the memory of the 379 bank employees who fell in the Great War.

A memorial plaque will be erected at the headquarters of the Bank shortly; listing those employees who fell in the service of their country.

§§§§§§§

21/1/1919 letter to Dorice Annaheim from Major R T Baxter 1st RMF

Dear Mrs Annaheim,

Very many thanks for your kind letter and especially your husband's photo and the lovely frame in which you sent it. We shall prize both very much indeed. I am so sorry that I have been so late in acknowledging the receipt of them and I hope you will forgive me for being so slack. I am glad George's kit arrived safely from Cox, and I am glad also that you found the money he had drawn the day before he was killed, as I know he could not have spent it where we were.

I am afraid there are not many now in the old battalion whom I know, and feel like a stranger in it. We have an officer from the Royal Irish Regiment in Command of us, and Major Nightingale is second-in-command still, and he is now the only officer whom I know rather well.

I am now on leave, while the men are still in France where they had a rather fine Christmas Dinner. I understand just how especially sad this Christmas will have been for you, but I hope you are continuing to be brave in your loss of my dear friend. I miss your husband very much; we were such good friends. I still can scarcely think that he has gone for ever.

With kindest regards from Mrs. Baxter, my daughter and myself.

May God Bless you and keep you well
Yours very sincerely
R T Baxter

§§§§§§§

31/1/191

The District Probate registry at Bristol,
BE IT KNOWN that GEORGE HERBERT ANNAHEIM of 1, South Parade, Bath, a Lieutenant 1st Battalion Royal Munster Fusiliers who at the time of his death had a fixed place of abode at 1 South Parade aforesaid within the district of Bristol died on the 4th day of October 1918 in France while in actual Military Service intestate.

Be it known that therefore that His Majesty's High Court of Justice at the Probate Registry at Bristol granted to: DORA ALBERTHA ANNAHEIM the lawful widow and relic of the said interstate, the estate amounting to 801 pounds 17 shillings and 5 pence.
Dated 31st day of January 1919

§§§§§§§

21/2/1919

Director of Graves Registration and Enquiries
WAR OFFICE
21st February 1919
London S.W.1.

Madam,
I am directed to inform you that a report has been received which states that the late Lieutenant G.H. Annaheim, 1/Royal Munster Fusiliers is buried in Anneux British Cemetery, South West of Cambrai.

The grave has been registered in this office, and is marked by a durable wooden cross with an inscription bearing full particulars.

I am, Madam,
Your obedient Servant,
Stowell
A.A.G. for Major-General, Graves Registration

§§§§§§§

1/3/1919

THE WAR OF 1914-1918
Royal Munster Fusiliers.
T. Lt. G. H. Annaheim, 1st Bn. (killed in action)
was mentioned in a Despatch from
Field Marshal Sir Douglas Haig, KT GCB GCVO KCIE
dated the 8th November 1918
for gallant and distinguished services in the Field.
I have it in command from the King to record His
Majesty's high appreciation of the services rendered.
Winston S. Churchill
Secretary of State for War
War Office
1st March 1919

20/4/1919

ENTRY OF BIRTH*: Registration district: BATH*

1919 BIRTH in the sub district of Walcot in the County of Bath

1. When and where born:	Eleventh April 1 South Parade
2. Name, if any:	Marguerite Sybil
3. Name & Surname of Father:	George Herbert Annaheim
4. Name, surname and maiden surname of mother	Dora Albertha Annaheim formerly Hookway
5. Occupation of father	Asst. Bank manager Lt 1st Battalion Muster fusiliers (deceased)

L.G. 31085. E/1675.

The War of 1914-1918.

Royal Munster Fus.

T. Lt. G. H. Annaheim, 1st Bn. (Killed in action.)

was mentioned in a Despatch from

Field Marshal Sir Douglas Haig, K.T., G.C.B., G.C.V.O., K.C.I.E.

dated the 8th November 1918

for gallant and distinguished services in the Field.

I have it in command from the King to record His Majesty's high appreciation of the services rendered.

Winston S. Churchill

Secretary of State for War.

War Office
Whitehall, S.W.
1st March 1919.

26

EPILOGUE

Family ties remain strong, though not many recall 'Anna', or his WW1 exploits. But the letters and journals will still bring recollections to those of us still alive, and who can remember some of the key characters appearing in this 'ghost autobiography'.

Anna's wife, Dorice Annaheim: following her husband's death on October 4th 1918, Dorice gave birth to their daughter, Marguerite Sybil Annaheim, in April 1919.

Dorice remarried a cousin, Louis Croydon-Fowler, in 1922 – a kind man with whom she had four children: Peter, Robin, Michael and Shirley.

Dorice became a singer and concert pianist, and, together with Michael and Shirley, ran the Croydon-Fowler School of Dancing, based in Victoria Place, Bath, teaching ballet and organizing tableaux and pantomimes for scores of years, until her death in 1971. She was outlived by Louis Croydon-Fowler, a dentist, who passed away in 1978. Three of Dorice's children and a number of grandchildren and great grandchildren are living today.

Anna's daughter, Marguerite Sybil Annaheim ('Anna'): was brought up and schooled in Kent, Wiltshire and Bath, and remained especially close to her grandparents, Bertha and Henry Hookway. Temp. Capt. Cecil Marsden MC attended her Christening, as her Godfather in late 1919 after having left the Army in August that year.

She was always very close to Anna's sister, her 'Aunt Dais', both being Annaheims by birth. In 1939 she joined the Women's Royal Naval Service (Wrens) and was always thereafter known as 'Anna', just like her father. She worked in Naval intelligence in WW2 and met and married RAF officer, Ewart Wilson, later having two sons, Andrew and Roger Wilson. She worked as a school secretary for many years, and lived in Kent, Surrey, Spain, Switzerland and California. She passed away in Salisbury, UK in 2013, aged 94. It was she who asked the author, her younger son, to "write something that will bring these letters of my father alive".

Anna's father, James Annaheim: was in born 1853 in the village of Losdorf in the Canton of Soleure, Switzerland. He arrived in the UK in 1878 after having studied languages at Basel University.

He taught French and German in schools in Middlesbrough, married Sophia Farley in 1882 in Drogheda Ireland, and settled in Bath in 1900, in which year, he was naturalised as a British citizen. He ended his teaching career as professor of modern languages at King Edward's School, Bath.

He suffered from poor mobility in his later years, and died in 1922.

Anna's mother, Sophia Farley: was born in Drogheda, Ireland in 1854, and later lived and studied in Middlesbrough, where she met her language professor, James Annaheim. They married in 1882 in the protestant Church of Ireland in Drogheda.

Her eldest child 'Dais', (Christened; Mary, Sophia) was born in 1884, her first son Edward Charles ('Eddy'), was born in 1886, and the youngest; George Herbert ('Bubbie' or 'Anna') in 1892. She died in 1927 in Bath.

Anna's sister, Dais Annaheim: was born in Middlesborough, the eldest child of three, later living with her parents at 8, Belgrave Place, Bath. She studied in Bristol to become a pharmacist, and met and married Sidney Carpenter, a solicitor in Bath.

Sidney Carpenter was called to the Colours in 1917, and became a Captain in the ASC in Woolwich and Portsmouth. In the 1930's he became a City Councillor and, later, a popular Mayor of Bath with his wife Dais as Lady Mayoress.

They lived for many years in 'The Towers' at Lansdown, Bath. Sidney and Dais Carpenter had two sons, Jim and Jack, who kept in touch with their cousin Marguerite 'Anna' Wilson throughout their lives.

Anna's brother, Edward Charles Annaheim ('Eddy'): attended King Edward's School, Bath where his father taught modern languages. There, he excelled at sports and mathematics. He joined the Navy aged 17 in 1904, serving on a number of naval cruisers and destroyers on the China station, the Channel and Mediterranean Fleets, as well as in the Home Fleet, as a paymaster officer. He married in

1919, and retired from the service as Captain instructor at Dartmouth Naval College in 1936.

In WW2 he was reemployed as Paymaster Commander of the shore base HMS Wildfire, retiring in 1945. Edward and his wife had a son, Patrick Annaheim, who joined the Navy from Marlborough College to become a naval aviator, only to lose his life when his ship was torpedoed in 1941. Edward Annaheim died in 1960.

Anna's mother-in-law, Mary Bertha Hookway ('the little Mater'): was born in Devon and came from a large family. A very slight woman, she met and married solicitor, Henry Hookway, and settled in Bath at 1, South Parade, a substantial house on the corner of Pierrepont Street.

After her husband Henry Hookway ('the auld Man') died in 1941, she lived at Victoria Place, Bath, until she died in 1972 aged 100 years.

The Royal Munster Fusiliers (RMF): withdrawn on October 11th 1918, from the sector of Cambrai, the 1st Battalion RMF was moved north and took part in a victorious march through liberated Lille.

After the Armistice, demobilisation started, and Battalion strength was soon down to fifteen officers and one hundred and twenty other ranks.

During 1919, 1920, and 1921 the Battalion was reequipped and retrained, while stationed in Plymouth, until ordered to join an inter-allied force in Silesia, Poland.

In June 1922, and as part of retrenchment of the British

Army, this historic Regiment was formally disbanded at a ceremony at Windsor Castle, and its colours handed-over to King George V.

TO THE OFFICERS, WARRANT OFFICERS,
NON-COMMISSIONED OFFICERS AND MEN
OF THE ROYAL MUNSTER FUSILIERS.

It is with feelings of no ordinary sorrow that I address you for the last time; for I know that I am taking leave not only of a fine regiment, but of great memories and great traditions which hitherto have been kept alive and embodied in you.

It is a hard fate to dissolve a corps, which after seventy to eighty years of existence in independent companies became a regiment in 1756 and had for its first Colonel, Robert Clive. Under him you fought at the Battle of Plassey, and not only Clive, but all the old heroes of India knew of what stuff you were made.

Moreover, you have shown in three different centuries that time could not change you, whether in India or in Europe.

Your deeds, extending in all over two hundred and sixty years, are written too clearly in the history of the Empire for anything lightly to efface them.

You have thought fit to entrust your Colours to me for custody and I am very proud to take charge of them to be preserved and held in reverence at Windsor Castle as a perpetual record of your noble exploits in the field.

Meanwhile be very sure that, with or without external

monument, the fame of your great work can never die.
I thank you for your good service to this Country and
Empire, and with a full heart I bid you – Farewell.

George R.I.
12th June, 1922

The colours hang in St. Georges Hall, Windsor Castle to this day.

That ammunition box and valise with their evocative contents of letters, photographs and wartime ephemera, are also kept safely.

They remain mementos of a man, born into a time that brought total War to the world, but who found true Love, and who left an everlasting legacy.

"We do not mourn him,
but we are glad he lived".

1914
1918

AUTHOR'S NOTES & ACKNOWLEDGEMENTS

My deepest acknowledgements go to every soldier who fought for their liberty in the Great War, particularly those from Britain and Ireland, and all the families and loved ones left behind. It is largely because of the courage of these men and women that we are who we are today.

In developing this story, I have drawn on my fifty years of study and readings of military history.

Many classic factual and fictional books have been written about WW1 that I have admired, read and reread over that time.

For 'Anna Uncensored', I have drawn on the War diaries of the relevant Battalions and Divisions, as well as my dog-eared copy of 'History of the Royal Munster Fusiliers' published in 1927 by Captain S McCance for private circulation.

These, and sources in the National Archives in Kew, The British Library, The Public Record Office, and librarians at The Imperial War Museum and The National Army Museum, have allowed me to build an accurate picture of people, places and times. Thanks are due to these organizations.

Especial thanks are due to Adrian Foley as well as the President and Chairman and other members of the

Royal Munster Fusiliers Association for information and inspiration over fifteen years of membership. A walk with a group of Association members along paths of the 'Great Retreat' in March 2018 was particularly important and moving.

I am pleased to be able donate the Ammo box and Anna's valise and their contents, to the Cork Public Museum in Fitzgerald Park, Cork. Here, memories of the brave fighting men of the Royal Munster Fusiliers will be maintained thanks to the enthusiasm of the curating staff.

Thanks also to Cara Wilson for editing and the cover design, and to David Powell and his team at Lighthouse Publishing Ltd for realising this project.

In formally acknowledging the quotes and pictures used in the text from plays, poems and newspaper cuttings, the source was the letters themselves, written in pencil or ink from Egypt and the Western Front, or from cuttings found in the Ammo box and valise. I have endeavoured to contact rights holders wherever possible. Any errors are my own of those of 'Anna' himself in all those letters and diaries.

Roger Wilson

ABOUT THE AUTHOR

Roger Wilson has had a busy creative life, working in marketing and communications for several of the world's most admired Companies.

During that period of his life, he produced scripts and copy for films, videos, brochures and collateral material for iconic products like the Ford Fiesta, Xerox Copiers, HP Printers and Dell Computers.

He previously lived in Weybridge Surrey, Geneva Switzerland and Moscow Russia. He now lives in Surrey with his wife, a successful artist, Claire Hardwick-Wilson.

From an early age, Roger's keenest interest has been the study of military history.

This 'ghost autobiography', which merges the classic memoir format with colourful and evocative novelized reminisces of his own Grandfather before and during WW1, is the first of his non business-oriented publications.